# GUGGISBERG

WEST AFRICAN HISTORY SERIES

General Editor: GERALD S. GRAHAM

*Rhodes Professor of Imperial History, University of London*

# Guggisberg

## R. E. WRAITH

LONDON
OXFORD UNIVERSITY PRESS
IBADAN NAIROBI
1967

*Oxford University Press, Ely House, London W.1*

GLASGOW NEW YORK TORONTO MELBOURNE WELLINGTON
CAPE TOWN SALISBURY IBADAN NAIROBI LUSAKA ADDIS ABABA
BOMBAY CALCUTTA MADRAS KARACHI LAHORE DACCA
KUALA LUMPUR HONG KONG TOKYO

Preparation and publication of this series has
been made possible by the generous financial
assistance of Overseas Newspapers Group,
Freetown, Lagos, London and West Indies

PRINTED IN GREAT BRITAIN BY
WESTERN PRINTING SERVICES LTD BRISTOL

# CONTENTS

## Part I
### *1869–1919*

## Part II
### *Governor of the Gold Coast: 1919–27*

## Part III
### *1927–30*

# ILLUSTRATIONS

*(between pages 14 and 15)*

# ACKNOWLEDGEMENTS

ALTHOUGH no biography of Sir Gordon Guggisberg has ever been written, a short account of his governorship is to be found in Chapters III and IV of *Ghana, The Road to Independence*, by F. M. Bourret, a revised edition of a previous book, *The Gold Coast, 1919–51*; and a great deal of unique information is to be found in Professor David Kimble's definitive *Political History of Ghana*; Professor Kimble was fortunate in having access to the Ghana Archives before the fifty-year rule was enforced. I have drawn a good deal on this work in Part II, and again where specific reference is made the authority is quoted; but there is a good deal for which only a general acknowledgement is possible. I am grateful to Professor Kimble and to his publishers, the Clarendon Press, for their permission to make use of this material. I must also thank Mr. Anthony Glyn and Hutchinsons for their kind permission to quote from *Elinor Glyn*.

As is fitting in a personal memoir, however, much reliance is placed upon the reminiscences of those who knew Guggisberg personally. Unfortunately these are far too numerous to mention exhaustively, and I must confine myself to acknowledging the help of a few who went to special trouble on my behalf. To two of them I owe a very special debt.

Lieutenant-Colonel J. H. Levey, a director of Offin Rivers Estates Ltd., and one of Guggisberg's closest friends, told me a great deal about him that is, to the best of my knowledge, unknown to anyone else; and Mr. F. P. Cobb, who had done a great deal of research into the story of Guggisberg, Fraser, and Aggrey, was good enough to hand over to me the whole of his material, which included some valuable personal letters from Fraser and from Colonel R. F. A. Butterworth, who had known Guggisberg at the turn of the century at Woolwich and later on the Somme. Mr. Cobb's papers also included a document compiled by the Librarian of the Royal Military Academy, Sandhurst, on which most of the war-time narrative in Chapter 3 is based.

I have also been greatly helped by Margot, Lady Davson, and her sister, the late Lady Juliet Rhys-Williams, D.B.E.; and by Mr. A. Duncan-Johnstone, Lord Hemingford and Sir Andrew Jones.

In Ghana I owe much to conversations with Dr. Susan Ofori-Atta, Mr. Archie Caseley-Hayford, the late Dr. J. B. Danquah, Sir Tsibu Darku, Mr. J. W. de Graft Johnson, Sir Arku Korsah, Mr. H. H. Malm, Sir Leslie M'Carthy, Miss Ruby Quartey-Papafio and Dr. C. E. Reindorf.

With regard to Guggisberg's career in British Guiana I owe a particular debt of gratitude to Sir Ralph Grey, who gave generously of time which, as Governor of the Colony, he could ill afford; and to Sir Frank McDavid and Mr. Malcolm Laing for illuminating conversations. A number of distinguished people in British Guiana helped me, at Sir Ralph Grey's prompting, with written recollections, and their names are acknowledged on page 297.

Mr. H. B. Thomas gave me unsparing help in Bexhill-on-Sea in tracing the events of the closing months of Guggisberg's life. Sir Gordon's daughters, Miss Nancy and Miss Rowena Guggisberg, have been most kind and encouraging. Professor John Fage, who had done some preliminary research into Guggisberg's life with a view to writing this book, kindly handed me the fruits of his labour. Finally, I am grateful to the Editor of this series, Professor Gerald S. Graham, who invited me to write the book, and when obstacles accumulated refused to let me abandon it.

# ABBREVIATIONS

The following abbreviations have been used in footnotes:

*Political History*    The Political History of Ghana: Professor
David Kimble

*Events*    The Gold Coast: A Review of Events of
1920–1926

*Debates*    The Gold Coast Legislative Council Debates

*A.R.P.S.*    The Aborigines Rights Protection Society

# NOTE

This book was written before the military *coup d'état* of 1966 in
Ghana and a few references to the existing Government need
to be read in this light.

In February 1966 it was arranged in Parliament that public
records would be made available immediately up to the end
of 1922, and that the Government's intention was in due course
to amend the 50-year rule to 30 years. The records for three
years of Sir Gordon Guggisberg's governorship of the Gold
Coast are therefore available already, and the rest may become
available soon. At the relevant time this book was already in
production, and the author and publisher decided to continue
with publication in its present form. Certain passages which
refer to the public records need to be read in the light of this
fact.

# Introduction

'GORGIE, Gorgie, Gorgie—Gorgie Number One!' Thus cried the young Edward Asafu-Adjaye, running barefoot after Guggisberg's motor-car through the streets of Accra in the 1920s, with other small boys of his time. So Sir Edward told me, sitting in the Ghana High Commissioner's beautifully restored office in Belgrave Square and looking back over the years. Ghanaians of his generation always speak of Guggisberg with affection and respect, though they do not always garnish their reminiscences with such piquant detail. Often the response to Guggisberg's name is more solemn than this. Since I first visited the Gold Coast in 1946 the words 'Governor Guggisberg, of blessed memory' have been uttered in a special, reverent tone of voice more often than I can remember. This book tries to reach some understanding of what sort of man it was who thus impressed a generation of Africans at a time when they were not—or at any rate their leaders were not—well-disposed towards governors, or to any other manifestation of the imperial power.

Guggisberg was Governor of the Gold Coast during the aftermath of the First World War, a mild forerunner indeed of the aftermath of the Second, but equally a time of questioning, of nascent nationalism and of the opening of windows on a wider world than Gold Coast Africans had known before. As we shall see, he never achieved complete *rapport* with the nationalists; even to his remarkably unprejudiced and forward-looking mind their claims to leadership were suspect and their hopes of self-government exaggerated. Yet their tribute to him in retrospect is as heart-felt as was that of the chiefs and common people at the time. Though he was a more complex character than at first appears, the motives which animated him were basically simple, and one of them was a belief in the British Empire and a pride in being an imperialist. Yet I have heard a contemporary Ghanaian Minister, most irascible of nationalists in the 1940s, leap to the defence of Guggisberg in discussion with the words 'But Guggisberg was *not* an imperialist.'

After the Second World War such a man might well have failed, for he was no diplomatist or politician, and was conservative from head to toe. He was one of the last pro-consuls who was, or could hope to be, a Father to his People; but this was not realized in the Gold Coast in the 1920s, and has since been excused by modern nationalists, because of the immense benefits he brought to 'his' people. He was the founder of the modern Gold Coast as surely as Kwame Nkrumah was the founder of Ghana, and is still gratefully remembered by Ghanaians across the smoke and dust of Independence.

That a British Governor should evoke these feelings in a colony that was more sophisticated than most at the time, and which has latterly led the world against colonialism, is a phenomenon worth studying in itself. What makes it peculiarly fascinating is that Guggisberg had none of the orthodox qualifications for the job, which raises the question of whether the orthodox qualifications were necessarily the best. Until the age of fifty he was an officer in the Royal Engineers, and though his connection with West Africa had by then been long and intimate, it was a surveyor's and engineer's experience, and the natural summit of his career would have been as a Director of Public Works, to which post he was in fact appointed in the Gold Coast at the outbreak of the 1914–18 war, but the war prevented him from taking it up. One of the characteristically theatrical touches in his life was that, having been appointed head of the Public Works Department he took office, after the interregnum of war, as Governor, a feat of hurdling which astounded and dismayed his able predecessor, Sir Hugh Clifford, who never got over it. For this sapper and bush surveyor was not out of the Colonial Service stable at all; his origins were obscure, he had been to no university, even his name was open to suspicion. It would be agreeable to record that the Colonial Office, with unique prescience, had seen the possibilities which lay beneath his unpromising pedigree, but, alas, it was not so. As we shall see, there was more than a suspicion of back-stairs petticoat influence in the manner of his appointment.

Sir Hugh Clifford, who never spoke to him again if he could avoid it, was in intellect, in subtlety and in administrative skill an abler man. His experience had been vast,[1] his outlook was liberal; both in the Gold Coast, where he criticized H.M.G.'s economic policies, and later in Nigeria, where he expressed himself with unusual and original vehemence on the administration of the Northern Emirates (the pride and joy of the Colonial Office in those years) he showed himself to be independent, forward-looking and courageous. Guggisberg indeed built on a good deal of Clifford's work, a fact which in the author's view he did not adequately acknowledge. Yet in Ghana today Clifford is forgotten, while the Guggisberg myth has survived Positive Action, 'S.G.', democratic centralism, Nkrumahism, and other triumphs and vicissitudes.

The fact is that Guggisberg did without effort what most public men today would recruit an expert team of public relations officers to do for them—he put himself across. He could not have done this—as a European *vis-à-vis* African subjects—if he had not been completely sincere, and if the advancement of the Gold Coast, materially, educationally and spiritually, had not been the mainspring of all his actions. Whether he was a natural public relations officer, or whether he consciously employed artifice, is not clear at this distance of time. He was fortunate enough to live in the days before we spoke of a man's 'public image', but it seems improbable that he consciously fostered a public image of himself and projected it by deliberate means. Perhaps he did not need to do so. He was

---

[1] British Resident, Penang, 1896–1903: Colonial Secretary Trinidad and Tobago, 1903–7 and of Ceylon, 1907–12; subsequently Governor of Nigeria, Ceylon and the Straits Settlements.

tall and strikingly handsome, precisely the man Ouida would
have chosen for a governor, had she worked in that field; Elinor
Glyn seems to have done just that.[1]

As a professional soldier he believed in ceremony, order and
protocol, and appeared more frequently in uniform than later
governors have done. A disciplinarian, he left no-one in doubt
as to who was in control. All this was impressive, and was understood and appreciated by an African people at that time who
liked both authority and display. But this was incidental; what
really projected the image was his identification with African
progress, his systematic assessment of what needed to be done,
his determination to do it, and his concrete achievement in
endowing the Gold Coast with a deep-water harbour at Takoradi, the finest hospital of the time in Africa at Korle Bu, Accra,
and above all, since education was almost more important than
life itself, with Achimota. Approaching his problems with the
method of an engineer, advancing upon each objective with the
precision of a commander in the field, he convinced the Gold
Coast people that they had a champion. Alongside his immense
practical achievement he took up from his predecessor the
torch of constitutional advance and carried it farther and faster
than previous governors had done. Here his achievement is
more open to question, as he worked within the limitations both
of his own nature and of the general colonial *ethos* of his day.
Later generations would consider his assessment of the nationalist movement to have been faulty, his deference to tradition
too unquestioning, his reliance on the chiefs too partial, and his
faith in 'native institutions' too uncritical. Even so he was the
first Governor to introduce even the mildest element of elected
representation into the administration of the country, and
although the Constitution of 1925 in which this was embodied
could scarcely be considered democratic today it is still not
uncommon to meet Ghanaians who feel more warmly towards
him because of his political contribution than because of
Takoradi, Korle Bu and Achimota; and even the surviving
members of the 'intelligentsia' of the time, who were not in

[1] See p. 65.

accord with him in 1925, and with whom he himself was in imperfect sympathy, do not allow this to detract from their admiration of him today.

Enough has been said about his achievements, perhaps, to justify an attempt to write a biography, however incomplete the records. But the human story provides an added incentive. Few men can have become so well known for a mere eight years' work out of sixty-one years of life. Behind the correct façade of public achievement, few can have had their private lives so surprisingly lit by romance and shadowed by failure and pathos. He made a runaway marriage with a girl of seventeen, resulting in early and complete disaster after the birth of three children; and a subsequent marriage to a well-known musical comedy actress, from which came unhappiness of a different kind. He failed at any time to build a domestic life or background, and died without roots. He failed, more understandably, to win the unreserved confidence of the Colonial Office. After his eight creative years in the Gold Coast he remained unemployed, finally collapsing in harness as Governor of the then minor Colony of British Guiana. His brief career had reached bitter anti-climax. He died obscurely and alone, away from family or friends, in an English seaside boarding house, and it was left to his Gold Coast friends, led by Nana Sir Ofori Atta, to erect a fitting tombstone over the bare and untended grave.

Perhaps he should never have been a soldier or colonial governor, for he was a born headmaster. The annual Budget Sessions of the Gold Coast Legislative Council were in fact, from 1919 to 1927, Speech Days in all but name, at which the Head, at inconsiderate length, spoke of the School's achievements in the preceding year, and commended the promising pupils, black and white, by name and form. The whole subject of education, both in practice and theory, became a passion to the point of obsession. The headmaster *manqué* had presumably been bottled up for fifty years, and when supreme authority gave him the opportunity he made up for lost time.

No biography of Guggisberg has been written, nor can be written, until the records become available in the Public

Record Office and the Ghanaian and British Guianaian archives between 1970 and 1980. Unfortunately none of his own
papers have survived, with the exception of a small scrap book
which he kept after his retirement from the Gold Coast and
during an American visit in the autumn of 1927. He was indeed
an indefatigable keeper of papers, and these followed him in
packing cases to his last assignment in British Guiana. Why he
took them there in preference to leaving them in England is
obscure; perhaps because he never had a home in England,
perhaps because he was intending to write an autobiography.
Be that as it may, when he left British Guiana suddenly through
illness he charged his private secretary, Malcolm Laing, most
solemnly to see a large consignment safely back to London.
'There is not a single scrap of paper in my room that may not be
of great value to me';[1] to which, incidentally, he added the
exhortation not to let his wife get hold of them. Mr. Laing's
wife duly shepherded them home, and they were stored late in
1929 in the attic of the house in Hampshire which had served as
his British *pied-à-terre*. During the 1939–45 war they were
destroyed.

In January 1960, I was given provisional permission by the
Ghana Government to study the official papers in the Ghana
National Archives; the proviso being that the Colonial Office
and Commonwealth Relations Office should agree. Predictably,
they declined to depart from the fifty-year rule, and after a con-
siderable delay—three and a half years to be exact—the Ghana
Government finally gave its own *non possumus*. The Colonial
Office also effectively blocked my efforts to see official papers in
Georgetown, British Guiana.

In the absence of documents, other than public ones such as
Legislative Council debates and Sessional Papers, it seemed
doubtful whether a biography was worth attempting. Moreover
it is more than thirty-five years since Guggisberg died, and those
who knew him become fewer as the years pass. I am indebted
to a number of these, both in the United Kingdom and in
Ghana, for their recollections of him, and have acknowledged

[1] Private conversation with Mr. Laing.

their names below. But few aspiring biographers can have had so little straw with which to make their bricks, and for this reason I do not pretend that what follows is satisfactory biography; it is simply an appreciation, or at most a biographical sketch, of a man who deserves more substantial recognition than I am able to provide. I trust that some future scholar in the 1980s will find the forbidden pastures in Chancery Lane, Accra and Georgetown as alluring as they now appear to me.

It has been particularly exasperating to try to tell the story of the Gold Coast Governorship with the help only of official documents, for these describe the happenings of the day but fail to bring them to life; they throw little light on the motives and manners of the characters in the drama. In talking to those who were active in the Gold Coast in Guggisberg's day one is frequently struck by the contrast between their knowledge of certain events, including the background, and the account of those same events in the public documents. For example, to read available accounts of the progress of Achimota is to read a worthy but essentially dull story of success—dull in the sense that an account of the building of a wall would be dull, with each brick being put in its proper place so that the wall grows higher and higher. Nowhere is it possible to verify, what one knows to be the fact, that in creating Achimota Guggisberg fought a hard running battle on two fronts; with his own officials in the Education Department who, in the manner of experts everywhere, mistrusted the gifted amateur, deeply resented his authority over them and thought his ideas about education misguided; and with officials in the Colonial Office, who mistrusted enthusiasm, disliked official despatches which were in the nature of sermons, and whose natural reaction to the flames of Guggisberg's imagination was to pour cold water on them.[1] An historical account must therefore await the opening of the files; this narrative is more personal in its intention, and for

[1] For example, I have seen a Guggisberg despatch, of glowing enthusiasm, on his conception of the Achimota buildings as a kind of temple of higher education, to which the reply of the Secretary of State was largely concerned with the excessive amount of money to be spent on the clock.

want of evidence cannot give a complete or always coherent account of Guggisberg's life and work.

Up to a point Guggisberg himself has provided basic material. In his Gold Coast days he was the last man to hide his light under a bushel. It was his custom at each Budget Session of the Legislature to deliver a considerable speech on the prospects for the coming year which was in effect an account of his stewardship for the last. There was nothing new in this; Clifford had done it before him and it was normal practice in most colonies. But Guggisberg, who had a well-developed sense of occasion, endowed it with the solemnity of a religious cermony, and elevated his annual speech into what he was pleased to call a *Message*, delivered at inordinate length. The Clerk of the Legislative Council of the time, Mr. H. H. Malm, has described to me the reserves of physical stamina which were necessary to members of the audience. The Governor, absorbed and happy, would read on and on, drinking a glass of water from time to time from the cooler at his hand; the legislators, denied even this modest refreshment, could do no more than wait for the next break, with perhaps the prospect of a similar day tomorrow.

These annual progress reports are Guggisberg's documentation of himself. But on the last of such occasions, on 3 March 1927, little more than a month before his final departure, he excelled even himself, for to his usual Budget Speech he appended a *Review of the Events of 1920–26*. This extraordinary document is his testament to his own governorship in its entirety. It is a substantial volume of some interest to historians, though to listen to it must have been an unenviable experience. It naturally skims the surface of events, and tells little of how they came to pass, but it provides a useful stopgap until such time as the files are open. At a number of points the narrative goes back briefly to the year 1900, which helps to put events in perspective. The style is characteristic of the born instructor, who delighted in the presentation of facts, and tried to reconcile the normally disparate aims of being both exhaustive and concise. Key sentences or phrases appear in heavy type, reminding the reader of the type of school textbook whose primary aim was to get him through examinations; or possibly of the letters of Queen Victoria.

Today Britain is accused by her former colonial wards of past exploitation and neglect. Sometimes these accusations are unfair, as they take too little account of the problems presented to colonial powers by pre-literate tribal societies which had only mastered their own environment in the most rudimentary ways. Sometimes however they are uncomfortably true, and Britain's record in developing her African colonies for their self-government which was her implied, if lukewarm, purpose does not always bear examination. But Guggisberg's objectives for the Gold Coast in the nineteen-twenties accord closely with those of the statesmen of the developed countries for the whole of the underdeveloped world in the nineteen-fifties. He was thirty years ahead of his time. Such men do not have a comfortable passage during their lives, and when, after they are dead, the world has caught up with them, some tribute is their due.

# PART I

## 1869–1919

# I

# The First Thirty-three Years

ADMIRERS of Frederick Gordon Guggisberg generally suppose, from his name, that he was Jewish, and that his singular success as a British Colonial Governor was either because of, or in spite of, this fact. It is a curious half-truth, for although he was in fact of Jewish descent this had nothing to do with his name. His forbears were Jews of a quite different name, who lived in Russian Poland. At about the turn of the eighteenth century his great-great-grandfather was a youth in his late teens, facing conscription into the Russian Army. Knowing that as a Jew his military service would consist of the most menial tasks, he decided to make a bolt for it, and managed to cross the frontier by night, carrying with him only the tools of his trade, which were those of a glazier. He then proceeded to walk across Europe in search of work and security, and these he ultimately found in the village of Guggisberg, in the Bern Canton of Switzerland. The man who employed him was a prosperous market-gardener, whose greenhouses were constantly in need of the glazier's skill, and the young refugee prepared to settle down. His effect on the market-gardener's daughter, however, was profoundly unsettling, for she fell wildly in love with his dark good looks, and they proposed to marry. The outraged father promptly sacked him, but upon his daughter declaring that she would follow him wherever he went he beat a retreat, and agreed to the marriage on two conditions; first, that the young man should change his religion and become a decent Protestant; and second, that he should change his name so that the Russians wouldn't find him. The question of a new name caused some difficulty, but his future father-in-law solved it by suggesting that he should adopt the name of the village. This he did, in the manner of a people in whose country his great-great-grandson was later to serve part of his African apprenticeship; which accounts for the other supposition among Gordon Guggisberg's friends, that in origin he was German-Swiss.

The sons of this marriage emigrated to Canada, and in the 1830s the two brothers, John and Frederick, are recorded as having settled in Preston, Ontario.[1] The elder, John, who was Gordon Guggisberg's grandfather, became the local butcher, and out of the profits of his business he built a tavern known as the 'Black Bear'. This building survived until 1930, by which time it had become a 22-bedroom hotel; but Progress cannot be stayed, and its site is now occupied by the Knotty Pine Kof-E-Bar.

The younger of the two brothers, Frederick, appears to have earned his living as a carpenter and joiner. He also seems to have been a good business man, for by 1841 he was building his own chair factory, which prospered sufficiently for him to be described by 1857 as a 'cabinet, chair and furniture manufacturer'. By 1884 the family had moved to Galt, in whose Directory appears an advertisement for 'Guggisberg Brothers & Company, Furniture Manufacturers. Established 1838. Factory at Preston.' Evidently his sons had gone into the business, which continued to develop, and which is today the Canadian Office and School Furniture Company, part of which occupies the original site. Only the stone family house has vanished, having been demolished in 1960 to make way—in this case—for a service station.

The son of the butcher and inn-keeper was named Frederick after his uncle, and is recorded as having followed the occupation of 'inspector and dealer in dry goods'.[2] Whatever this may have involved it does not stir the romantic imagination; his own son, Frederick Gordon Guggisberg, born in 1869, was to make good this deficiency.

[1] For the subsequent details I am indebted to Mr. Andrew W. Taylor, President of the Waterloo Historical Society, Galt, Ontario.
[2] Mr. Carl Guggisberg, Sir Gordon's second cousin, and now living in Gaylord, Michigan, has described him to me as a 'retail dry-goods merchant'.

Guggisberg when Governor

# The T-model Ford, the railways and imports in Guggisberg's day

A District Officer on Tour
*Royal Commonwealth Society*

The touring lorry of the Gold Coast Medical Department
*Royal Commonwealth Society*

The railway station at Odaka (sic)
*Royal Commonwealth Society*

Imports
*Central Office of Information*

Under construction
*Sir Robert McAlpine Ltd.*

Takoradi Harbour

Completed
*Central Office of Information*

General view
*Central Office of Information*

Korle Bu Hospital

A corridor
*Central Office of Information*

# Achimota

View from air c 1930. In the background is
Legon Hill, now covered with the buildings of the
University of Ghana
*Charles Deakin*

The
administrative
block
*Charles Deakin*

The Official opening. Guggisberg has his right hand on Aggrey's
shoulder. Fraser is on the Governor's left. Casely-Hayford is standing
behind Aggrey.
*Charles Deakin*

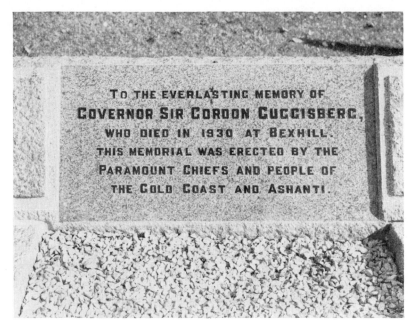

Guggisberg's grave at Bexhill-on-sea

## Memorials

The council chamber at Dodowah
*Central Office of Information*

GUGGISBERG MEMORIAL HALL

Guggisberg and Ormsby-Gore, Secretary of State for the Colonies,
during the latter's visit to West Africa in 1926. Taken in the
courtyard of Christiansborg Castle
*Charles Deakin*

## Visits

American Visit. The British
Ambassador, Sir Esme
Howard, on Guggisberg's
right and Canon A. Phelps-
Stokes on his left. Taken
outside the White House

# Wife and Home

Guggisberg's second wife,
Decima Moore, as Casilda
in *The Gondoliers*
*Radio Times Hulton Picture
Library*

Christiansborg Castle,
Accra, the official residence
of British Governors of the
Gold Coast
*Central Office of Information*

Guggisberg's forbears, then, were small-town pioneers, who came from a foreign country, struck Canadian roots, prospered in the hotel and furniture trades, developed into local worthies, and in a manner common to all countries and ages moved away from the place where they had originally made their money to another residential town. Guggisberg himself was always oddly reticent about this background, and sketchy though these few particulars have been (they are all that long-distance research can bring to light) few of his friends knew even so much about him. There was an occasion after he had become celebrated when he was placed next at dinner to Lady Vischer.[1] A good cosmopolitan European, she leaned towards him remarking 'Guggisberg—that is a good German name . . .?' 'Swiss, Madam,' he corrected coldly, 'and the connection is very distant.' That closed the conversation, and he turned somewhat abruptly to his other neighbour. This reticence continued throughout his life, for though he became content to describe himself as a Canadian, he was by inclination, and in some measure by achievement, an Englishman of the governing class, a class in which conformity in family, school and university were an advantage, and an unconventional ancestry and upbringing something to be deprecated. It was this, no doubt, that disposed him to be more English than the English. Certainly devotion to cricket, King, Empire and the older universities, in roughly that order, were the contemporary hall-marks of the English upper class whom he admired. Meanwhile the only hereditary skill which seems to have persisted was his love of the carpenter's bench, inherited no doubt from his great-uncle who had secured the family fortunes by starting to make chairs in Preston. In his declining years it was his principal hobby.

When Guggisberg's father died in 1873, he was four years old, and the family was in fact substantial and prosperous. His widow moved to Toronto, where she met and married an Englishman, and in doing so forged a remarkable link between

[1] Widow of Sir Hanns Vischer, known in Northern Nigeria, and later throughout the Colonial Empire, as an educational pioneer. The story was told to me by their son.

the family and the Royal Navy, for her second husband was
Paymaster R.N. Admiral Ramsey Dennis, and of the four
daughters of this marriage three also married admirals, Sir
Frederick Tudor, Sir Percy Scott and Keighley Peach. This
Senior Service connection proved to have a very direct in-
fluence on her son's career, for in 1879 she found herself in
England with his education to provide for. Nothing was
more natural than that he should be sent to Burney's School,
Gosport, otherwise known as the Royal Naval and Military
Academy.

This school had been founded in 1790 by a Dr. William
Burney, and its purpose, in the agreeable idiom of the time, was
to provide private education for the sons—and presumably the
step-sons—of gentlemen, especially those intending to enter the
Navy or, as a second best, the Army.[1] When William Burney
died in 1832 his son, Henry, who had been associated with his
father for some time, took over and was later joined by his
brother, the Rev. Edward Burney, who was the sole principal
at the time of the ten-year-old Guggisberg's arrival. In its day
Burney's was a place of some importance, and had numbered
among its pupils H.R.H. the (then) Duke of Edinburgh (afterwards the Duke of Saxe-Coburg Gotha), Prince Henry of
Prussia, H.R.H. the Duke of York (King George V), and
Prince Louis of Battenberg (father of Lord Mountbatten). In
an obituary notice of the Rev. Edward Burney in the *Portsmouth Times and Naval Gazette* of 11 August 1888, the writer
claimed that it had been 'the largest private school in England,
and the only one that had ever been under the immediate
patronage of H.M. the Queen'. An article by an old boy of the
Academy, Frederick Hamer, appeared in the *Portsmouth Evening
News* of 20 May 1952, in which he said, 'We took great pride
in being "Royal" and in being allowed to fly the Union Jack and
to wear the royal crown on our caps. These distinctions were
conferred on us by Queen Victoria as so many members of
the Royal Family had been educated there.'

[1] In 1830 it had been advertised as an 'academy for the education of young
gentlemen destined for the navy, army and the East India Company's service'.

A much earlier writer, in the Portsmouth Guide of 1823, described the Academy in these terms:

To the north of the High Street is Cold Harbour, a fine square, one side of which is open to the Harbour, of which it commands a pleasing view. In this square is the celebrated Academy conducted by Dr. Burney, from whence have emanated so many of those distinguished characters whose deeds have done themselves and their country honour.[1]

The descendant of the Polish emigré, the German-Swiss market-gardener, the Canadian butcher-cum-innkeeper, and the small-town dry-goods merchant, thus received his education in an atmosphere which would have surprised his ancestors. Britain was not yet conscious of her African Empire, which she was accumulating unwillingly and sporadically, but Burney's was at the heart of the older imperial tradition, and devotion to the Queen, the Royal Navy and the Army shaped his thoughts and determined his future. It would be satisfactory to be able to say something of his school career, but nothing is now known of this. The Academy migrated to Shalford House, Guildford, in 1904 and seems to have fallen into decay, for the House had become a hotel by 1910; no recollections survive in the minds of local people and the Academy's records have disappeared.[2]

Neither is anything known of Guggisberg's record during the next stage of his education, which was, predictably, at the Royal Military Academy, Woolwich; save that he entered it in 1866 and was gazetted 2nd Lieutenant Royal Engineers on 15 February 1889, at the age of twenty.[3] Surviving evidence does suggest, however, that he found it extremely congenial, for when he returned there in the capacity of an Instructor in 1897 his devotion to his *alma mater* found expression in the writing of his first book. The writing of books, be they good or bad,

[1] I am indebted for these details of Burney's to Mrs. E. Cottrill, the Hampshire County Archivist, and Miss Betty Masters, the City Archivist of Portsmouth.

[2] Information supplied by Miss Enid Dance of the Guildford Muniments Room.

[3] The personal records of Army officers are withheld for a hundred years, by which time it is thought safe for them to be read.

involves persistence, self-discipline and drudgery, and is an exercise not readily embarked upon by young army subalterns. The fact that he wrote it at all marks the beginnings of emergence from the rut; the manner of his writing it, which was characterized by leaving nothing out, foreshadowed the driving industry and didactic tendencies of later life. It is called *The Shop—The Story of the R.M.A.*, and is an account of the history, traditions, daily life and general *ethos* of the Academy, told with a simple enthusiasm and devotion and in a singularly repellent style. To be able to write, at the age of thirty:

The meal over, the 'swanker' hies him to his room and spends the few remaining hours of gaslight poring over pages of 'swot', 'stinks' or 'G.D.'

suggests, in view of the crisp, soldierly and occasionally imaginative writing of subsequent years, the 'late developer'; yet all his clichés cannot quite spoil a nostalgic vignette of Woolwich in the days of the old Queen:

The gym is transformed into a veritable palace of delight, where the fairy slippers of the beauteous maiden and the glossy wellingtons of the bold G.S. glide smoothly over the well-polished floor to the dulcet strains of the gunners' band.

But after all few of us would wish to admit to the authorship of our own *juvenalia*.

In what might be called a sports supplement to this early work there emerges another love which was to be powerful and life-long—his love of cricket.[1] The prowess and vicissitudes of the R.M.A. team are lovingly recorded, and the full scores and bowling analyses of the matches between Sandhurst and The Shop are set out in full. He was at one time a member of the R.M.A. XI and later became—as far as his career allowed—a playing member of the M.C.C. He joined other fashionable Clubs, including the Free Foresters, and valued his member-

[1] It is said, apocryphally or not, that when as Governor of the Gold Coast he was called on to sign the indent for next year's cadet entry to the administrative service he wrote, 'The Secretary of State is requested, other things being equal, to assign to the Colony a reliable slow left-handed bowler.' This, if said at all, could have been said without intended humour.

ship and enjoyed sporting their ties; these, which lean towards the spectacular, became one of his foibles, and he enjoyed being chaffed over his 'rainbows'.

The book was published in 1900, three years after his return to The Shop from service overseas. For in 1893, shortly after being gazetted Lieutenant, he had been posted to Singapore, where he remained for three years. He was in charge of the Local (Malay) Submarine Mining Company of the Royal Engineers, and seems to have enjoyed his work.

He also enjoyed life in other ways, for he gained a colony-wide reputation for his cricket and for his love affairs. His cricket reputation was considerable, both as batsman and bowler, and he and another Sapper were the mainstay of the Straits Settlements side in a triangular tournament with Hong Kong and Shanghai. As to his love affairs, these seem to have been innocent enough, and may not all have been of his own making, for he was an incredibly handsome young man over whom young women tended to lose their heads; as indeed did older women in later years, for even as Governor of the Gold Coast he was apt to become the focus of their ardent attention.

One affair, however, developed into his first serious essay in romantic love; this never brought him domesticity or lasting happiness, for in the intimacy of marriage he seems to have been a difficult man, in youth as well as in middle age. With typical panache he fell in love with the seventeen-year-old daughter of his Commanding Officer, Colonel Wilfred May, a lovely fair-haired girl but of singular inexperience, whose knowledge of the world did not extend beyond protective parental care, and who was ill-equipped to set up house for a junior officer on a restricted income. The Colonel strongly disapproved, but her more susceptible mother enjoyed the romance, and helped them to elope in the French mail-boat homeward bound via Colombo. Here they were married, and Ceylon was the scene of their honeymoon. This was in 1895; she did not leave him until 1902, by which time three daughters had been born of the marriage, the eldest of which died in infancy.

By 1897 he was back at Woolwich, as 'Instructor in Fortification and Geometrical Drawing', and there he remained for
five years. This period of his life was characterized—as was a
later period—by absorption in his job, marred by growing
domestic unhappiness.

The duties of an Instructor in Fortification seem somewhat
remote in this atomic age, but it is known that he revelled in his
work and thought himself fortunate to be on the staff of the
place he loved. His enthusiasm for his profession and his natural
energy of mind found expression in a second book,[1] which was a
mild curiosity in its way, and about which a word will be
said presently.

But his marriage went steadily to pieces. He was at this time
of his life a meticulous, slightly humourless man, inclined to be
pompous. A tidy and methodical husband was married to a
woman who could not manage the house and who got in a
muddle with the tradesmen's bills. To make matters worse, she
was having to bring up two small children on a lieutenant's pay,
and friction inevitably developed when she bought clothes for
them out of money which had been given her to pay the butcher.
With a husband who loved precision and worshipped method
the constant disorder was bound to lead to an explosion.
Guggisberg's method of dealing with the situation was to give
her lectures on domestic economy and to take the payment of
the household bills out of her hands. Finally he did an incredible
thing. He brought his mother into the household to run it for
her.[2]

This would seem to disqualify him from performing any task
which required sensibility, tact or judgement, and one can only
suppose that the qualities needed to govern a colony are less
exacting than those required to be a successful family man.
No lively young girl could have been expected to stand for it.
Others over the next forty years must have suffered from his pre-
dilection for holding forth *de haut en bas*, and for deciding what

---

[1] *The Shop*, published in 1900, was already on the stocks, or had possibly been
written in Singapore.
[2] I owe these domestic details to the first Mrs. Guggisberg's younger sister.

was good for them, but these had not her remedy, which was to run away with a clergyman of the Church of England. She seems to have been a girl of spirit, with a penchant for elopement, in spite of her careful upbringing. Thus ended the episode which *Who's Who* records as 'm. 1st Ethel Emily Hamilton Way'. Guggisberg was left with two small girls.

His other activity during these five years was to apply his mind to the profession of soldiering and the defence of his country, and in 1903 there appeared, published by Thomas Nelson, a very odd book indeed. Its original title was *Modern Warfare*, and the author modestly hid behind the pseudonym of 'Ubique'.

The opening paragraph reads:

In the month of May, nearly thirty-five years after the great war between France and Germany in 1870, it is evident to the whole world that the two great military nations are preparing to fight each other.

Eventually war is declared, and on the 15th June over 350,000 German troops cross the boundary and invade France between Nancy and Belfort. . . .

The fictional setting of this book anticipated very closely the events of August 1914. and the fictional note is sustained throughout as the author follows the fortunes of a battalion and its officers over the Flanders fields on which he was to fight himself during the First World War. But the fictional device is used only to allow him to describe, in detail, the mobilization of an Army Corps and its operations against the enemy in the field. The book is liberally inset with maps, diagrams and sketches drawn by his own hand. Maps in fact abound, and the reader, who is addressed in the second person, is urged forward to their proper use, to the point of being told where he must keep his finger in the pages if he is to get the full benefit of the text. With the memory of the Second World War behind us, and the possibility of intercontinental nuclear warfare ahead, the actual operations smack by comparison of G. A. Henty or the *Boys' Own Paper*, with reconnaissance patrols and charges by cavalry presented in an aura of excitement and romance; doubtless they were a serious description, and a contribution to popular knowledge in their day. They reveal a strengthening of his lifetime's foible of purveying information and of allowing no detail to escape his readers'—or in later years his listeners'—attention. In 500 pages he makes sure that one misses nothing.

But the curiously prophetic quality of the book's fictional setting was sufficient to persuade Nelsons to republish it in a shilling edition after the outbreak of the First World War. Their preface is worth quoting:

This book was first published, under the title of *Modern Warfare*, in 1903, at the close of the South African War. The author is an officer of the Royal Engineers. He has succeeded in presenting in these pages the best popular description ever published of the organization of a modern army and its operations in the field.

When the book first appeared, it was commended by Marshal Oyama of Japan, and other distinguished soldiers.

In issuing a cheap edition at the present crisis, the publishers have not forgotten that since 1903 some minor details of military organization have been changed, and that motors and aeroplanes have been added to the engines of war. At the same time this book, with those qualifications, gives a true description of war as it is fought today.

The volume is of special interest at the present moment, from the fact that *it describes in detail a struggle in Belgium almost identical with that now raging*. Not only is the theatre of strife the same, but the combatants, the forces, in some cases the very generals whose operations are described in the pages of this book, are those actually engaged in the present Belgian campaign.

In 1900 he had been gazetted Captain. In 1902 his term as Instructor in Fortification came to an end, and he took the decisive step of his life. He was seconded by the Royal Engineers to special employment under the Colonial Office, on a Survey of the Gold Coast Colony and Ashanti, of which he was to be Assistant Director.

Army officers' personal records are not available, so that it is not known exactly how this came about. There is an obvious temptation to speculate about the connection between this move and his broken marriage. It was an age when men of his kind, a the end of an unhappy love affair, went to the African jungle to shoot lions. He possibly sublimated his pain by burying himself in professional work—he was essentially a surveyor and field engineer in spite of his devotion to the Army—and this took him to the West Coast of Africa. At the age of thirty-five he forged his first link with the country which was to hold him in thrall for the rest of his life, and of which, unforeseeably and probably to his own great astonishment, he was to become the greatest Governor.

# 2

## West African Surveyor 1902–14

AT the turn of the century the Gold Coast was largely un-mapped, as were all Britain's West African dependencies. Internal and even international boundaries were of the most tentative kind, dependent on crude landmarks, while dividing lines between chiefdoms and family lands were carried in the head, and rested on such disputable evidence as a particular tree, a bend in a stream or an empty gin bottle stuck in the mud of a river bank. Before the age of gold this had not mattered very much, for memories were tenacious, and when they failed or were challenged the resulting boundary disputes were greatly enjoyed by all concerned. But these pleasures could not persist into the industrial era. Disputes became too frequent, too complicated and too bitter to continue unchecked.

What happened in the absence of a map, said Guggisberg, was this:[1]

Mr. Prospector Smith would find good evidence of gold at a place say one mile south-west of a certain village. He would lease a block of land about two miles square from the chief, who would receive a substantial sum down on account of future royalties and rents. The lease would be drawn out in the most correct and verbose legal style, filed in the European judge's court by Mr. Smith, who would then sail for England to do business over his find. In his absence, along would come Mr. Prospector Brown, who would find gold a mile *south* of the village, and then go through the same procedure as Mr. Smith, not forgetting the substantial sum on account to the village chief. When Mr. Brown brings his lease to the court, the European judge naturally allows him to file it, as in the absence of a

[1] Lecture to the Liverpool Geographical Society, 3 March 1910.

map the man of justice cannot tell that most of the new concession has already been taken up by Mr. Smith.

The fun began—for the legal profession—when Brown's and Smith's respective companies begin developing the same piece of ground. And as this sort of thing was happening in scores of places, the law courts soon assumed a festive aspect. The native chiefs and their attendants, mothers, cousins, brothers, and aunts, loving a law case like natives do all over the world, turned up in force. The unfortunate mining companies paid heavily in fees, and the black barristers and solicitors began to grow fat and prosperous.

The problem had begun to be serious as early as the 1870s,[1] and by the end of the century had caused the Gold Coast Government to be dragged through a painful and humiliating experience. The Government's intentions were wholly proper and benevolent. They wished to protect the people of the Gold Coast both from 'unscrupulous prospectors and concession-mongering chiefs'.[2] Their solution was to draft legislation, in the Crown Lands Bill of 1894, modified to meet African opposition in a Bill of the same name in 1897, which proposed a tidy and sensible solution in terms of European concepts and on the evidence as it appeared to European eyes. African concepts, and the facts as known to Africans, were another matter. Had the two parties understood the way each other's minds were working the measure of disagreement between them might not have been so great. As it was there was no meeting of minds, the Government was thought to be expropriating ancestral lands, and the Aborigines' Rights Protection Society went into battle as the first organized opposition to the Colonial Government.

But the problem itself got steadily more acute, since prospectors continued to come not as single spies but in battalions, and were now being reinforced by large-scale capital, in turn assisted by the start of the railway from Sekondi in the direction of Tarkwa, which it eventually reached in 1901. The huge, unsavoury camps of the mining companies began to appear in the

[1] Gold mining among the Akans had of course been going on for centuries, but it was not until about this time that the survey problem became acute. See Professor David Kimble: *A Political History of the Gold Coast*, p. 15. The whole problem is admirably described in Ch. IX; see also pp. 30–1.

[2] Kimble, *Political History*, p. 355.

bush, and their steel dredgers would be encountered unexpectedly in inland rivers. Moreover timber began to supplement gold as a profitable extractive industry, which created
identical problems of concession and ownership, with the added
hazard that the bush would be denuded, with no plan or prospect of replacement, of its proudest trees.

Eventually good sense prevailed, and in 1900 a Concessions
Ordinance was enacted which gave the Government the substance of the powers it needed, while not too greatly outraging
African susceptibilities about land. Concessions were to be
controlled, and limited in extent, but the right of Africans, and
not of the Crown, was recognized in the granting of lands to
concessionaires, and the explosive concept of 'waste' lands, to
which the Crown would have an automatic right, was abandoned.

It was not a bad solution, however painfully reached. But it
was based on a premise of major importance, namely that the
land would be mapped, and that it would be possible to say
with precision who owned what, and which were the exact
limits of any concession. But systematic, as distinct from *ad hoc*,
survey work had not even begun when the Ordinance became
law.

The appointment of a new Governor in 1900 was to a large
extent owing to Governor Hodgson's inept management of the
Golden Stool controversy and the siege of Kumasi.[1] The choice
of his successor may well have been influenced by the urgent
need for a survey, for although he became one of the Gold
Coast's most statesmanlike governors in his own right Sir
Matthew Nathan was also a Royal Engineer, and in spite of his
preoccupation with the aftermath of the Ashanti disturbances
he began to put 'teeth' into the Concessions Ordinance by em-
ploying, in 1901, the services of a brother officer, Major Alan
Watherston, who had previously been in charge of surveys in
Nigeria. With the assistance of a party of 'sappers' Watherston
made a preliminary survey of the Survey problem itself, finding
incidentally that of the large number of individual concessions

---

[1] Kimble, op. cit., p. 320.

which had been mapped by private individuals or companies about 80 per cent had been wrongly demarcated and needed re-cutting. He returned to the Gold Coast in 1902 with the recent divorcé as his second-in-command. Under the aegis of the new Mines Survey Department they tackled the problem of mapping the Gold Coast in earnest.

It is appropriate here, at the risk of underlining the obvious, to refer to the Gold Coast's debt to the Royal Engineers. In these early years of the century there were three creative men working in harness together—Nathan, whose reputation as a Governor is still growing after more than sixty years; Watherston, who later became Commissioner for the Northern Territories of the Gold Coast and died there in 1909; and the young Guggisberg, who was destined to outstrip them both in reputation and achievement. This raises a curiously contemporary issue. There is evidence in the newly independent African States that among young, and necessarily inexperienced, administrators, holding down jobs in their twenties to which their European predecessors aspired in their forties, the best have frequently been trained not in administration but in a profession or a scientific technique. The training of an agricultural, co-operative or forestry officer is more rigorous and specific than that of a general administrator; it is in both the academic and colloquial sense of the word a 'discipline'; training in administration has not reached a comparable stage, for although the landmarks of a 'science' are being discerned it is doubtful whether in its present stage of development it is providing, on the ground as distinct from in the lecture theatre, the confidence which goes with the possession of one of the less ambiguous skills. We shall return to the point later, in considering Guggisberg as a Governor, but meanwhile it is an interesting reflection that it was engineers in the first decade of this century, and professional and technical officers in the sixth, who set the pace in good administration.

The next six years of Guggisberg's professional life were spent in a hard routine. From October to May, during the dry season,

he walked all over the forest country of the Gold Coast and
Ashanti, living in tents, huts and bush rest-houses. Each rainy
season he returned to London and worked on the results in the
Survey's drawing office there. A month at sea—to England and
back—was almost his only relaxation.[1]

In those days it was obligatory for European officers in the
public service to tramp all over the vast areas they helped to
administer. Their terms of employment compelled them to
spend much of their lives 'on trek', and in countries like the
Gold Coast, where the tsetse fly made it impossible to travel on
horseback except in a narrow radius from the coastal cities, and
where in any case the principal highway was a narrow, winding
bush track, there was literally no way of moving from place to
place except on foot. The worst rigours could sometimes be
avoided, or exchanged for the traditional imperial carriage, the
porters' hammock, but a surveyor had to work on his feet as he
navigated his way through the bush, and in these six years
Guggisberg must have trodden an astonishing amount of country.

It is now considered somewhat old-fashioned to speak of the
need for a government officer—and especially an administrative officer—to tour in this way, to sleep rough in villages and
to 'get to know his people'. Bureaucracy has sucked its victims
out of the bush, motor-cars and all-weather roads have turned
touring into a series of day trips or night stops, and needs and
circumstances have changed. The paternalistic government of
black men by white demanded that the priests of the cult should
know their people in a pastoral sense, visit them in their villages
and homes, speak to them in their own language and hold
palaver with them on their own ground. This was perhaps inclined to become something of a fetish, and the benefit which
the people and country derived from a good deal of long, elabor-
ate and extremely expensive touring has not always been articu-
lately expressed, nor could it always be said to have represented
a good day's work; nor indeed were many of the 'intelligence

---

[1] These and other details are largely taken from Guggisberg's lecture to the
Liverpool Geographical Society, already quoted; from an article he wrote for the
*Government Gazette* for 3 August 1907: 'A Brief History of the Mines Survey Depart-
ment; and from the Report of the Director of Surveys, 1906'.

reports', which were the most tangible fruit of these peregrin-
ations, always distinguished for sensitivity.[1] In general, however,
and with wise selection, the point of touring was obvious. Unhappily the priests and devotees have turned into civil servants,
and indigenous ones at that; the villages have become more
sophisticated; there is not the same need for an African administrative officer to 'get to know' Africans in the pastoral sense,
though in a country of social extremes he can drift very far
away from the common people; and the business of government nowadays can be conducted in a more bureaucratic way.
After all one would not in one's own English village welcome
the knock on the door which presaged the visit of a local civil
servant, paying a pastoral call; and in any case the romantic
element in touring, which counted for a lot with British officials,
means nothing to their African successors, who do not like
touring and do not see the point of it.

But in Guggisberg's day continual touring was a great advantage to an administrator and was of course at the very heart of a
surveyor's work. To the former the elusive pastoral concept of
'getting to know the people' was apt to seem an end in itself;
to the latter it was a by-product of his daily work. The point to
which this leads is that those six years of walking about the Gold
Coast undoubtedly helped Guggisberg to know the ordinary
people of the country very well, and that without this experience
he could never have become the Governor he was. On the one
hand he travelled the country with some 500 'natives'; although for the most part these were bush-clearers and carriers
there were a number who did more advanced work as survey
assistants, record keepers and foremen, and as time went by
Guggisberg gave rein to his schoolmasterish tendencies by going
out of his way to improve the skills of some and to teach others
the rudiments of what was going on.

At the same time he was in daily touch with village communities, on whom he was dependent for much of his food, for

[1] On the other hand in 1948, the year of revolution, the British Administration
was found to be completely out of touch with what people were thinking, and it was
argued at the time that this was due to the post-war decline in trekking.

local advice and for information about ancient boundaries and
new concessions; in these six years he had to get down to business with countless chiefs, which taught him how their minds
worked, how local communities were organized and how people
earned their living. And in all these contacts, whether with his
own carriers and clerks or with chiefs and farmers, there began
to develop within him a certain quality that in time distinguished him from many other able expatriates of his day—
an apprehension of the latent and unrecognized potentialities
of the people of this country. He was always, and quite sincerely, a greater optimist in this than the general run of Europeans; even the best-intentioned and most forward-looking of
them were never able to take the Gold Coast African quite as
seriously as Guggisberg did. It was an outlook which would have
been even more valuable to the Government at this point in
time (round about 1906) than in 1919–27, when he ultimately
found himself with supreme authority. Even the extra dozen
years of a more realistic outlook on African abilities might have
given the little extra momentum to the 'run-up' to Independence and have ensured a safer 'take-off'; though this is a
foolishly optimistic speculation, since in the year of revolution,
1948, twenty years after Guggisberg's Governorship, Europeans
of influence were still talking much as they had talked in 1906.

Something ought now to be said about the nature of Guggisberg's work as a surveyor. The country which the survey team
had to tackle was among the most unpromising in the world
from a professional surveyor's point of view, and Watherston's
and Guggisberg's achievement had a pioneering quality.

The usual way of surveying a country is by triangulation, which,
described roughly, is a system by which points 10 to 50 miles apart
are fixed accurately by measuring the angles of the triangles which
they form. These points are usually on high hills, and if from anywhere in the country you can see one of these points you can fix your
own position with accuracy. Triangulation, therefore, necessitates
obtaining a good view, and a good view is unobtainable in the Gold
Coast without the expenditure of great labour, and large sums of
money, in clearing the forest.

He was writing of country—the tropical forest belt of West
Africa—which has fascinated some Europeans and repelled
others. Guggisberg came to love it and thought it beautiful.
He liked the trees, particularly the odum, cotton-wood and
mahogany, which ran to heights of well over 200 feet, 'as clean
as the masts of a ship, and then from the top springing out huge
branches covered with orchids, fungus and parasites, the trunks
joined together by a matted, entangled mass of rope creepers,
varying from the size of a cord to that of a hawser'. He does not
actually speak of the 'impenetrable jungle', but he would have
been well justified in doing so, for his party had to hack its way
with axe and machete through a confusion of creeper, thorny
bush and matted undergrowth, day after day and month after
month, in order to get their survey traces, for which the winding bush paths were useless. The country is undulating, even
hilly in parts, but so dense is the forest and bush that to European eyes, accustomed to vistas, it gives the illusion of being
flat. To reinforce the impression of suffocation by the bush there
is the damp tropical heat, averaging 86 degrees, with high
humidity, all the year round, and as even Guggisberg says at
the height of his physical powers 'sapping the strength of the
strongest man, both mentally and physically'.

All this sounds sufficiently unattractive, but as those who
have experienced such country know this is only the beginning
of tribulation; the thing which is apt to swing so many Europeans' love-hate attitude to the African bush towards hate
rather than love is, quite simply, insects. Guggisberg's own
words on this subject may be quoted, not only for what they say
but for how they say it; for from about this time his cliché-
ridden style had begun to fall away, and his English becomes
cleaner and more agreeable to read.

In this cutting and measuring we encountered every variety of snake,
poisonous scorpions and other biting insects, pestilential swamps,
wide groves of thorny bush, and mosquito-haunted rivers. The work
was very dreary, the eternal green and gloom of the forest, un-
relieved by flowers, getting on the nerves after a few months. A little
relief to the monotony of the days was furnished by occasional

swarms of gorgeous coloured butterflies, in deserted sunlit clearings,
or by armies of verminous ants, several millions strong.

Or again:

Astronomical work was not very pleasant. The observer usually tied
a mosquito net over his head, well tucked into the collar of his coat,
and tied his sleeves tightly round his wrists with string to prevent the
numerous flying ants and other bugs crawling in. This added greatly
to the intense damp heat. As the instrument was kept coated with a
thin layer of very fine oil to ward off rust, it was usually half an inch
thick, shortly after you began observing, with writhing insects,
attracted by the light from the electric torch. In this writhing mass
one's fingers mechanically worked the screws as, with eye glued to the
telescope, one followed the stars in their courses.

Apart from all this, there was the question of malaria, and
occasionally of blackwater fever. During Watherston's preliminary survey of 1901 two British N.C.O.'s had died and one
officer had been invalided home. During subsequent tours of
duty it was common for all Europeans to be incapacitated by
'fever' during the closing months, and in one year Guggisberg
had ten attacks during one working leave in England. There
were no doctors available, and surveyors on active service had to
treat themselves, which could mean little more than dosing
themselves with quinine.

The method of surveying which had to be used in the absence
of open views was an extremely laborious one, which had been
employed in the United States Survey, and was known as 'long
traversing'. We mention it briefly merely to show that the entire
country had to be trodden—and cleared—step by step; there
could be no rapid progress from one point of eminence to another. At some identifiable place, usually a village, an astronomical bearing was taken; the party then set off in the general
direction required until it encountered an obstacle which prevented further progress in a straight line; this spot would be
marked, and the party would proceed to hack its way forward
at an angle to its previous line of progress, measuring with a
steel tape as it went; this would go on for five or ten successive
days without a break, until another village or identifiable place

was reached, completing a subsection of the traverse. Distances and angles would then be calculated so as to give the distance between the two villages in a straight line, and this calculation would be checked at night by an astronomical bearing, the delights of which have been described. No careless work was permitted. 'We went in for great refinements, such as taking the temperature of the tape every time it was laid down, and correcting for the expansion of metal due to heat. . . .'

Even the layman can see that the greater part of the work was exhausting and extremely monotonous. The cutting was done, with axes and machetes, by gangs of fifteen to twenty men. With a party in good working order 'a mile a day was very good work, and that meant continual cutting from sunrise at 6.0 a.m. until 5.0 in the afternoon, with an hour's break for the mid-day meal'. Today the imagination boggles at traversing the forest belt of the Colony and Ashanti, from north to south and from east to west, at the rate of a mile a day. The Europeans found the usual consolations of men who choose to do that kind of work—the open-air life, if that is not a misnomer in tropical forest, the hard physical routine, the relaxation of the evening camp, the well-earned wash, drink, meal and smoke; they had little else to enjoy.

Leadership in these conditions is a severe test of character, and the technical supervision and co-ordination a test of ability, for several parties would be working simultaneously on different parts of the survey, and there were in one season six Royal Engineer officers, fifteen N.C.O.'s, thirty Australian and New Zealand surveyors and no fewer than 600 Africans on the Survey's strength. The average number of Europeans, however, was about thirty-five during the first three seasons, tapering off sharply as the Survey approached its conclusion.

At home, in the English summer, Guggisberg's work was hardly less arduous, for although he was nominally on leave he was at work in the London office within a few days of arriving and gave himself very little rest. There is unfortunately more than a suggestion that he already belonged to the noble army of martyrs, who enjoy being the slaves of duty while others are relaxing, and such people can be very irritating. There is for example a hint of smugness in his statement that during the wet season 'the Director and Assistant Director are at work in the London office, the remainder of the staff being on holiday'. On his first leave after he himself had become Director the 'loads' which had to be taken from his house to the waterside were so excessive that the P.W.D. sent him a bill for the cost of transport over and above the normal entitlement for an officer going on leave. This produced from him an extremely angry letter in which he pointed out self-righteously that most of the loads in question were things he required for his work in London, adding that for him leaves were merely an extension of his work. Such 'holier than thou' attitudes are rarely popular, though they can be forgiven more easily in some people than in others. They rarely occur among men with demanding family ties, and this was probably part of the explanation in his own case. It is probable that he was happier immersed in work he loved in the drawing office than wrestling with an intractable family problem.

On the other hand, the work had to be done, and one can only sympathize with Watherston and Guggisberg over the way they had to do it; for not only were they expected to work while others rested, but for the period of their leave they were on half pay. In his report for 1906 (to anticipate) Guggisberg draws attention to this in a dignified and—to do him justice— relatively uncomplaining way, pointing out that the only solution would be a significant increase in staff; which was, in the context of the time, impossible. One notes, as so often, the wide gap between what was expected of the early pioneers and of their pampered successors in the early days of independence.

Such was Guggisberg's life for his first three years on the Coast. The next three had a different flavour, partly because on his return for the 1905–6 season he became Director of the Survey (at the age of thirty-six), Watherston having been appointed Chief Commissioner for the Northern Territories, partly because he brought out his second wife.

In 1905 Decima Moore was a musical comedy actress and concert singer of some reputation. At thirty-four she was two years younger than Guggisberg, though professionally she may have been 'over the hill'. She had been born into a theatrical family, being as her name implies the tenth child, the daughter of Edward Henry Moore and Emily Strachan. Two of her sisters, Ada and Eva, achieved modest fame on the legitimate stage. Decima was the musical one, possibly the last 'Savoyard' to survive.[1] She had played the first Casilda in *The Gondoliers* at the Savoy in 1889, at the age of eighteen. 'One of the several newcomers to the Savoy Company for *The Gondoliers* was delicious Decima Moore', writes Leslie Baily in *The Gilbert and Sullivan Book*, and page 309 is graced by a contemporary sketch of Decima looking indeed delicious. It is interesting that her first appearance on the stage was in the lead, and on a major theatrical occasion. At seventeen she had written to Sullivan for an audition, got it, and had impressed both him and Gilbert. In Mr. Baily's book she describes rehearsals under Gilbert's stern discipline and tells how a sympathetic smile from Sullivan rescued her at the last moment from stage fright on the opening night. By the time Guggisberg met her she had also sung at some of London's principal concerts, at the Queen's, St. James' and Albert Halls.

It is not known how they met. Although Guggisberg was almost excessively devoted to his work, and his business in London was to draw maps, he was entitled also to some leave, and the tradition of the Army in Edwardian days, especially for an officer who had worked for eight months in the circumstances we have just described, was to go on the Town. As a younger man Guggisberg did not disdain the bright lights, nor the charms of attractive women; these for their part were disposed throughout his life to be more responsive, and their propensity to meet him more than half way was, even in the days of his Gold Coast Governorship, the source of gossip which probably did him an injustice. It is not difficult to see him (though this is mere speculation) as the Edwardian stage-door gallant. At any

[1] She died in February 1964.

rate he appears to have repeated the whirlwind tactics of Singapore, or possibly to have had them practised upon him, for by
the next dry season Decima was in Accra, and by the New Year
she was with him under canvas, sharing the ants and mosquitoes,
in the Ashanti bush, an odd circumstance for a London actress
on the fringe of fashionable society. This marriage, unlike his
first one, dogged him for the rest of his life. The phrase is not
inept, as will become clear.

The wedding was a civil one, and was held at the Registry
Office at Staines on 15 August 1905. Decima, although
she disregarded the fact in *Who's Who*, was not in fact Decima
Moore, but Decima Walker-Leigh, divorced wife of Cecil
Ainslie Walker-Leigh, by whom she had had a son.[1] The fact
that both parties to the contract were divorced no doubt ex-
plains why a wedding tailor-made for Hanover Square took
place in a suburban registry office. The two witnesses were
Decima's sister Ada and, a little surprisingly, Arthur Conan
Doyle. Conan Doyle was a close friend of Guggisberg at the time;
among other things they had played cricket together, appearing
at Lords on one occasion for the Authors versus the Actors, one
of the more curious dividends of *The Shop* and *Modern Warfare*.
With the onset of the dry season Captain and Mrs. Guggisberg
were on board an Elder Dempster vessel from Liverpool to
Accra.

With Guggisberg's promotion to the Directorship of the
Survey the base of operations was moved from Sekondi to Accra.
There seem to have been two reasons for this. First, the so-
called Mines Survey was gradually developing into a normal
territorial survey, and once the back of the work had been
broken in the principal concession areas, centring on Sekondi,
the capital city was its natural headquarters; and secondly because Sekondi was in those days unhealthy, and the sickness
records of the survey teams, even at base, had been bad; the
Report of the Mines Survey for 1906 reports a dramatic improvement after this move.

---

[1] He entered the Royal Navy, and in later years was friendly with Guggisberg's
own daughters.

The party was housed in the old officers' mess and some of the soldier's living quarters on the Accra Cantonments. Money was tight and the work went forward on a 'do-it-yourself' principle; for example, even the skilled members had to spend many months adapting the buildings, and making shelves, pigeon-holes and map drawers out of old packing cases or anything else they could lay their hands on. This rather parsimonious principle, as it would appear in these more affluent, or perhaps more extravagant, days, extended to the Survey's London office, for one learns that in 1906 the Director himself had to hire an empty flat at 68 Buckingham Gate, furnish it with hired furniture and to start work within a few days of arriving home.

Not far from the new headquarters of the Survey he and Decima set up house in a bleak and ugly spot. Today the Accra Cantonments are a normal garden suburb, their only unusual feature being that a name so redolent of the British Raj should survive in this contentious *milieu*; perhaps nobody in Ghana knows what it means. Shrubs, lawns and flowers are sustained, at a high cost in man-hours, by the hoses and watering cans of countless garden-boys; cars purr along a curious maze of tarred roads in which the novice can get lost almost as easily as in the Ashanti bush; the only pedestrians to be seen are domestic servants and their numerous progeny. In 1905 it was otherwise. The low ridge some five miles from the town was bare and red, with the eternal laterite of West Africa. The few houses looked at each other across featureless scrubby grass. The only hint of suburbia to come was to be found in the lightly adumbrated compounds, the principal feature of which was a large circle of white-washed stones outside the front door, as of a Wimbledon villa retired from the road, within which a few African mari-golds fought the sun. The great days of the T-model Ford lay ahead, which was perhaps as well, for otherwise the Canton-ment residents would have lived their lives in a cloud of red dust; suburban traffic was based on the horse and the ox. The only relief to the eye lay in a distant glimpse of the ocean, beyond and to the east of the town.

In this uninviting spot Decima set up house with astonishing zest and delight. Indeed, she was at her best on this first tour, when everything was fresh and interesting to her. There were no regrets, no looking over the shoulder to metropolitan pleasures. She took each day as it came and enjoyed them all. She delighted in improvising furniture out of packing cases, disguising the worst eyesores with cheap cottons purchased in the Accra market and disposing their few possessions to look as attractive as possible. Her only active misery was not for herself but for her piano, which had to endure the damp heat and mould of the coast. She created a home as charming as the place allowed. It was the only home they ever had.

All this we know from *We Two in West Africa* (Decima Moore and F. G. Guggisberg),[1] which was published by Heinemann in 1909, when their first spell in the Gold Coast was behind them. The book is what its title might imply—a very feminine and slightly rapturous account of a new experience, when her delight in her new husband was echoed in her pleasure in all that she saw and heard. The title is a little misleading, as is her husband's introduction:

This is a most irritating book to read.

My wife wanted to write an account of her travels—I wanted to write an account of mine. My wife was a newcomer and saw the novelty of things. I was a fairly old inhabitant and had grown accustomed to living in strange surroundings. My wife kept notes— I did not.

This book in fact may either be described as experience looking on things through new glasses, or as a fresh receptive mind regarding the 'Coast' with the eyes of experience.

'Misleading' because the book seems to be Decima's entirely; but this does not detract from it, for it shows both Decima and the marriage at their best. She probably owed some of her shrewder comments, and there are a number, to her husband, but it is obvious that she was observant, interested and as Guggisberg says 'receptive'. Though the style would not be acceptable in these days of tauter and more disciplined writing,

---

[1] She could never bring herself to renounce her public name, and in later years called herself, with dubious authority, Decima Moore-Guggisberg.

there are excellent descriptions not only of such matters as fetishes and funerals, but of the processes of mining and surveying. For although we hear all about the voyage from Liverpool to the Coast, and the home-making on the Accra Cantonments, most of the book is an account of a three-month trek from Sekondi to Accra, via Kumasi. In the conditions of the time this was quite a formidable journey for any European woman to undertake, and in a number of places she was the first white woman the local people had ever seen. Even in Kumasi she was only the third.

The purpose of the trek, so far as the Survey was concerned, was to align district administrative boundaries with tribal affiliations; to delimit a number of gold-mining companies' concessions; and to determine the boundary between the Colony and Ashanti. The party started off from Sekondi by train, but left it at Tarkwa and took to the bush, from which point Decima lived very much as her husband had done during his first three years, except that she was usually carried by hammock over the worst parts. They made their way through Dunkwa and Obuasi to Kumasi, turned south, spent some time at Bimpeta, crossed the river Prah and settled down in a bush rest-house for four weeks at Abetifi. This was one of Guggisberg's principal objectives, and from this centre he carried out an exciting pioneer survey of the Kwahu mountains. Moving on, they eventually emerged into relative civilization at Aburi, where Decima comments, 'When Accra possesses a few motor-cars Aburi will probably become a popular week-end resort for Europeans.' She could hardly have foreseen that it would become such for the Ghanaian Osagefyo.

Tracing the route on the map today, and imagining the circumstances of 1905, it was a considerable feat for someone whose life until a few months previously had been in metropolitan society and on the London stage. But she was always a woman of initiative and determination, as her later career in war-time, which she fashioned for herself, was to show, and in 'her' book she writes with no hint of the self-centredness and self-aggrandisement which was subsequently to wreck the marriage. In

West Africa she was the simple and admiring enthusiast, for
her husband, for the men who worked for him, for the ordinary
people of the country and above all for the Empire whose
benevolent might sustained the whole enterprise.

At this time no one—not even his ambitious wife—could
have remotely imagined that Guggisberg would become Governor of the country he was mapping out. These, however, were
the crucial years which made the unexpected outcome possible.
The exercise of responsibility and the employment of a considerable skill gave him authority and stature; but this has
happened to thousands of men. The more significant aspect of
the preparation was his growing awareness of the people of the
country and a deepening conviction that their potentialities
were underrated by the colonial power.

In the first place he liked them. One engaging aspect of his
feeling towards them is that he thought they deserved to be
taught to play cricket, and he sent home for the very considerable apparatus required for this new *ju-ju*. Ostensibly, according to his own account and Decima's, he thought it would
counteract the boredom of his own party with the idle evenings
in the bush and that, in a wider context, it would sublimate the
pronounced tendency of tribes and villages to bicker with one
another. Inwardly no doubt he was worshipping his own gods.
Anyway he got Africans playing cricket against each other, and
both his wife and some of his surviving friends seem to have
believed, a little naïvely perhaps, that this was a powerful
weapon with which to keep the *Pax Britannica*.

But the schoolmaster began to appear in more serious aspects
of life than house-matches. He was not content to see the
'natives', as he called them in accordance with the usage of the
time, as mere labourers or 'hands'. His itch to educate found
its first expression on the members of his own survey gangs. He
eyed them sharply, picked out the promising ones, and started,
while still on trek, to instruct them in his own craft. 'Several
. . . became quite good surveyors, and one or two went as far as
picking up a little field astronomy.' As time went by he became

more selective in recruiting, and tried to catch them young, just after they had left the Government schools, 'where', he remarks sadly, 'they had acquired a large amount of learning, often, however, of a parrot-like nature'. Thus began one of his abiding dislikes—of education which was not rooted in vocation; and one of his most insistent determinations—to draw African education away from the literary and largely meaningless form in which the mission-schools had cast it. Meanwhile there was a strictly practical aspect—'By means of these natives we were able to fill in the details of the country between the framework lines by means of compass surveys very cheaply.' He did not stop at the promising educated boys. Among the labourers he was equally careful in picking out potential foremen of gangs, and giving them as much responsibility as they could carry.

None of this sounds very startling today, but it was unconventional in the West African colonies in the early 1900s, and caused a certain amount of head-shaking among Europeans. As we shall see later, he never accepted social equality as between Europeans and Africans, any more than a good housemaster accepts equality with his boys. None the less, he was ahead of his time.

Before he left the country he submitted a Report on the need for 'a Survey School for West African Natives from all Colonies', which would serve not only the Survey Departments but the P.W.D., Railways and Marine. He was not impressed with Africans who had received their training overseas.

I received a considerable number of applications from Natives who had been trained in England and regret to say I found the majority of them I tried quite unreliable, their work by no means corresponding to their certificates.

By contrast he developed a high opinion of the men he had trained himself:

On embarking for England in July I left three Native Surveyors each with a party of 8 carriers with instructions to fill in certain blank spaces existing on the map with accurate compass surveys. One . . . . not only did first-class compass work but got over an unexpected amount of country.

His appointment ended at the close of the 1907–8 tour of duty. After he became Director the emphasis of his own work had shifted from surveying (apart from the long trek recorded in *We Two in West Africa*) to map-making, which had previously had to be neglected because of the urgency of sorting out the muddle over the concessions, which 'precluded serious attempts at map-work until 1906'. He accords very high praise to a certain Captain Symons, who 'took over the management of field survey work and left me free to tackle the production of the Colony map'. Rough provisional maps had been drawn by Guggisberg himself on earlier tours, but he claims no merit for these, saying that they were 'rapidly put together at home by a tired and overworked staff'. His work had been both assisted and complicated by the establishment of the Colonial Survey Committee, which drew up a comprehensive plan for mapping British Africa; assisted because there was now the satisfaction of knowing that he was working within a master plan; complicated because the Survey Committee decided on a scale of 1/250,000, whereas his previous work had been on 1/100,000. He approved the change from a technical point of view, but remarked that it was 'unfortunate that the only people the change should have bothered were those who had made most progress'.

After he and his staff had put their results on paper in the drawing office, the map-makers, Messrs. W. & A. K. Johnston of Edinburgh, were able to engrave and publish over forty sheets of maps in four colours on a scale of one inch to two miles. It was by far the greatest achievement of its time in any African colony. In addition to mapping nine-tenths of the Colony and one-quarter of Ashanti, and laying down a framework for the rest, over three hundred mining or timber concessions had been surveyed, and delimited by eight-foot avenues cut through the bush or forest. Every one was marked with iron posts and name plates, bearing the company's name. 'We charged the mining companies £50 per thousand fathoms for cutting their boundaries, which was far less than they could have done it for themselves, and we tied the survey of each concession on to the framework which I have previously described. . . .'

The entire cost of the six seasons' work was £135,000, of which £50,000 was recovered from the mining companies; even the smallest item of expenditure was accounted for by a triple receipt.

This net expenditure of £85,000 is a big sum for a Colony the size of the Gold Coast. That a considerable amount of expenditure was necessary for the sake of the mining interests goes without saying, but that this Colony should have at once combined the mines survey with that of the whole country, instead of deferring the latter to a later period for the sake of present £.s.d., but at a greatly increased ultimate cost, was surely a wise and far-seeing step. The result is that the Gold Coast is in the proud position of being the first of our African colonies to possess a complete and modern map.

In the year before he left the country the connection with the Mines was in fact officially ended, and a new Survey Department was formed, which he was able to leave as a fitting memorial to his six years' work. It was based on proposals which he himself had submitted. His work had originally arisen from the urgent, but narrow, purpose of surveying the mining concessions, but it quickly became apparent that expert surveying, with appropriate equipment and training schemes, was a national necessity for a variety of other purposes. There was need for a normal topographical survey, quite apart from the concessions; there were the large towns, in which he became increasingly interested and to which in his last year he gave a great deal of time; and traces needed to be cut for such purposes as water supplies and roads. On his return to England the Colonial Office recognized his services by the award of the C.M.G., and the Army by promotion to the rank of Major.

There follows an interlude of rather less than two years at home, of which little remains on record. Professionally, he was returned to regimental duties and posted to Chatham, where he was put in charge of a survey of a very different terrain, and for a very different purpose. The terrain was the mild and un-emphatic countryside round Chatham, and the purpose was the coastal defence of England as envisaged in 1908–10. Clearly he did his work well, for on 31 March 1910, the Commander-in-Chief, Eastern Command, minuted to the Secretary of the War Office:

As the reconnaissance work executed by Major Guggisberg of the country round Chatham is much above the average I submit his name for record if considered desirable.

Domestically, things were more complicated.

In the first place he was the father of two small girls, and this was not an easy situation for a man of thirty-three on the staff of the R.M.A., still less for one spending eight months of the year in the forests of the Gold Coast. A home had to be found for them. This was achieved through the interest of a brother officer, who introduced him to a Mrs. de Winton Corry and her daughter. The Corrys lived in a large country house near Farnborough, called Yateley Hall, and an arrangement was made whereby the girls went to live with them.

This *ad hoc* plan, made after his first wife had left him and before his departure for the Gold Coast, struck roots, and Yateley remained their home until shortly after his death. It also became his own home, in so far as he ever had one and in the absence of the home-making instinct in his wife, and it remained so under Miss Corry's regime, after her mother's death. Not that it was ever much more for him than a *pied-à-terre*, even after his retirement from the Gold Coast, when he used to visit it more frequently. For during the whole of his working life, from the age of thirty-three, his bases in England were in London, either in some London office of the Gold Coast or Nigeria, or in the Army and Navy Club. His spiritual home, of course, was in West Africa.

It cannot be denied that he fought shy of his responsibilities as a parent. He visited his daughters when they were young and entertained them in London when they were grown up. But they did not much occupy his mind, which was given almost exclusively to his work. He never took them to the Gold Coast, even when he was Governor.

So far as his second marriage was concerned, the honeymoon tour of 1905–6 was soon forgotten, and it provided no foundations. Decima was ambitious for him, and as we shall see played a large part in his advancement to a governorship. But they were both difficult people to live with, alike in their energy and egotism, but differing largely in their interests and wholly in their attitudes. For all his faults, which were those of the pedant and 'do-gooder', his general approach to life was one of service, and embraced a genuine love and understanding of a 'backward' people. She for her part was in the beginning genuinely keen on his work, as well as his career, and she was, as genuinely, fond of the Gold Coast people. But she stood in her own light, and in his days of eminence she stood, or tried to stand, in his. She had to take centre-stage, and friction was inevitable. How soon this developed it is now difficult to say, but by middle-age the relationship had turned completely sour, and she hated him.

But this is to anticipate. In his days as a surveyor all we know is that their absences from each other were prolonged, that they never bought a house or settled down even to the limited extent that West African expatriates could hope to do in those days, and that she and the children of the first marriage never accepted one another. The component parts of his domestic life never fused, and he, his wife and his daughters lived in relative isolation from one another. A younger brother had died in Canada and he had no near relations. Gordon Guggisberg was in fact a lonely man.

Early in 1910 the Colonial Office offered him the post of Director of Surveys, Southern Nigeria. Negotiations with the Army Council were successful, and Guggisberg himself accepted with alacrity; he was accordingly appointed with effect from 1 April 1910 at a salary of £900 p.a. plus £180 duty allowance. The Colonial Office wrote to him officially on 21 March saying, *inter alia*:

Your appointment, to which it has been ascertained that the Army Council will raise no objection, would be for five years in the first instance, and during this period would carry no claim to pension or gratuity under the local regulations.[1]

The pension difficulty was to recur, and towards the end of his life was to become a source of bitterness.

His five years were cut short by the War of 1914–18, but the period during which he actually served was significant for two things—a growing professional competence and reputation; and the clear emergence of personal ambition, which brought him up against the formidable Lugard, who with the instinctive appreciation of the pot for the kettle thought him an 'empire builder'.

Professionally his task was perhaps more onerous and certainly more disagreeable than in the Gold Coast, where he had started with a clean slate and taken part as second-in-command, and later as Director, in a pioneering job. In Nigeria he inherited an unsatisfactory Survey Department, of whose standards he thought little and much of whose work he scrapped and did all over again. The new broom is rarely a popular figure with the majority, but in this instance Guggisberg seems to have reinvigorated the Department without meeting undue opposition or unpopularity except at the top of the Administration, i.e. from Lugard. He had never lacked self-confidence, and now at the age of forty-one he took hold of the Directorship of Survey with the same authority and aplomb which he later brought to his two governorships.

His horizons were widening, and his growing knowledge of his own powers was soon to bring restlessness and frustration. But for the moment he got on with his work with his usual single-minded devotion. Few men who have done a job well in one place can resist the temptation to apply the same methods in another, and the Department under Guggisberg came to bear a strong family resemblance to the Mines Survey in the Gold Coast. This was no disadvantage, however, as the southern Nigerian terrain was similar and the technical methods of sur-

[1] This part of the chapter relies largely on Guggisberg's personal file, happily discovered in a Lagos Ministry, there being nothing about him in the Nigerian Federal Archives. See also an article by Peter Cobb in *West Africa*, 7 October 1961 which does not however give its sources.

veying such country had been brilliantly justified. (He was less successful, years later, when he applied what he had learnt in the wider sphere of governorship in the Gold Coast to a West Indian Colony. There his job involved human awareness rather than a specific skill.) He re-equipped the Department, re-organized its work and brought out a party of Royal Engineers to stiffen it; above all he conveyed his own energy and enthusiasm to the existing staff, and got them out of their offices and into the bush. From his own office there began to pour a stream of memoranda, instructions and exhortations which were finally brought together in the form of a Handbook, which was perhaps his most significant written work.

The *Handbook of the Southern Nigerian Survey and Textbook of Topographical Survey in Tropical Africa* is Guggisberg's professional testament. In a brief character study such as we are attempting here it would be out of place to summarize or comment upon the technical substance of the book, which is in any case imperfectly understood by the present writer. Its technical excellence may be taken for granted and is supported by professional colleagues.[1] What is impressive to the layman is the perspective in which the technical work is now seen, the realization that 'administration' is an indivisible whole and that it must be rooted in sociological fact. Guggisberg's own introduction to his *Handbook*, written in August 1911 from the Southern Nigerian Survey Office, Carlton House, Regent Street, is engagingly modest:

As a textbook it does not pretend to be complete, but rather to adapt existing systems to what may fairly be described as very different local conditions, both climatic and topographical.

But the Director-General of Ordinance Survey at the Colonial Office (Sir Charles Close, another ex-Royal Engineer) is more generous:

The duties of all members of the staff were strictly defined and, in particular, sensible rules were laid down as to the relationship of Survey Staff with the Civil Administration. Much attention was

[1] Mr. Vincent Roth, O.B.E. (see p. 296n.), in sending me some general information about Guggisberg's Governorship of British Guiana, paid tribute to the immense help this Handbook gave him when he was himself a surveyor in that country.

paid to the treatment of villagers; unpaid labour was forbidden; all goods were to be bought and paid for at the recognized rate, and great care was to be exercised not to damage crops. On the technical side emphasis was laid on the standards of accuracy, on tests and reliability and on the uniformity of the work. *They were model instructions and the Survey of Southern Nigeria was a model survey*, and the results fully justified the care and ability which the Director of Surveys exercised in every detail of administration. (Author's italics.)

The code of professional ethics, hinted at by the Director-General, was in fact an important feature of the book. The Headmaster may be heard again in such words as these:

It cannot be too strongly impressed on all members of the Department that every consideration should give way to the one great and paramount object of turning out good work, which can be thoroughly relied on by the public. . . . The surveyor should resist all temptation to gain fictitious credit by departing from the strict line of duty. It may be difficult for him to refrain from injudicious haste when he knows that some of his brother surveyors are working with greater rapidity than himself, and are likely to gain more credit than himself because they happen to have a greater show of work, but his duties appertain to his own work only, and if he is careful to make it as good as possible it will always be a credit to him and to the Department.

Moralizing of this kind is no longer as acceptable as it was in 1910. A more materialistic and cynical world is made uncomfortable by such censures, and thinks it knows better. Guggisberg's sermon to surveyors, delivered shortly before the First World War started to erode such an approach to life, is characteristic of the Victorian moralist, a role which he himself sustained unflaggingly throughout his later years. What was needed to make a whole man of him, and what alas was conspicuously lacking, was a solid Victorian family background. Meanwhile he was developing every attribute of the Victorian family man except the domestic pulpit. Decima was living her own life in London, and would hardly have appreciated his efforts to improve her any more than his first wife had done; and his children were growing up as strangers to him.

Within a year he had got the Southern Nigerian Survey

organized to his satisfaction, and his thoughts began to turn to new worlds to conquer. It is clear that he was beginning to suffer from a special kind of frustration, familiar to many professional and technical officers before and since, namely a feeling that he could run the country better than the administrative élite. That the Colonial Administrative Service was a privileged élite there can be no doubt. In terms of modern management selection their qualifications were nil. Their presumed professional skill was administration, but they had no training in this; indeed no such training was available in Britain.

They learnt administration from their seniors on the spot, who had not been taught it either. Equipped with the prejudices of the first Resident or District Officer under whom they served, they made their way in their profession by intuition and personal qualities, and governed the natives according to the tenets and attitudes of their public schools and universities, the imponderable attributes of which had been the cause of their selection. Some wise, humane and occasionally great men emerged from this odd process, but the colonies also suffered, then and until the end, from men who governed them because they themselves came from the British governing class, and found a satisfaction, which would have been denied to them elsewhere, in being fathers to their people. Men are not, of course, trained to be fathers either—they pick it up, with good results and bad, but a procedure which is acceptable in the ordinary relationships of the human race is not necessarily appropriate for the public service, and as many indifferent fathers emerged in the Colonial Administrative Service as in normal family life.[1]

Such men were infuriating to skilled technicians like Guggisberg, who had acquired an expertise by long training and were using it with visible results for the betterment of the countries in which they served, but who were excluded from the ranks of the 'heaven-born'; who indeed looked down upon them. For

[1] This is perhaps an inappropriate argument in a life of Guggisberg, who, as we have seen, was the most indifferent of fathers, though a magnificent 'Father to His People'.

there is no doubt about this either. It is a matter of recent re-collection that the departmental officer ranked as an N.C.O., and that commissioned rank was virtually unobtainable except by the mystical process that the Colonial Office considered appropriate to the needs of developing countries. In the fading years of the Colonial Empire professional and technical officers came into their own, and with political independence emerged as the men who really mattered. But in 1912, when Guggisberg was beginning to get restive, he was beating at the doors of a very tightly closed corporation.

In his heart of hearts Guggisberg knew two things; first that he believed in the potentialities of the native races whom Britain governed more than did the Administrative Service; and second that he was a more competent administrator than most of them. He was also ambitious, and somewhere in the back-ground he had an ambitious wife. Early in 1912, on the prin-ciple presumably that 'if you can't beat 'em join 'em', he applied for transfer to the Administrative Service. He received an acknowledgement from the Colonial Secretary's Office, Southern Nigeria, dated 22 April 1912:

Referring to your application for transfer to an Administrative appointment, I am directed to inform you that your application has been noted in the Colonial Office and will be considered with those of other candidates on the occurrence of suitable vacancies.

How many such vacancies occurred is not known, but two years later the War interrupted the presumed cogitations of their suitability for Guggisberg, and he finally joined the Ad-ministrative Service at the top, and by an unconventional route.

Meanwhile he set about the unedifying task of trying to improve his personal status in the position for which his superiors did consider him suitable. His opportunity came in the same year (1912), when he was asked to supervise the new Survey of Northern Nigeria in addition to his duties in the South. This task he took in hand on 1 August, shortly before going on leave; he was proposing to recruit new staff in England and return with them by boat on 27 November; their first assignment was to be in the tin-mining areas of the Jos Plateau, a high, bleak and occasionally cold part of the world as different from the gold-mining areas of the Ashanti forest as it would be possible to imagine.

As soon as he got home he wrote to the Secretary of State asking for financial recognition of these increased responsibilities, a detail which the authorities had apparently overlooked. He received this reply, dated 14 September:

I am directed by Mr. Secretary Harcourt to inform you that in consideration of your supervising the survey staff employed in Northern Nigeria and advising and assisting the Government of that Protectorate in all survey matters, he has, on the recommendation of Sir Frederick Lugard, approved of your being paid a temporary non-pensionable allowance of £15 per month as from the 1st November, 1912, pending consideration of the amalgamation of the Survey Departments of Northern and Southern Nigeria.

Guggisberg digested this for a week, then wrote protesting. The proposed allowance, he thought, was inadequate; it should be £25 a month. Further, he asked for the rank of Acting Surveyor-General of Nigeria (or alternatively of Northern and Southern Nigeria). 'I spoke to Sir Fredk. Lugard on the subject on Wednesday at Liverpool and he told me that I could say in my letter that although at the present time he was not prepared to recommend any permanent titles, yet he had no objection to my receiving the rank of Acting Surveyor-General.' He pointed out finally that he had been actively engaged on the Survey in the North since 1 August, and that the allowance should date from then and not from 1 November. In such disputations did the Colonial Office in London engage with its technical officers in 1912.

The Office turned down his financial demands flat, but yielded in the matter of a title, since Lugard had no objection. As a consolation prize they wrote to him on 5 November expressing the Secretary of State's appreciation of his services 'in connection with the recent Commission for the Demarcation of the Boundary between Southern Nigeria and Dahomey'.

In the event Guggisberg did not return with the minefields

party on the boat leaving on 27 November. He had to be given sick leave until 22 January 1913, and the reason was an ominous one. At the age of forty-three he was crippled by a thrombosis of the leg, and this was to recur and to cause him much misery in later years.

When he did return his efforts to advance his own position brought him into collision with Lugard, who liked to control his own empire and was not well disposed to others engaged in building theirs. Matters were made worse by Lugard's dislike, common among officers of line regiments, of the Royal Engineers. Mr. Peter Cobb quotes from Lugard's diary a comment on a visit to Lokoja, as early as 1898, to inspect a survey camp in charge of Watherston, Guggisberg's old chief in the Gold Coast:

This is not what I want. The fact is that like so many R.E.'s he thinks he can go one better than his orders. He seems to think that God made the R.E.'s first, and then, if not with their approval, made the rest of the world. I am therefore of the poorer clay, but I will have my orders obeyed nevertheless. . . .

Now, fourteeen years later, he turned an equally baleful eye on Guggisberg's activities. Although he had appointed Guggisberg and had approved, no doubt reluctantly, his title of Acting-Surveyor-General for the whole country, he resented his attempts to dig himself in in the North and to turn his acting position into a substantive one. He wanted to eject the R.E.s from the North and to replace them with civilian surveyors; and he wanted to cut Guggisberg down to size.

In a long and aggressive minute dated 4 November 1913 (on a document which has unfortunately been removed from the file) he writes:

I naturally proceed on the assumption that the Head of the Southern Nigerian Survey has plenty of work to do. He does no surveying at all as I understand, and this seems to me a pity. If he has his hands *full* as they should be in S.N. I cannot impose fresh duties on him in N.N. without detracting from his work in S.N. I do not wish to do this. I wish him to carry out the duties he was engaged in before, but at his strong desire I have secured for him the title of Surveyor-

General and the position of Advisor to the Government of Nigeria on Survey matters. I do not intend that this position should be a sinecure, while it must not interfere with the already full programme which presumably he has as Director of Surveys in S.N. . . .

The hostile note in this can scarcely be mistaken. Possibly he was annoyed with himself for having given way to Guggisberg's importunities, on the occasion when the latter had apparently pursued him to the boat in Liverpool and buttonholed him there. It is interesting that, assuming Lugard's observation to be correct, Guggisberg had at last withdrawn from field surveying; none the less, the minute is to say the least ungracious in view of the *Handbook* and the Director-General's encomiums upon it. But Lugard had not yet finished; he went on to reiterate the argument against giving Guggisberg the extensive powers in Northern Nigeria for which he had apparently been asking:

This is to constitute him Head of the N.N. Survey and is incompatible with the discharge of the duties of working Head in S.N. It would also make the Chief Surveyor in N.N. a mere subordinate. . . . If the Surveyor-General has time to undertake this, the work of his Dept. in S.N. must be quite inadequate to employ his time. Or he must turn over a part of them to someone else, which I do not desire.

Guggisberg was apparently shown this minute, for he comments on it in a letter to the Colonial Secretary (Lagos) on 15 January 1914, in mild and reasonable terms which carry more conviction than Lugard's petulant words:

In bringing the foregoing points to the notice of His Excellency I trust I have made it apparent that the Surveyor-General cannot hold himself responsible for seeing that identical surveys are followed, that surveys are co-ordinated, or that economy is observed, unless he is given general central control of the Survey of Nigeria.

This trivial battle dragged on, but was soon to be put in perspective by a greater one, for by the time Guggisberg's next leave came round the war clouds were gathering over Europe, and he never returned to Nigeria. And when he next met Lugard he could speak to him, as Governor of the Gold Coast, man to man.

.       .       .

In Guggisberg's career the spotlight is turned so brilliantly on his eight short years as Governor of the Gold Coast that one is tempted to see the whole of his previous life as a preparation for it. What did his time in Nigeria contribute to the process? It seems to have stirred his personal ambition; it gave him a taste of administrative responsibility on a larger scale than hitherto, for Nigeria is nearly five times the size of the Gold Coast; it caused him to measure himself against the Colonial Administrative Service, at a time when he was not daily, weekly and monthly tramping through the bush or working in a drawing office. It broadened his perspectives.

More intimately, and deeply involved with the question of ambition, it brought him to his mid-forties, and to a stage in his career when he either had to extend his reach or remain a surveyor all his life. He had the Army to fall back on, but regimental duties had lost something of their glamour in comparison with nation-building in Africa, with its colour, its responsibility and its *mystique*. In the background there was also Decima, born to be the centre of attraction and no more willing than he in her early forties to be cast in the part of a surveyor's wife. Her public, and her ego, expected something better.

But there was little he could do about it, and the War rescued him, as it rescued many a lesser man, from a personal dilemma. A dilemma heightened by an offer of supreme irony from the Colonial Office, to whom no suitable administrative appointment had occurred but who now, in mid-1914, proposed that he should become Director of Public Works in the Gold Coast Colony. He went on leave in 1914 on the assumption that this would be his next step, and he cannot have felt very cheerful about it; for though it represented promotion and was an established post it would have brought him no nearer to his administrative ambitions. Not in his wildest dreams could he have imagined that on his return to Africa he would indeed step ashore at Accra, and with Governor's plumes.

# 3

## The War and its Sequel

GUGGISBERG started his war ignominiously, by falling off a motor-cycle at Hyde Park Corner and injuring himself quite seriously. It happened on a lovely morning in late July, soon after he had got back to England on leave, when he had been to his Club to write two letters—one accepting the Directorship of Public Works in the Gold Coast, the other, as a corollary of this, resigning from the Army. With these letters in his pocket he set off to spend the rest of the day at Lords, using what was really an ordinary bicycle with one of the early 'auto-wheel' attachments. As he rounded Marble Arch the handlebars came loose and he was pitched into the road, sustaining a fracture of the base of the skull. He was taken unconscious to a private nursing home.

At the time he lost consciousness there was, of course, talk of war with Germany but the possibility was remote enough to have allowed him to resign his Commission and accept a civilian job; when he regained full consciousness, so slow was his recovery, the Retreat from Mons was already over. He at once became an extremely difficult patient, furious at having to lie helpless at this moment of supreme challenge, and when the nurses' backs were turned he risked serious injury by crawling out of bed and forcing himself first to stand and then to walk. So impossible did he become, and so successfully did he hoodwink the medical staff—professing to be in no pain when he was actually suffering agony—that he was discharged before he was fully recovered. His last act on leaving the nursing home was to tear up the two still unposted letters that he had written on his way to Lords.

It was not until 8 September, however, that his personal problems were solved, or at least shelved, by a letter from the Colonial Office:

I am directed by Mr. Secretary Harcourt to inform you that he has learnt from the War Office that it is desired that your services should be placed at the disposal of the Army Council, as soon as you are physically fit for service. Mr. Harcourt therefore regrets that it is not possible for him to proceed with your appointment as Director of Public Works in the Gold Coast Colony, and he is causing a communication to be addressed to the War Office with a view to your immediate restoration to your Corps.

In the circumstances you will be paid half the salary of your Nigerian appointment from the 23rd August inclusive, pending reabsorption into the Army.

But the spirit could not wholly overcome the weakness of the flesh, and it was not until 5 October that he was passed fit for service at home, or until 11 January 1915 that an Army Medical Board at Bournemouth finally declared him fit for active service. His accident had set him back five frustrating months.

Between these dates, however, he had been appointed Officer Commanding the 94th Field Company, Royal Engineers, of the 19th Division, one of the Divisions which made up Kitchener's new volunteer Army. It was a very junior appointment for an officer of his seniority, and of his responsible West African experience, but he appeared to accept the position with good grace and threw himself wholeheartedly into the work of transforming a couple of hundred civilians, without uniforms or equipment and lacking the most elementary amenities of Army life, into soldiers who could dig trenches and dug-outs, deal with barbed wire in the dark, and build emergency roads and bridges. Not until the early spring of 1915 did the Division receive its uniforms, equipment or arms; by 23 June, after an inspection by Kitchener himself, it was ready to go overseas. In fact, it embarked for France on 18 July, almost exactly a year after Guggisberg had fallen off his bicycle. Apart from the months of September and October 1916, when he was invalided home as the result of a serious illness, he spent the rest of the war with the British Armies in France, living out the imagined events of *Modern Warfare*, though in conditions of horror which no imagination could have encompassed in 1905.

His own baptism in war was bloody and brutal, though in the following years blood and brutality were to become the normal *milieu* of existence. No battle conditions in the Second World War approached the sub-human degradation of trench warfare, of life lived in a wilderness of mud and in the companionship of rats, or of 'losses' in terms of tens and even hundreds of thousands in apparently pointless attacks and counter-attacks over a few hundred yards of useless earth. Forty years later official historians were to justify some of the battles and losses in terms of overall strategy, and within the terms of the corporate madness which overwhelmed the human race in those years they were possibly correct. At the time, all that was apparent was the madness, unrestrained and indescribable.

The 19th Division, as part of the Indian Cavalry Corps, took part in the Battle of Loos in September 1915. On this occasion the role of the Corps was to stage a 'holding' attack on the northern flank of the main attack, while another Corps put in a similar holding attack to the south. Their task was thus subsidiary to the principal operation, but they lost over 4,000 men, mown down by machine-gun fire on the enemy's barbed wire, or just outside their own trenches. In the year 1915 the human mind had somehow to adjust itself to gruesome massacres of this kind, and in the Battle as a whole there were 60,000 casualties. Nothing was gained, and it was later reckoned a regrettable failure.

The enemy wire had not been adequately cut by the British artillery, and Guggisberg actually had some part to play in preventing an even worse shambles. He had personally surveyed the wire in front of his own brigade—an act requiring courage in the face of enemy sniping—and had reported to the Brigadier that the attack would be suicidal and should not be made; this advice was overruled. In spite of its utter failure orders came down that the attack was to be renewed, and late on the afternoon of September 25, the Commander, Royal Engineers, held a conference with the commanders of his field companies. Guggisberg protested in the strongest terms against any resumption of the attack, insisting that it would be simple murder. The C.R.E. was shocked by this and said it was no responsibility of the R.Es, but Guggisberg, with considerable moral courage, insisted on seeing the Brigadier himself, and so impressed him with the urgency of his protest that the attack was cancelled and a resumption of the massacre averted.[1]

This futile battle was followed by one of the wettest autumns within memory, which turned the whole sodden plain into a quagmire and flooded the trenches south of Neuve Chapelle. The Germans were superior in artillery and mortar fire, and in the monotonous daily attrition of trench warfare the job of the R.Es turned into one of repairing, at the dead of night, defences which were as rapidly destroyed the next day. These conditions were a test of physical and spiritual endurance, and Guggisberg, now in his late forties, was never really fit. The old trouble in his legs had caught up with him again, as had West African malaria. In this situation he began to reveal the qualities of leadership which were to win him rapid promotion in the next few years. He gained a reputation for severity, even for harshness, but as a slave-driver he drove himself hardest of all. It was always noticed that he never swore, in circumstances when a constant stream of bad language was the norm of conversation, for he appeared to feel that it was an unnecessary breach of good manners. But within the limits of these austerities, which set him a little apart, he was regarded as a human and friendly man, and was liked because he was constantly trying to check the Staff's enthusiasm for costly futile raids, which were supposed at the time to be useful for 'keeping up morale'.

In late November he was promoted C.R.E. of the 8th Division with the rank of Lieutenant-Colonel, and said good-bye to Kitchener's Army (one Company of which he had trained

---

[1] Information supplied, in a letter to Mr. F. P. Cobb, by Colonel R. F. A. Butterworth, who knew Guggisberg both in Singapore and on the Western Front. Colonel Butterworth adds: 'I am positive that his brave and independent action saved his Brigade from an appalling disaster.'

from its civilian days) to take command of the R.Es in a regular Division with a proud professional spirit.

This 8th Division had been in France since November 1914, but from the time Guggisberg joined it until the opening of the Battle of the Somme on 1 July 1916 it was not in any important engagement, though it was continuously employed in the static trench warfare of the time. Guggisberg seems, characteristically, to have used this period of comparative calm to devise a *R.E. Programme of Work to assist the Infantry in a Brigade Sector* which was later to receive commendation in the *History of the Corps of Royal Engineers*. He was always a man who believed in filling in his time usefully.

But behind the apparent lull vast preparations were going forward in the opposing armies for the opening of the Somme battles. Everybody knew that these were building up, and there was an undercurrent not only of subdued excitement but of eager optimism, which Guggisberg fully shared, for it was rumoured that this was to be the beginning of a major break-through. Unfortunately the Germans were equally busy, and as events proved somewhat more effectively, if the word is not out of place in describing the perpetual stalemate of the war on the Western Front.

The 8th Division, as part of III Corps, was to be involved in that part of the Battle of the Somme known as the Battle of Albert. On the opening day it was given the formidable task of an assault on a gentle spur crowned by the village of Ovillers, which German competence and thoroughness, unknown apparently to British Intelligence, had transformed into a fortress. The Division was engaged in the Battle for one day only, but it was a day of ugly tragedy which decimated its ranks, for in spite of incredible gallantry the attack failed with crippling losses.

Although in places the troops of the Division got into the German trench system, they were driven out again, and by evening the whole Division was back where it started. Guggisberg's own plans had been based on keeping his R.Es together, ready to move quickly to any captured trenches and to 'reverse' them against their late owners, but these plans had to be abandoned as his men were needed for emergencies. One of his field companies had to be sent up to hold the front of the 70th Brigade, which had been almost wiped out, with only a hundred men left alive; and in the evening his other two companies, which till then had not left their positions of assembly, were sent up to the front to assist in bringing in the wounded. The Ovillers spur remained in German hands, occupied only by British dead and dying.

That night the Division was pulled out of the line.

In a single day's fighting on 1 July 1916, it had lost over 5,000 men. The Battles of the Somme dragged on until 16 November, by which time the British had suffered *400,000* casualties. Whether the gains compensated for these appalling losses—if indeed such macabre arithmetic has any meaning— is still a matter of opinion among military historians.

On 22 July, Guggisberg, temporarily a physical wreck, fell seriously ill with pneumonia and pleurisy, complicated by malaria, but was sufficiently recovered to go back to England on sick leave for the months of September and October. On recovery he was appointed C.R.E. of the 66th Division.

The 66th (2nd East Lancashire) Division was a Second Line Territorial Division raised in the autumn of 1914, and when Guggisberg joined it was stationed at Colchester. He went with it to France in February 1917, and his ability as a trainer of troops is recorded in the *History of the East Lancashire Royal Engineers*:

On arrival in France the field companies got their first chance to practise the long, detailed, but well thought out maxims of the C.R.E., Lt.-Col. F. G. Guggisberg.

This was wholly in character. Whenever he had made his appreciation of any set of circumstances, in military or civilian life, it was not long before he put pen to paper, in the form of principles, maxims or instructions. They were usually 'long, detailed, but well thought out'.

This Division was also employed in the normal engineering

work of trench warfare, which was by now second nature to Guggisberg, at first near Ypres and then in the Dunkirk area, but it took part in no major battle before he left it in July, after serving with it for nine months. The occasion for his leaving was promotion of a new kind, for he ceased to be a Sapper and became Commander of the 170th Infantry Brigade, with the rank of Brigadier-General.

On appointment to this new command he attended an Army Corps Training School for Senior Officers, where for the first time he met Lieutenant-Colonel J. H. Levey, who was its Commandant. Levey knew the Gold Coast well, and he was to become a director of the Offin Rivers Estates Ltd, and this encounter, as we have seen, was to be the beginning of a life-long friendship.[1] According to Levey '. . . this promotion from the Royal Engineers to the Command of an Infantry Brigade was rare. He must have possessed unusual commanding ability to have been selected for it. . . . Without any doubt he was the keenest officer of all those attending the course.'[2]

The course in question lasted only a week, but Guggisberg made a practice of dropping in on Levey in the late evenings, ostensibly to discuss the training demonstrations which had taken place during the day, but in reality to indulge in nostalgic talk about the Gold Coast and Nigeria. He spoke to Levey of his hopes of returning to the Gold Coast, if he survived the war, but his talk was not of Public Works, to whose Directorship he had been appointed, but of the possibilities of building up the cocoa industry, and of the prospects which this could open up for Gold Coast education. He was thinking of what he could do in command, though he had of course no suspicion that he would ever have supreme authority.[3]

The 57th Division, like the 66th, was a Second Line Terri-torial one raised in the autumn of 1914, and it too went to France in February 1917, where it became part of Gough's

[1] See p. 9 and several other parts of this narrative, especially in Chs. 1 and 15.
[2] Private communication to the author.
[3] Towards the end of the war he actually applied for the Chief Commissionership of the Northern Territories. See p. 74.

Army holding the flank in north Flanders. Although it had experienced the full measure of the dangers, casualties and discomforts of trench warfare, it was not engaged in a major battle until 26 October 1917, the opening day of the Second Battle of Passchendaele. Here, as part of the XIV Corps, it attacked with its three Infantry Brigades in line, and in spite of appalling weather and mud, some advance was made before the attack was held up. That same night it was relieved by another Division and took no other important part in the Battle, which finally ended about 10 November, by which time the Canadian Corps had captured and held the objective, the dominant high ground round Passchendaele itself. But in the attack on 26 October Guggisberg's Brigade lost half its strength, and the total casualties of the 57th Division amounted to about 1,600.

Between the two World Wars a vast volume of emotion centred on this insignificant Flemish village. Passchendaele cast its shadow over a whole generation; it became a symbol for the mad folly of the Western Front, for the horror of its degradation and slaughter, and for the alleged incompetence of the British High Command in general or of Earl Haig in particular. Recently, during the fiftieth anniversary of the outbreak of the First World War, it has lived again in the consciousness of the British people. The Battles of Passchendaele were in fact part of a series of battles which together constituted the Third Battle of Ypres, which was believed by an angry post-war generation to have been fought in impossible conditions of rain and mud, to have been futile in conception, conduct and result, and to have sacrificed 400,000 casualties for nothing. The British Official History of the Great War covering 1917 was not published until 1948, but in it the official historian takes a very different view. In the Third Battle of Ypres he says the weather conditions were only really bad during the last month, i.e. in the actual Battles of Passchendaele, and declares that the Canadians especially overcame them brilliantly. From official returns he shows that the casualties in the whole of the Battle from 31 July to 10 November were 230,000 and not the 400,000 or more estimated by previous writers. Next he emphasizes that the strategic object of the Battle was to contain the German forces in the north lest they moved south and overwhelmed the French Army which had not yet fully recovered from the mutinies of the summer of 1917. Finally he contends that the Battle was a British strategic victory which probably prevented the loss of the war in 1917 and helped to prevent a complete German victory in 1918 as a result of the March offensive. He shows that these contentions are supported in the German Official History. Thus there are two diametrically opposed schools of thought on 'Passchendaele'. Which is correct still remains a matter of individual opinion.

This is a digression which may seem to have little to do with Guggisberg, but it is worth recording since it recalls how he and millions of others were caught up, almost as though they were insignificant insects, in events of incalculable horror which appeared to have no meaning, but which the perspective of history may show to have been part of a purposeful design. Guggisberg, between his forty-sixth and fiftieth birthdays, experienced the holocausts of Loos, the Somme and Passchendaele, and the long periods of squalid boredom in between. But Passchendaele also saw, for him, the end of active combat, for the 57th was not again engaged in battle until the middle of August 1918, by which time he had left it.

The last six months of the war brought Guggisberg work which was not only congenial but for which he was ideally suited. The fearful casualties had left the war in the hands of a new army, sadly raw and inexperienced, whose leaders were quite unable to keep up with the continually changing techniques of fighting. Accordingly, in the early summer of 1918, the Commander-in-Chief of the British Armies in France decided to set up a new establishment under an 'Inspector-General of Training', and appointed Lieutenant-General Sir Ivor Maxse, Commander of the 18th Army Corps, as Inspector-General. (Maxse was later to become Lord Milner's brother-in-law.) It happened that Colonel Levey was appointed his

Chief Staff Officer, and he immediately proposed to Maxse that Guggisberg should become one of the three Deputy Inspector-Generals who were to be on the establishment. Maxse, who had known Guggisberg from an early training days on Salisbury Plain, very readily agreed. From then until the Armistice, Guggisberg's duties took him to all five Armies in France.

A picturesque detail of his activities is supplied by Colonel Butterworth. The Deputy Inspectors tried to promote interest and rivalry in the training exercises by drawing on the sporting instincts of the troops, and Guggisberg naturally turned to the game which was almost part of his religion. At a machine-gun training school at Etaples for which he was responsible he instituted what he chose to call 'net practice'. Soldiers on the flank of the range were enjoined to bowl empty tins across the machine-guns' fire path, which the gunner had to pick up with his stream of bullets and drive high over a distant bank. A macabre perversion, no doubt, of a game of placid, civilized associations but an engaging sidelight on the man.

Such, in bare outline, was Guggisberg's war. He was five times mentioned in despatches, was awarded the D.S.O., became a Chevalier of the Legion of Honour, and attained the rank of Brigadier. In December 1918, the British Armies entered Cologne, and the Inspector-General and his staff moved with them; and in Cologne Guggisberg became reunited with his wife.

The war had given Decima the great chance, which she had seized with both hands, of building a second independent career. Throughout the whole period of hostilities she did remarkable work in France, which was recognized in 1918 by the award of the C.B.E., and by a French decoration, the Médaille de Reconnaissance Française, Première Classe. Her chosen field was a Leave Club for the Forces in Paris, of which she was, in her own words 'Honorary Organizer and Director-General'. This was a recreational club for officers of the British Navy, Army and Air Force, though her energy also overflowed in

1915 in an attachment to the French Army, for which she served as a 'Directrice de la Cantine'. All this was work admirably suited to her drive, her enthusiasm and her vivacious personality. It made her a person of some importance. Her husband too had become important. Neither of them was going to be exactly at home in the Department of Public Works in Accra.

After the Armistice, the need for the club in Paris diminished and she turned her attention to the Army of the Rhine. And in Cologne, whither she had gone on her husband's heels, she established a 'British Empire Leave Club.'

But by this time a more urgent need was to re-establish her husband's career, and not on the lines envisaged by the Colonial Office. She knew a great deal about life in a tropical African colony, and although her love of Africa at the grass-roots had been sincere she was not, in her late forties, a woman who was likely to be content with a position some way down a colony's social scale. A Director of Public Works was an important man; indeed, by the modest standards of achievement which Britain then set herself in her colonial dependencies his work was of more significance than that of many of his colleagues. But British colonial society was a complicated fabric of unspoken assumptions about status and prestige, and rested, in the ultimate analysis, upon caste. Professional and technical officers were not yet acceptable as equals in Government House; and it was from the windows of Government House that Decima now mentally surveyed the Gold Coast. In her club in Paris she had been a reigning queen. She fully intended that this state of affairs should continue.

Regrettably, few men are restrained by inhibitions in advancing their own careers, and ambitious women appear to have none at all in advancing those of their husbands. Decima looked round for someone who had the ear of the great. She did not have to look far, for the Secretary of State for the Colonies was by now Lord Milner, and she herself had made the acquaintance of Elinor Glyn.

Elinor Glyn did not enter deeply into Guggisberg's life, though she and her daughters remained on terms of friendship with him for many years; but her impact on his career was significant, even decisive. Bluntly she played a significant part in getting him the job of Governor of the Gold Coast.

It is not easy to imagine her equivalent in contemporary public life. Beautiful, passionate and exotic herself, she had risen to fame and made a great deal of money as a best-selling novelist. Her books, which would not be regarded favourably today, dealt with romantic love in high places; their eroticism shocked a generation, though nowadays they would be considered sexually innocent. She was the high priestess of sex-appeal and glamour, and through her millions of ordinary folk escaped from the narrow restrictions of their own lives into a more voluptuous world whose inhabitants could bring them the vicarious joys of splendour and unbridled love. Lest this should sound unpromising, she had qualities, other than her peerless physical qualities, which raised her above ordinary mortals.[1] One was character, which could more appropriately be described as 'guts'; for years she had to be the financial mainstay of an erratic and often difficult marriage, and she drove herself mercilessly to sustain her family and keep the place in the world which her talents had won for them in easier days. Another was to be found in the stature of the men who loved her. Notable among these were Curzon and Milner. To Curzon she herself had an avowed, almost abject devotion, and the words of glowing love in which she wrote of him are, to say the least, embarrassing. Milner, for whom she had a less passionate regard, gave her the more steadfast devotion, and greatly respected her intelligence and judgement. When Elinor Glyn was in Paris as a war correspondent Milner, a member of the War Cabinet,[2] visited and helped her there, and often wrote to her from London. His regard for her never wavered.

The value of this friendship was not lost on Decima when,

[1] Her story is told in *Elinor Glyn*, by her grandson Anthony Glyn, Hutchinson. 1955.

[2] And in 1918 Secretary of State for War.

in 1919, Milner, by a most fortunate circumstance for Guggisberg, became Secretary of State for the Colonies. She had come to know Elinor at the Paris Leave Club, and now went into action on her husband's behalf.

Maria (Elinor Glyn's maid) . . . would often go, on her afternoons off, to help at the forces' leave centre in Paris which was run by Mrs. Guggisberg (later Lady Moore-Guggisberg), and through this connection Elinor became acquainted with Mrs. Guggisberg, who mentioned one day that she feared her husband, who in peace time was an officer in the colonial service, had been passed over for a governorship of a British colony.

Elinor expressed sympathy but said she could do nothing to help until she had met the husband. Accordingly, a few days later she travelled to Amiens for the sole purpose of meeting and lunching with Brigadier-General Guggisberg (later Sir Gordon Guggisberg). She returned to Paris that evening, greatly impressed by his personality and capabilities.

On the first suitable opportunity she spoke about him to Milner, who was by then Secretary of State for the Colonies. Milner, treating as always with respect her views about personalities, went into the matter carefully, summoning Brigadier-General Guggisberg to an interview. The result was that Guggisberg was shortly afterwards given the governorship of the Gold Coast, an outstandingly successful appointment.[1]

The author is a little astray in accepting that Guggisberg had been 'passed over'. As we have seen, he was not even an official starter in the gubernatorial race. It is clear that the right decision was made, and we may assume that Milner's judgement in making the appointment would be unclouded by his natural desire to please his friend. Nevertheless it seems reasonable to say that in some measure, Guggisberg owed his appointment, and the Gold Coast its greatest Governor, to the most celebrated *femme fatale* of his generation; and, of course, to his wife's ambition. In this particular case no one could deny that the end justified the means. The means by which Governors were normally appointed is obscure; it is clear from this episode that they were not necessarily the best means.

This, almost certainly, is not the whole story. Indeed Decima

[1] Anthony Glyn, op. cit., p. 252.

herself claimed the lion's share of the credit for his appointment.
She certainly knew Milner, though how well it is impossible to
say:

Lord Milner was a good friend of mine when I was working and
started my British Army and Navy Leave Club in Paris in the first
Great War—and in Cologne.[1]

But in a letter of June 1931,[2] she writes quite specifically:

I have all the correspondence relative to my getting Gordon the
Governorship of the Gold Coast. Neither Lord Milner nor others
connected with it considered that it involved 'scandalous wire-
pulling methods'. In fact, quite the opposite.

What this letter was in reply to has been forgotten, and the
correspondence to which Lady Guggisberg refers has not survived. It seems clear, however, that she had a lot to do with it,
and that some people were upset in the process.

It would be unreasonable, however, to suppose that Guggisberg was a mere puppet, whose affairs were arranged for him by
Elinor Glyn and his wife. His war career had brought him to the
notice of the men who moved in Milner's circle, and indeed
Milner himself was at least acquainted with him. There is some
evidence[3] that Milner had met him on one of his visits to the
Leave Club in Paris, and that he had actually discussed his
future with him, though this may simply have been one of a
hundred similar conversations with other officers. But Maxse
also was a good friend of Guggisberg, and a relative of Milner,
and L. S. Amery, then Milner's Parliamentary Under-Secretary,
knew Guggisberg and thought well of him.[4]

On incomplete evidence it seems reasonable to say that by the
end of the war Guggisberg was too distinguished a man, in terms
of rank, authority and personal reputation, to fit harmoniously
into the Department of Public Works in the Gold Coast Colony;
that he might in his own right have been appointed by the
Colonial Office to one of the higher administrative posts for

---

[1] Letter to Mr. F. P. Cobb's mother, 23 July 1953.
[2] To Mr. A. Duncan-Johnstone.    [3] In the recollection of Sir Andrew Jones.
[4] Fraser thought that Amery's influence was possibly the decisive one.

which he had previously been considered inadequate, and that the combined efforts of these two formidable women ensured that this happened, and that there were no half measures in the process.

It has often been said that when Guggisberg came out of the furnace of the 1914–18 War he made a solemn vow to dedicate the rest of his life to the service of his fellow-men.[1] This is not as improbable as it may sound. To our more sober and cynical generation such high-sounding resolves seem priggish and embarrassing, but they were in accord with the mood and sentiment of 1919. The scale of the slaughter, the horror of the blood and filth, and degradation of existence in the Flanders mud produced a reaction to which the sober relief of 1945 cannot be compared. After years of apparent peace and security the flower of a generation had been killed and maimed, and men generally were gripped by a sense of obligation to those who had been sacrificed. The world was then more innocent in its hopes, and noble resolution was in the air. Men believed quite sincerely that they had fought a war to end war, that madness would now give way to sanity, and that a new world was theirs for the building. The deep comradeship of the trenches inspired the survivors with hopes, unprecedented among Englishmen, that class bitterness, jealousy and self-regard could be overthrown, and that a lasting memorial could be built in honour of the dead, and worthy of their sacrifice. This mood survived, in spite of growing disillusionment, until the economic slump of the late 1920s.

Guggisberg shared the general intoxication, and caught the mood which caused men more prosaic and unsentimental than himself to dedicate themselves to the service of the 'elder brethren' who had fallen in battle. Though personally ambitious, he was the kind of man who sought to fulfil his ambition as leader in a cause rather than in simple self-advancement.

[1] This was accepted by Fraser, and was recorded by Dr. Edwin Smith in his *Aggrey of Africa*, published in 1929, p. 225. In his introduction Dr. Smith says that he had talked to Guggisberg, who had later read the relevant chapter.

The traumatic experience of the War sharpened this ambition; his latent, inarticulate religion fought for expression and fulfilment; his unexpected governorship gave him a glowing opportunity. Whether or not he actually vowed the vow which is attributed to him, he sailed for the Gold Coast in a spirit of high resolve and dedication.

PART 2

Governor of the Gold Coast

1919–27

# 4

## Guggisberg's Inheritance

A FEW men leave their mark upon the world by virtue of an achievement which is theirs alone; it is conceived in their imaginations, nurtured by their own minds and built with their own hands. In our own century Albert Schweitzer created Lambarene, John Flynn the Flying Doctor Service of the Australian outback, Baden-Powell the Boy Scout movement. These men were originators, owing little to others.

This could never be true of colonial governors, who received a torch from their predecessors and, in a pitifully few years, handed it to successors. However creative they may have been they built on what had gone before, and whether they received praise or blame from their contemporaries, or from the critics of later years, the credit, or the opprobrium, ought justly to be shared by others. A colonial governorship was an incident in an unfolding story, and none survived long enough to be able to say 'Alone I did it.'

Guggisberg has been over-praised as an originator. His virtues lay rather in a fantastic capacity for work, an orderly and systematic approach to his problems, and a drive and determination which could impress itself upon the stolid bureaucracies of the Colonial Office and the Secretariat. His most original qualities, worth all the rest, were an obsessional belief in the potentialities of the people whom he governed, coupled with a flair for putting himself across and appearing to them as the embodiment of their own aspirations. He gave his governorship glamour, and this enabled him to achieve more than many abler men. It was more valuable in the Gold Coast of his time than a university training in the intellectual disciplines, or a deep experience of 'political administration'.

He was doubly fortunate in his inheritance. In the first place the Colony was financially sound and commercially prosperous. This was partly because the War had curtailed development expenditure, since the future was uncertain and the staffs were depleted; the other, and more positive, reason was that through-out the War the cocoa industry was finding its feet and justify-ing the hopes placed in it by the pioneers of the early years of the century; manganese was also a profitable war-time export. Thus the revenue rose while expenditure fell, presenting Guggis-berg with a revenue surplus of £1,612,000 on his assumption of the governorship; this would have been very much larger if war-time shipping facilities had been able to keep pace with production. Moreover the years 1919 and 1920 were boom years of unprecedented magnitude, and the value of trade, even though still diminished by the bottle-neck of transport, was three and a half times that of the two preceding years. Judged by the relative standards of 1919 he took over a rich Colony.

In the second place, he succeeded Sir Hugh Clifford, who had not only husbanded the Colony's resources with care and skill during the War, but had probed deeply into its economic, social and (less surely) political problems and cleared the ground for advance by his successor. In this situation a more appro-priate successor than Guggisberg could hardly have been found.

It is a pity that Clifford did not think this himself, but un-fortunately he detested Guggisberg and was profoundly shocked by his appointment. He had reason to be, for towards the end of the War Guggisberg, still itching to get into the Administration, had asked to be considered for the post of Chief Commissioner of the Northern Territories, a part of the Gold Coast which always held a romantic appeal for him and which he believed to be capable of vast development. Clifford had opposed this on the ground that Guggisberg *lacked administrative experience*. This phrase was still being used by colonial administrators until the sun finally set on Britain's African Empire. Only in the last few years, when it was clear that the administrative service had no future, did a few outsiders penetrate the ranks. The loss of talent caused by the persistent belief that colonial administration was an art so esoteric that it could only be successfully practised by someone who had never done anything else is incalculable. It is not difficult to imagine Clifford's chagrin when, within months, he had to acknowledge Guggisberg as his successor.

From then onwards Clifford never lost an opportunity of denigrating him, and his conversational method of referring to him was 'that mountebank'. He did on one occasion bring himself to pay a duty call at Christiansborg Castle when he was passing through Accra on leave, and was doubtless relieved to find that the Governor was on tour; unfortunately someone had forgotten to put out the Visitors' Book at the Castle, and this gave Clifford the opportunity to create a disproportionate fuss, and to run the Governor down to various Accra acquaintances on whom he also called, and even to denigrate him openly in the Accra Club, to the resentment of Guggisberg's admirers. On another occasion Guggisberg was not so easy to avoid. They travelled on the same Elder Dempster mail-boat from Liverpool. This voyage, according to a well-attested story, had a farcical prelude. Guggisberg, learning by chance that he and Clifford were to be ship-mates, rushed round to the Crown Agents to confirm this, and on learning that it was true asked for his own passage to be transferred to the next sailing, a fortnight later. The same news shortly reached Clifford, who behaved identically.[1] There is wide agreement among their contemporaries that this actually happened, although it is not known whether the clerk at the Crown Agents was the same person on each occasion, and whether he maintained an attitude of non-intervention to gratify a sense of humour or from fear of embarrassing the Governor of Nigeria. However this may be, Guggisberg and Clifford met on board at Liverpool, and

[1] Students of Dr. P. G. Wodehouse will recall that the identical thing happened to Bertie Wooster's twin cousins, on a voyage to South Africa. See 'The Delayed Exit of Claude and Eustace' in *The Inimitable Jeeves*.

passed the entire voyage without speaking to each other.[1]

It is a little disillusioning to find that colonial governors, those bland and upright men of god-like aspect in their own domains, are no different from the rest of us. Yet pettiness apart, Sir Hugh Clifford was a considerable figure. Ghanaians who knew both men—a declining number, alas—freely acknowledge Clifford's greater intellectual quality, grasp and stature. A phrase that recurs in their conversation is that Clifford could 'think on his feet'; he had a quick and subtle mind, a vast administrative experience in Malaya and Ceylon, and a combative and liberal outlook.[2] But the same Ghanaians reserve their affection for Guggisberg; this Clifford could not command.

We are, however, concerned with Guggisberg's debt to Clifford, and by implication, since governors were like relay runners, to Clifford's predecessors. It is therefore necessary to summarize briefly the significance of Guggisberg's stage of the journey, and to see how far they had started him on the road.

The achievements of those eight tremendous years were of different kinds. First, there were those which were expressed in feats of engineering and in bricks and mortar. In his mind the key to all development lay in better transportation, and he was able in 1927 to look back on road and railway extensions without precedent in so short a time, and to the enduring monument of Takoradi Harbour. He saw these developments always as a means to an end, an end which he never allowed to become obscured. Young men in Ghana today are apt to assume that the end was the well-being of the cocoa companies' shareholders, but there can have been few people who interested him less. What he wanted above all was education—secondary and higher education no less than primary—and he knew that

---

[1] Clifford and Decima, on the other hand, thought highly of each other. In later years she lamented the fact that no one had written Clifford's biography; this Life of her husband, on the other hand, she thought not worth writing, and declined to give the author any assistance with it. She did not help to mitigate the quarrel between Clifford and her husband, but rather exacerbated it.

[2] It is sad that in his later years his mental powers declined, and towards the end of his life he was mentally ill. The first serious symptoms of this became apparent during his Governorship of Nigeria; it may have accounted in part for his deplorable attitude towards Guggisberg.

it could never be paid for unless the cocoa, the timber, the manganese and the gold could be got to the coast more cheaply and shipped more expeditiously. There was, however, another intermediate aim, which was that the Gold Coast people should be healthier. Quite apart from the gruesome facts of infantile mortality he knew that unhealthy people were ineducable, and that the schools and colleges of his dreams would be of little service to the boys and girls who attended them if their minds were blunted and their stamina impaired by debilitating tropical disease. Civil engineering and administration were never far apart in his mind, so that he gave great impetus to improving piped water supplies in the major cities and to sanitary engineering in all the towns; and to crown his public health programme he brought to fruition the then magnificent African Hospital at Korle Bu, on the low-lying land to the west of Accra. And finally he built—and here the phrase is not an undue exaggeration—the Prince of Wales College at Achimota.

In all these things his touch was sure, for he was a soldier and engineer by profession, and was at home with communications, engineering projects and buildings. The second category of his achievements lay in the sphere of politics and administration in the more abstract sense, that is in representative government and 'native administration'. Here his work is embodied in a Constitution of 1925, the establishment of Provincial Councils of Chiefs, and the Native Administration Ordinance of 1927. These now have an air of antiquity, but in their day they were progressive. It was a less familiar field, in which his own objectives did not command unanimous African agreement, in which his political beliefs and prejudices inevitably played their part, and in which he was more susceptible to the influence of his European advisers, the majority of whom had little *rapport* with African aspirations and did not care for the 'educated native'. It was less easy for him to give orders, for he did not always know what ought to be done, and he was dealing with human beings in their most irrational aspect. Nevertheless he moved the country forward.

The third category of his achievements was not strictly a

separate category at all, for it lay in an abstract quality which informed the other two. It consisted in faith in the Gold Coast people, and in the belief that they were capable of, and should be trained for, the highest posts in all departments of the Administration. It had its paradoxical aspect, for though by temperament he was something of an autocrat, and accustomed to command obedience, he believed intensely in informing the people of the country what the Government was doing so that they would feel a sense of identification and partnership. It would be an exaggeration to say that he believed in consulting them overmuch, since he was not always patient of criticism, and had a lively sense of the beneficence of his own ideas. But at least he broke through the barrier of secrecy which was, and continued to be, the bugbear of so much colonial administration, and treated the people of the Gold Coast as intelligent adults, capable of understanding what was going on. He would have made little of the modern science of human relations, but would have understood the art of the Public Relations Officer, and was indeed one of the first colonial administrators to practise it. To this he owed a large part of his success.

But on what foundations did he build? And in particular what did he owe to Clifford? It is worth trying to answer these questions, since because so much came to final fruition under his hands he is apt to be credited with more than he deserves; and as we have said his way, financially, was easier than that of previous governors. Takoradi, Korle Bu and Achimota are thought of as Guggisberg's creations, but a good deal of the spade work had been done by the time he came to Christiansborg Castle.

The *sine qua non* of the achievement was communications. Throughout their own governorships Nathan, Rodger and Clifford had all addressed themselves to this problem. Nathan and Rodger had both been motivated by a desire to avoid trouble. The cocoa farmers were getting less, and the merchants more, than they deserved because of the utter dependency of the farmers on the buyers' agents for getting their crops to market. They believed that if they improved the railways and the roads, thus putting the farmer in a stronger position by reducing transport costs, they would be able to avoid political intervention in a commercial transaction.[1] A cocoa hold-up in 1911 forced Rodger to abandon this hope, and his successor, Clifford, became deeply involved in the dispute. In 1915 Clifford went so far as to convene a meeting of farmers and advise them to withhold their stocks until better prices could be obtained. The merchants, not unnaturally, took grave exception to this 'most dangerous' advice, which was indeed unusual advice for a Governor to give.

One of Clifford's earliest impressions of the Colony in 1912, in comparison with the West Indies or Ceylon, had been the endless stream of men, women and children carrying cocoa on their heads to the coast or the railway line; for example, at Mangoasase, the rail-head on the Accra–Akwapim line, they had walked as much as thirty miles. At that time the construction of roads appeared to offer no solution, as the tsetse fly made animal transport impossible and the few heavy lorries of the day battered both the roads and themselves to pieces. Their only advantage was that it was easier to roll a cask along them than along a bush path, until the rains and the lorries made even this impossible; but head-loading was still the principal means of transport, and for this roads were a positive disadvantage, for they robbed the unfortunate head-loaders of shade, the only thing which made their burden tolerable. Accordingly Clifford, like Guggisberg after him, had been concerned more than anything else with railway extensions, since at the time the development of transport could only be envisaged in terms of railways and of light rail or tram lines to feed them.

My earliest preoccupation, therefore, on my assumption of the Government of the Colony was to endeavour to find some means of relieving the crippling transport disabilities, the continuance of which threatened to render really rapid progress quite impossible.[2]

---

[1] Unpublished thesis by Mr. B. Kwaw-Swanzy in the Cambridge University Library. See also *Debates*, 13 December 1915, pp. 86–88.

[2] *Debates*, 1918–19, pp. 84–5.

This remark related to 1912, and in March 1913 he addressed
the Secretary of State at length upon the subject; proposing a
steady long-term plan of railway extensions intended above all
to open up new tracts of fertile cocoa-producing country; but
cocoa was not by any means the only consideration, for he
thought that the closer administration of the country, even the
'moral and intellectual advance of the people', depended on
transport development.[1]

In 1916 he was still saying:

It is my firm conviction that upon the rapid pushing forward of our
projected railway extensions, more than upon any other individual
effort that the Government can make, is dependent the immediate
and future development of the Gold Coast and Ashanti.[2]

and in a despatch to the Secretary of State of the same year
he had considered the development potential of the Northern
Territories so hopeless, in terms of the poverty, the scattered
nature of the population and the vast distances, that he recommended cutting down administrative expenditure in the North
and concentrating everything available on the extension and
development of the railway in the Colony and Ashanti, 'which
are capable of prosperous expansion and where capital development will be remunerative'.

The Government was not able to do much about railway
construction during the War, though at the same meeting of the
Legislative Council the Colonial Secretary was outlining plans
for the extension of the main line south from Kumasi to meet
the northward line from Koforidua and Tafo. It was skill rather
than money that was hard to come by in the Gold Coast in the
middle of the War, and Clifford was negotiating for the transfer
of engineers from Nigeria, where an economic depression was
rendering them idle.

But by this time a profound revolution was beginning to take
place in transport. The heavy lorry had reduced road transport
to an absurdity, since the combined cost of maintaining the
roads against the depredations of the lorries, and the lorries

[1] P.R.O., C.O. 96:528, GC Vol. 2—Clifford to Harcourt.
[2] *Debates*, 23 October 1916.

against the depredations of the roads, made their use more uneconomic than head-loading. The change came with Henry Ford's light chassis, standardized parts, simplicity of design and service organization. Here were vehicles which would run with safety not only on the main roads but on tracks which the local people could make themselves. Road-rail strategy now had to be re-thought, and both Clifford and Guggisberg have been blamed by subsequent critics for not having realized this sooner and drawn in their horns on railway construction. It would of course have been difficult at that stage not to complete the Accra–Kumasi main line; but more to the point is the fact that although the railway only advanced 26 miles from Tafo towards Kumasi during the whole of Clifford's administration, main roads constructed by the Public Works Department increased by 165 miles, and District roads capable of supporting the new Ford lorries by over 650 miles. The cost of all this was met out of current revenue or surplus balances, and Clifford was able to say:

Save in some special instances the tram or light railway, as a feeder of a main railway system, may be regarded as a project of the past, so far as this Colony is concerned. Roads in the Gold Coast have suddenly acquired a new and unprecedented value, since they can be used by vehicles which are far more efficient, and not much more destructive, than the bullock-cart of the East or the mule-wagon of the West Indies, and which are not affected by *tse-tse* or *trypanosomae*.

These points are mentioned because it is sometimes supposed that Guggisberg was the first to see the potentialities of road transport, and to develop feeder roads for the cocoa farmer on any considerable scale; indeed, that he was the first to give serious attention to the economics of transport in relation to the cocoa industry. This supposition is wholly misleading.

For the final link in the chain of communication, however— the deep-water port which would get the Gold Coast produce into the world market—Guggisberg deserves a good deal of personal credit, if only for his insistence on putting right the mistakes of the past.

A deep-water harbour in Takoradi Bay was no new idea. It had first been advocated in 1895 by consulting engineers employed by the British Government, who were interested in it both as a terminal port for the proposed railway to Tarkwa and as a strategic harbour for the Navy in time of war. When Guggisberg first came to the Gold Coast as Assistant Director of Survey in 1902 it was still a live issue, and his chief, Watherston, was firm in his professional opinion that the village of Amunful in the Bay was the only possible place for it; this he explained to him as they sat on the rocks at the shore end of the present breakwater. Guggisberg recalls this in *Events* (p. 86):

In August, 1919, before leaving England to take over the adminis-tration of this country, the late Lord Milner . . . asked me what my plans were with regard to development. My discussion with Lieutenant-Colonel Watherston seventeen years earlier came back into my memory, and I answered 'Build a deep-water harbour at Tadoradi.'

But in the intervening years matters had not stood still. The line to Tarkwa had been started in 1898, not from Amunful but from Sekondi, a few miles away, and this had led to the development of a small 'boat' harbour there, for surf boats and small lighters. Once committed the Gold Coast Government could not stop, and in the years before the First World War a quarter of a million pounds had been sunk in providing mini-mum, though hopelessly inadequate, harbour facilities in the wrong place. So serious had the position become by Clifford's day that in February 1918 he set an enquiry on foot as to the cost and technicalities of extending Sekondi Harbour into the desperately needed deep-water port, where ocean-going ships could come alongside instead of loading and unloading by the slow, costly and inefficient method of lighterage. In May of the following year his Committee submitted a detailed technical and financial report,[1] which Guggisberg inherited on arrival.

The idea of a deep-water port did not therefore originate in Guggisberg's mind; but his engineering knowledge told him that a mistake had been made in its proposed siting, and his drive and persistence got the error corrected and a new port built in the proper place.

[1] *Sessional Paper* No. 3 of 1918–19.

In the matter of public health Clifford and his predecessors had been inordinately concerned with the European problem, which was, of course, urgent and important at the time. It is largely irrelevant to the present discussion, though it deserves a side glance as an illustration of Clifford's good sense and balanced judgement. There had been some alarming facts, in the first decade of the century, but the remedy proposed by a meeting of Principal Medical Officers in Lagos in 1912 amounted to complete segregation of Europeans from Africans, and this struck Clifford as being almost worse than the disease. 'The preservation of the health of Europeans in West Africa is a matter of great concern and importance . . . but it appeared to me that we were in some danger of mistaking it for the principal, if not for the sole aim for which British rule is established in this country. . . . This attitude toward the health question appeared to me to be bereft of any due sense of proportion and to be calculated, if accepted, to work untold mischief in the Gold Coast'.[1] He worked hard for, and achieved, a compromise which, though repugnant to a later generation of Africans, was better than the *apartheid* proposed by the Medical Officers of Health.

Of more relevance is the fact that during his governorship plans were being laid for a reputable native hospital in Accra:

In order to facilitate the expansion of the native town of Accra, a considerable area at Korle Bu, on the western side of the lagoon, was acquired during 1916. It is proposed, when funds are available, to construct a causeway across the lagoon, and the new native hospital, which is so urgently required, will be situated at Korle Bu.[2]

This makes it clear that Korle Bu was not Guggisberg's creation, as is frequently supposed. Moreover, the Water Works at Accra and Sekondi were both completed during Clifford's time, and he acknowledged that Sir John Rodger deserved most of the credit.

In the matter of higher education for Africans, Clifford's

[1] *Debates*, 28 October 1918.
[2] *Debates*, 25 October 1917, p. 19.

predecessors cannot be said to have distinguished themselves, and Clifford himself was hesitant, though not inactive. This was notoriously the blind spot of expatriate governments. At the level of conscious thought, the Europeans believed that secondary education, in the only terms in which anyone then understood it, was inappropriate for Africans and of no service to the country. The same defect in their own education was not apparent to them, or was disguised by the fact that it was their environment and upbringing, rather than their formal education, which made them the superiors of all but a very few Africans in the ability to command, plan and administer. They believed also that secondary education was 'premature'; it continued to be premature until Guggisberg tore these ideas to shreds. Subconsciously, no doubt, they disliked the 'Black Englishmen' who had found their education abroad or in the Church secondary schools at Cape Coast, and who, despite their brashness and inexperience, were not noticeably different from themselves in basic intelligence and ability.

Their prejudices were rationalized also by the quite sensible belief that African education should be founded on a higher standard of straightforward literacy and on artisan and agricultural skills, a belief which Guggisberg shared to the full. The great fallacy, which they were certainly intelligent enough to see through and which they therefore must have avoided by some trick of the mind, was to suppose that lower and higher education were mutually exclusive, or that the one must be brought to completion before the other could be begun. Guggisberg was never guilty of this. A glance at the history of education in their own country would have told them that it was nonsense; yet Clifford, a highly intelligent man, could apparently take this view himself in the last year of his governorship, when he said:

The view, which I have expressed above, that the first object of the Government should be to render primary education accessible throughout the Colony, and when accessible compulsory, is not altogether popular in certain quarters; but I none the less adhere to the opinion that, in the matter of education, this is the first and most obvious duty.

The best that can be said of the British Administrations before Guggisberg was that in this particular field they believed
in progress when convinced that it was inevitable. Clifford was
prepared to go a little further and examine the proposition on
its merits, though without any predisposition in its favour.
Initiative in secondary education had of course come wholly
from the Missions, and was embodied at Cape Coast in the
Methodist and Anglican foundations of Mfantsipim and Adisa-
del; and in a more down-to-earth and less academic way by the
work of Basel Mission. The Government had demonstrated its
inability to disapprove by grant-aiding at least one missionary
secondary school, but early in Clifford's governorship he had to
face the demand from the educated African community that
Government should adopt a more positive attitude to their
responsibilities, and put secondary education on its own
agenda.[1]

Accordingly in 1915 he commissioned the Board of Education
to examine this matter. The members of the Board replied
individually by the end of the year, but it was not until 1917
that their replies were published by the Governor's instruction.[2]
They make fascinating reading, and a word should be said
in summary in order to convey the climate of thinking in the
Gold Coast a mere four years before Guggisberg's arrival as
Governor.

The two African members of the Board were Mate-Kole, the
Konor of Eastern Krobo, and T. Hutton-Mills. It goes without
saying that their support for a Government secondary school
was unqualified, and one notes how deeply they resented the
superior position of Lagos and Sierra Leone. Hutton-Mills had
some harsh things to say about the 'antipathy' of the Director
and Acting-Director of Education, and their persistence in
'opposing and discouraging' the foundation of a secondary
school. This odd attitude to their responsibilities was to become
familiar to Guggisberg. The representatives of the Basel and
Roman Catholic Missions were also favourable, though their
enthusiasm was tempered by the disillusion of experience and

[1] See Kimble, *Political History*, pp. 84–87.     [2] *Sessional Paper* No. 5 of 1916–17.

they were extremely down-to-earth in the matter of the curri-
culum. The Reverend Fred C. Cleaver, on the other hand,
writing from Bishopsbourne, Sekondi, seemed somewhat be-
wildered by the whole affair, and disposed to agree with the
Director of Education. Of the two European Unofficial Members of the Legislative Council one was for and one against. Of
the four Officials, the Acting Treasurer was the most favourably
disposed, as he wanted better clerks in the Treasury; the Attorney-General thought that there were not enough 'unofficial
vocations' for many educated natives, and that in any case
financial stringency put the project out of the question; the
Acting Principal Medical Officer, in a letter of two lines, agreed
with the Acting Director of Education that there was no need
for a secondary school; and the Acting Commissioner for the
Eastern Province believed that the time was not yet ripe.

With this measure of enthusiasm from his officials and co-
nationalists, it was to Clifford's credit that he did not give up
and leave it to some successor to cope with an enterprise about
which he himself was less than half convinced. However, in the
last year of his administration he appointed a Special Committee, with far stronger African representation, to have a look
at Gold Coast Education once more; their terms of reference
were wide, and did not mention a Government secondary
school specifically, but it is clear from the manner of their report
that it was in fact their major consideration.[1]

The Committee reported on 8 October 1919, by which time
Clifford had gone, so that Guggisberg on arrival was presented
with the contemporary Gold Coast view upon the topic which
was to dominate his mind for the next eight years. It gave him
little satisfaction, and one of his early acts was to appoint yet
another, and smaller, committee, know as the 'Educationists'
Committee to go over the whole ground again. Characteristically, and in sharp distinction to Clifford, he did not do so until
he had delivered his own views on the subject; these, again
characteristically, amounted to a directive. There was to be no
more nonsense about finding out what people thought; they

[1] *Sessional Paper*, No. 17 of 1918–19.

would do, at any rate in essentials, what the Governor wanted done.

The Committee of Educationists would investigate the past, and make proposals for the future, in accordance with principles, methods and policy as laid down in:

(*a*) The speech delivered by His Excellency the Governor to the Legislative Council on 23 February 1920.

(*b*) ...

But (*b*) to (*g*) hardly mattered. There was a new, and authoritative hand on the reins of education.

What emerges from this is that in education, if not in communications, public health and the African hospital, Guggisberg could lay claim to being an innovator. The long peace of the Directorate of Education was over, and the wind of change rose steadily to gale force.

Even so, Clifford's contribution, halting and inadequate though it was by comparison, must not be written off. His own Special Committee had recommended the establishment of a Government Secondary School for Boys to be known as the Royal College, Accra; its site was to be extensive and capable of enlargement; all the pupils were to be boarders; a gift of £5,000 from Cadbury's was to be applied to the building of a Natural Science Laboratory; European masters were to be resident on the site. Here was the germ, if no more, of Achimota, and Clifford's last words on the subject to the Legislative Council were these:

By this means it should be rendered possible for boys to acquire a sound secondary education, far in advance of that at present attainable, without being compelled to migrate to Europe for the purpose. Those who possess the means and ability to do so should then complete their studies in England (*sic*); but those who concluded their education with the Royal College course would be far better equipped for their future careers than are the majority of educated men today; and by no other means can the general standard of education and intelligence be raised throughout the Colony.[1]

[1] *Debates*, 19 August 1919, p. 120.

We turn to an aspect of Guggisberg's policy which, very understandably, won him higher regard than any other in the eyes of contemporary Africans, namely the promotion of Africans to higher posts in the public service than they had hitherto been allowed to occupy. This was thirty years before the terms 'Africanization' and 'localization' became current coin, and it represented a hard battle both with Gold Coast Europeans and with a suspicious and fearful Colonial Office. But this was a battlefield over which Clifford had also fought, and on which he had won some ground, and Guggisberg's work should be seen against this background.

It is a curious fact that Africans occupied posts of greater responsibility in the Gold Coast of the nineteenth century than of the first quarter of the twentieth.[1] It was a small and exclusive circle, including some failures, and one that gave little satisfaction to the African élite of the time. Yet undeniably the nineteenth century accepted in principle, and to an extent in practice, what the twentieth century colonial administrators rejected. The recruitment of Europeans to West Africa was becoming easier, with the success of the fight against tropical diseases, and the Colonial Service was building up an *esprit de corps* which had many admirable features, but whose less commendable side was that it almost inevitably became a vested interest, in which the basic premise that it was working for its own extinction was apt to be forgotten. Africans found themselves relegated to subordinate posts in the service, and discontent and frustration grew.

Clifford was shocked by this, as by many aspects of Gold Coast administration. He may have been misguided in measuring the situation by the yardstick of Ceylon, from which he had just come, or of Trinidad, which he also knew, but he was undoubtedly right in believing that local talent was being wasted and ignored, and that expensively imported Europeans were doing a good deal of work below their proper level of responsibility. In particular he shared the Africans' own

[1] The theme is developed by Richard Symonds in *The British and their Successors*, Ch. VI. See also *Political History*, Ch. II.

exasperation that qualified doctors and lawyers were kept out of the public service; not that they were doing badly in private practice, from their own material point of view, but this was a matter in which material considerations were not always para-mount in their minds. Clifford pledged himself openly to put this right, and the leading Africans of the day believed him as they had not believed previous governors.[1]

He first tackled the thorny question of the doctors. Previous governors had admitted the injustice of the prevailing situation but had shirked effective action, in deference to the prejudices of Europeans, who would not contemplate being treated by black doctors—a prejudice, of course, which was never fully broken down. It was a prejudice also that the Colonial Office had felt bound to support, in compliance with a recommendation of their own Medical Advisory Committee in 1911, the result of which had been that Africans were restricted to the subordinate medical services.

Clifford openly challenged this ruling in a despatch of March 1913, shortly after he had transmitted a petition on the subject from the Aborigines Rights Protection Society.[2] He quoted his Ceylon experience and argued against the principle of exclusion—an illustration of how African dependencies could benefit from the more advanced ideas normally accepted in India and the East. It requires some courage for a governor to reopen a matter which has been officially closed only a year or so previously, and the Colonial Office must have thought him a nuisance to do so.

But he succeeded, at any rate in part, for in 1914 he was able to say:

During the early months of my first tour in the Gold Coast my attention was engaged with the most important question of em-ploying native medical practitioners in the Medical Department, and the views which I held from the start favoured their employment. I had an opportunity of discussing the matter at length with the

[1] Several administrators who came to Africa from India or Britain's Eastern dependencies received a comparable shock on realizing what a small part was played in the governmental process by natives of the country.
[2] P.R.O., C.O. 96.528 GC Vol. 2, 3 March 1913. Despatch No. 133.

whole Advisory Committe while lately in England, and although I
have failed to obtain a whole loaf I have secured a small piece of
bread. . . . The Secretary of State has agreed to the creation of
six posts in the Gold Coast Medical Service which shall be open to
natives of West Africa possessing qualifications current in England.[1]

Under Clifford's régime also an African (E. C. Quist) became
the first indigenous Crown Counsel.

Quite apart from the select categories of doctors and lawyers,
Clifford was assiduous throughout his governorship in improving the terms of service of the mass of Africans in subordinate
positions in government service. Accordingly it is no disparage-
ment of Guggisberg's more far-reaching efforts in this direction
to point out that he built on these foundations. Professor Kimble
has a sentence which is intended to assess the relative contribution of the two governors in this particular sphere, but which
has in fact a far wider application:

Guggisberg simply added his own characteristic drive to the policy
already initiated by Clifford; but his approach captured the public
imagination in a way his predecessors had never done.[2]

In the field of political administration, both men fumbled a
good deal. It must be remembered that they were facing something new in the African Colonial Empire—a nationalist
movement which was approaching maturity and talking sense.
Africans themselves, at this stage, were deeply divided. Outwardly there was a rift between the traditional rulers and the
'moderns'; the latter included, on the one hand, the 'youngmen'
who were in rebellion against old authority, and on the other
the educated élite; though the two classes were not mutually
exclusive, since the so-called 'youngmen' might themselves be
educated and indeed wealthy. This rift was growing deeper
every year. Nevertheless, within the conflict there existed strong
ties of sentiment and kinship which joined the participants on
the different sides, so that neither wished to destroy the other,
but to come to an accommodation. Such was the suspicion

---

[1] *Debates*, 1 Febuary 1914, p. 73.
[2] *Political History*, p. 106.

between them, however, and between all of them and the British Government, that the situation was always tense and brittle, and called for diplomacy of a kind in which colonial governors were not then as experienced as they were later to become.

In such situations a colonial government was not necessarily a catalyst, as it ought to have been, but could equally well force the various political elements further apart instead of causing them to seek accommodation. It was always a tenable, if risky, theory that in the absence of a colonial government the various factions, instead of manoeuvring for advantage by trying to impress the ruling power, would be forced to reach a workable compromise; risky, because if this failed to happen the result might well be anarchy. But the risks of holding the ring and pleasing no one were equally considerable. Already the British power had inadvertently[1] acted in this way pursuing the policy of indirect rule, thus conferring on the chiefs more power than custom had accorded them, and opening a rift which ought never to have existed.

Both Clifford and Guggisberg were what would now be called liberal in outlook, but both were heirs to the Lugard tradition, and when placed in the position of having to adjudicate on the spot, or to make an appreciation of the position to the Colonial Office, it was inevitable that their judgement should be given in the light of the major premise that the authority of the chiefs should be upheld,[2] and that forms of government should be encouraged which reflected the indigenous, and not the alien western, tradition. They were also pioneers in the sense that they grappled in its difficult adolescence with the nationalist uprising with which their later successor Arden-Clarke had to treat in its maturity. Political scientists and social psychologists had not yet descended on West Africa, and their books and

[1] An alternative theory is that they did not act inadvertently, but deliberately followed a policy of 'divide and rule'.

[2] Clifford, however, thought that the Government should give greater support to the chiefs, who were now frequent victims of 'destoolment', because their unpopularity was due to the fact that *they were more enlightened and progressive than their people*.

theses, which were later to crowd the bookshelves, were not written; indeed, their authors were yet to be born. Colonial governors could only act in accordance with their instincts and upbringing.

But Clifford, in spite of these limitations, was far ahead of his time. In the field of 'Native Policy' he was advocating in 1916 a reform which was not brought about until 1951. In a despatch to the Secretary of State in which he noted the economic revolution caused by the progress of the cocoa industry he reiterated the Administration's policy of developing the country through the traditional chiefs and of preserving native custom in every way, but added that the economic revolution had set up a social movement among the young men against the customary land system, towards individualization of land tenure and towards insubordination to tribal authority. He thought, however, that this could be remedied by persuading chiefs to admit *young men representatives on to the State Councils*. This was not done until the Local Government Ordinance of 1951.

The young men of today . . . are beginning to acquire the influence which is wont to accompany wealth, and unless this new power is recognized and made use of in time, it may end by destroying the tribal constitution, and with it the natural system of administration.

This is precisely what happened; 1951 was far too late to prevent it; whether the 'natural system of administration' ought to have been preserved is, of course, another matter.[1]

In a speech delivered in a wider context later in the same year, concerned with the introduction of a new Constitution, he was to say:

I foresee that the very partial application of the democratic principles *on which the theory of native constitutions rests* [authors's italics] which has been accepted without demur in the past, is likely in the near future to be very seriously challenged, and I foresee the probability of the various tribal divisions experiencing during the next few years con-

[1] Mr. Kwaw-Swanzy (op. cit.) puts the other point of view, namely that the development of the cocoa industry had itself undermined native constitutions, and that economic development necessitated a change of political institutions. 'The Government's insistence on preserving native institutions, though well-intentioned, complicated the issue.'

siderable difficulty in adjusting the ancient machinery of tribal government to the changed conditions with which they are now beginning to be confronted.[1]

It was this speech which brought a remarkable tribute from T. Hutton-Mills:

... you know more of the country than myself ... [I wish to move] that in order that this day may carry reminiscences of a memorable epoch it shall be regarded and observed from henceforth as a Public Holiday and known as 'Clifford's Day'.

Guggisberg himself was to receive no warmer praise. The subject of the debate was the new Constitution which Clifford had brought back with him from leave, the effect of which was to increase African representation in the Legislative Council from two to six. Hitherto all the 'natives' on the Legislative Council had been barristers, except for Mate-Kole who had been appointed by Governor Thorburn in 1911 to represent the interests of the cocoa farmers, but now three places were allotted to Paramount Chiefs representing the Twi-, Fanti- and Adangme-speaking peoples. It has generally been assumed that Guggisberg was the first to institute this system of indirect representation through traditional chiefs, but the germ of the idea was clearly Clifford's. The other three Africans represented the educated classes, and they were in the first instance J. E. Caseley-Hayford, E. J. P. Brown and T. Hutton-Mills.

We should not consider this to be particularly forward-looking today, and Clifford explicitly rejected the idea of *elective* representation; indeed, in his speech he defended the Crown Colony system of government and affirmed his belief in paternal rather than democratic government at the centre in the circumstances of the day. But the speech also reveals that even if the reforms were limited they were introduced on his own initiative and as a result of his thoughtful observations of what was going on around him. It is full of references to the depth and far-reaching character of the social revolution, and to the political genius of the Gold Coast peoples in their traditional constitutions, which he thought were 'based on democratical,

[1] *Debates*, 25 September 1916.

and not on autocratical or oligarchical, principles, as is usually
the case with forces of government that have been evolved for
themselves by other tropical races'. Although he could not
accept that the time was ripe for democracy in the Legislative
Council he got as far as saying that as a result of his study of the
cocoa revolution:

I felt that the Administration should have at its command a much
larger measure of advice from far more varied sources than was then
available.

Here again Guggisberg continued, and quickened, his predecessor's work.

The cocoa industry fascinated Clifford, not only because of
the economic revolution which it brought about, and of the
social and political consequences in which his analytical mind
revelled, but as a technical achievement by family farmers, or to
use his own words, 'native peasant proprietors'. This was partly
a reaction stemming from surprise, for he had been familiar all
his professional life with estate agriculture, financed by European capital and under European management, in the West
Indies, Malaya and Ceylon, and had come to take for granted
that this was the only road to progress. But the more he examined the economics of the cocoa industry, the more convinced
he became of its superiority in relation to the Gold Coast, and
in relation to that particular crop, and even his early despatches
to the Colonial Office argue this point of view in careful terms.
He was not uncritical, and as he found his way about the subject he had some hard things to say. His speech to the Budget
Session of 1916, for example, was in large part a penetrating
lecture on the state of the industry. He discussed the loss entailed
in slovenly cultivation, examined the consequences of substituting permanent 'gardens' for shifting cultivation, and gave
weight to the role of the Agricultural Department in teaching
improved methods. He also, more far-sightedly, urged the
formation of what were virtually co-operatives—'Farmers'
Associations'—which would work to approved qualities, collect

and market the crop in bulk and deal direct with the merchants without the intervention of the cocoa buyer.

This was not the only instance of his championship of the peasant proprietors. In the last year of his office he firmly opposed a Mineral Oil Bill which the Colonial Office had sponsored, the effect of which would have been to transfer the granting of oil concessions from the Concessions Court, a judicial tribunal of the Supreme Court, to the Governor himself. He knew that the Concessions Ordinance was regarded by the people of the country as the main rampart of their rights in connection with their land, and was uncompromisingly opposed to this extension of his own powers.

Finally, in assessing Guggisberg's debt to Clifford, it must be remarked that Clifford was as dissatisfied with the state of the Gold Coast when he succeeded as Governor in 1912 as was Guggisberg in 1919. The diaries of his early tours in the Colony show the stupefaction—the word is not too strong—of a man accustomed to the highly developed conditions of Ceylon at what appeared to be crude and haphazard administration:

Only a very small beginning has been made in really administering the Colony . . . . British rule in many parts of the Gold Coast has, so far, done little more than effect a change on the surface of things.

Except in the towns in which Government headquarters of some kind or other have been established, the administration of the Colony is to a great extent theoretical rather than practical, and exists on paper rather than in fact.[1]

Towards the end of his term he was deploring the ignorance on the part of Government officers both of native institutions and of the political aspirations of the Gold Coast people. Intelligence reports were in his view too subjective to be of any consequence.

The War prevented Clifford from doing very much to remedy this state of affairs, but it is impossible to believe, in the face of such evidence, that he can have left behind him an administration which was wholly complacent. Although Guggisberg, fresh

[2] P.R.O., C.O. 96.528 GC Vol. 2 (Encl. with Despatch of 3 March 1913.)

from the War and bursting with idealism, found the position of
the Colony deplorable enough by his own standards (except
financially), he was not the first Governor to disturb the peace;
his immediate predecessor had done his best, and Guggisberg
took over the kind of opportunity for which Clifford had longed.

Guggisberg succeeded therefore to a man whose stature
was comparable to his own, and who on at least one occasion
drew a spontaneous and glowing tribute from one of the leading
nationalists of the day. Clifford's limitation, and Guggisberg's
genius, lay in popular appeal. Clifford's speeches are often
elaborately, even tortuously, reasoned; his subtleties and shrewd
analyses clearly appealed to the coastal lawyers, but the mass of
people had no idea of what was going on in his mind. Guggisberg by contrast was simple, forceful and direct, and—though
not in any pejorative sense—a showman. He was a people's
Governor, while Clifford was a Governor for the élite.[1]

Could any man in the Governor's position have succeeded in
pleasing Africans and Europeans alike? It is a cogent question,
because at the time the task of giving leadership to the expatriate community, who were themselves the real leaders in every
practical sphere, was as vital in its way as that of winning the
confidence of the mass of ordinary Africans. In this Guggisberg
was only partly successful. It cannot be said that his popularity
with Europeans was broad-based, for many—possibly the
majority—resented him, as people everywhere resent the 'new
broom', and believed his faith in the prospects of the African
to be starry-eyed and dangerous. Throughout his time of office
there was backbiting, gossip and cynical comment on the probable collapse of his hopes and plans; even when the buildings
of Achimota were rising from the ground the worldly-wise,
behind his back, said what excellent premises they would make

[1] In justice to Clifford he had not been wanting in the sphere of public relations,
short of exploiting a personal appeal. It was he who initiated the practice of publish-
ing the proceedings of Legislative Council, although verbatim reports were not published until 1916 or Sessional Papers until 1917.

'While the War lasted Clifford had little time to develop his [public relations]
policy to the extent he had hoped. It was Guggisberg who after the War worked out
the details of the policy.' (Kwaw-Swanzy, op. cit., p. 192.)

for the Accra Asylum, whose gruesome condition was a local byword. But among a minority of Europeans, and especially those in the political administration, he came to command a quite exceptional devotion. As one of its members has written to the author:

He managed to bring a spirit and feeling of adventure into the country and infuse, to an extraordinary degree, the feeling that we were a first-class team. He gave us something that I never felt under any other Governor. He brought a sort of renaissance spirit into the country.[1]

[1] Mr. A. Duncan-Johnstone.

# 5

## Foundations:
### The Ten Year Development Plan

WITH the passing of colonial rule some huge deficiencies have become apparent in the former British colonies. The colonial achievement, in terms of the welfare of the people who were ruled, was very far from discreditable, and those deficiencies have to be considered in the context in which the colonialists did their day-to-day work. Before the World Wars a 'developing' country in Africa did not mean a country which needed an injection of foreign capital and skill in order to raise its living standards; it meant one in which journeys from place to place had to be made on foot; in which the first step towards ordered government was to prevent fighting and raiding; in which every device of development was unknown. The problem was not unlike that which faced the Roman legions in Britain. In such circumstances a long time was needed to gather momentum, and for the first quarter of the century development meant pacification, the establishment of law and order and the compiling of rough maps. Today, when the frailty of the new African nations is mercilessly exposed before the world gaze, critics are apt to ask what the British were doing all these years, since in the 1960s there was so little of the apparatus of material civilization, so few men with modern qualifications. The answer is that they were otherwise, and busily, engaged. Today economists speak of 'infrastructure' to describe the communications and services which are the prerequisite of development; the earlier colonialists were trying to establish the 'infra-infrastructure' of development.

But although the achievement was not so discreditable as is often supposed by those who have come later into the field, it seems, at any rate with the wisdom of hindsight, to have lacked an ultimate purpose. This was hardly the fault of the colonial service, which was a disciplined body, under general orders. But what were these orders from the Supreme Command in London? What was *their* strategic objective? It seems to have been the unambitious one of preserving a framework in which the natives could develop at their own pace and expatriate commercial enterprise could work in conditions of security. African education, health, agriculture and welfare were fostered, but only in so far as local colonial finances, or missionary resources, allowed. Colonies were declared to be political units and then expected to make themselves viable, and only a few which were especially small or primarily strategic were regarded as a proper charge on the British taxpayer. The Victorian horror of charity and the belief in thrift and self-reliance which characterized Britain in relation to her own poor was extended to these poor relations of the British Crown. It was possible to become a grant-aided colony by going bankrupt, but so fantastic were the British Treasury controls in this situation that it seemed to some who experienced them better to give up trying. The principle of 'less eligibility' was applied in all its rigour. The idea that 'countries' which had been pronounced to be political entities without knowing anything about it had a *right* to receive injections of capital was one that lay in the future, so far as the British were concerned. Although considerable achievements grew out of this situation, to the eternal credit of colonial officials working on shoe-strings, it was a modest interpretation of Chamberlain's doctrine of 'developing the estate'. The purpose of good administration tended to be better administration, rather than economic development, by the Colonial Power. Development was a marginal rather than a central activity; within the limits of British Treasury doctrine it could never have been otherwise.

Guggisberg, a military engineer rather than a political administrator, broke sharply with this stifling tradition. His

speeches, writing and actions show little apprehension of the
theory and practice of administration; they were about harbours, railways and roads, whose ultimate purpose was to
strengthen the economy to the point when it could support
schools, colleges and hospitals. This he made clear in the per-
oration of his first address to the Legislative Council, which
appears to have been composed under the influence of *Pilgrim's
Progress*, a book to which one imagines he was devoted:

Whatever decisions I may be called upon to make I promise the
people of the Gold Coast that I will always be guided by the fact
that I am an Engineer, sent out here to superintend the construction
of a broad Highway of Progress along which the races of the Gold
Coast may advance, by gentle gradients over the Ridges of Difficulty
and by easy curves around the Swamps of Doubt and Superstition,
to those far-off Cities of Promise—the Cities of Final Development,
Wealth and Happiness.[1]

More prosaically, he presented the people of the Gold Coast
with a *Ten Year Development Programme*. Development Plans are
now so commonplace that it is easy to overlook its profound
significance in the Gold Coast of 1919. It brought an invigorating breath of fresh air, and in spite of an economic slump in
the second year of its operation, it succeeded to a greater degree
than did many Plans of a more sophisticated era. He was the
first colonial governor to practise long-term planning, though
his economics, like his administration, owed nothing to instruction or experience.

The amount of homework which he must have done between
his appointment as Governor and his presentation of the Programme to his second meeting of the Legislative Council, at its
Budget Session, was fantastic; the work which he must have
made his officials do is awe-inspiring. For he sailed from Liverpool on 24 September and presented the Programme to the
Budget Session on 17 November.

The Plan itself[2] was concerned primarily with the basic
foundations of a developing country in the third decade of the

---

[1] *Gazette* No. 83 of 9 October 1919.
[2] Summarized on p. 125.

century—the infrastructure of the economists' jargon. Two-thirds of the capital expenditure was to be on the extension of the railway system and the completion of a deep-water harbour; expenditure on roads was to be trivial compared with that on railways, and Guggisberg has been criticized for this imbalance. It must be remembered, however, that roads, as a method of main arterial transport, were in their infancy at the time, and no one foresaw the development in motor transport which would make them serious competitors of the railway in a tropical country; and further that his Plan was to be supplemented by a considerable item which does not appear in the figures, namely the construction of local feeder roads by communal labour.

The principal theme of the speech in which he presented this Development Programme on 17 November 1919, was that without the harbour, and without the railway extension, 'we cannot appreciably increase our trade, and without an increase in trade we cannot hope to support the recurrent costs of a better system of education'.

So fundamental to his plans—indeed to his whole governorship—was this question of transportation that it will be appropriate to trace the story of the harbour, the railways and the roads during his period of office.

Although, as we have seen, Takoradi Harbour was not Guggisberg's own idea, it would almost certainly not have been built without him. He got the fact established, by further expert survey, that Amanful was in fact the proper place for a harbour, and that further expenditure on Sekondi would be uneconomic; he negotiated a loan to finance it, won African support for it, and piloted the project through the Legislative Council; he stood foursquare against powerful attacks on it, and proposals to abandon it, in 1922, when the economic slump plunged both Africans and Europeans, for different reasons, into a mood of pessimistic criticism; and he sustained his optimism through a dreary and discouraging experience with the contractors, who were constantly under-estimating both time and cost, and who

eventually withdrew from their contract altogether. He displayed throughout that undeviating faith in the future of the
country and the steady refusal to be shaken by misfortune which
were the essence of leadership in a situation of that kind.

He had not been speaking idly when he had told Milner on
his appointment that the first thing he would do as Governor
was to build a deep-water harbour at Takoradi. He repeated
it in a despatch to the Secretary of State in his second month
in the country:

So profoundly convinced am I of the unlimited potentialities of the
Colony if modern transportation facilities are provided that I unhesitatingly place the Deep-Water Harbour at the Head of my programme.

From long experience he knew of the congestion, the waste of
time, the loss, deterioration and high insurance rates which
resulted from shipping the produce of the Gold Coast—and
especially its life blood, cocoa—through the surf ports. Even as
late as 1926, the congestion at Sekondi, with its relatively advanced boat harbour and lighterage facilities, 'baffled description'. There were some 10,000 tons of cocoa stacked on the
beach, in every nook and cranny, and another 15,000 stored in
the town. The important manganese shipments could not get
through the chaos and imports of every kind were standing out
to sea for weeks on end.[1] At this time the adjacent harbour of
Takoradi was nearing completion, and the confusion at Sekondi
was an eloquent tribute to Guggisberg's foresight and persistence.

He had taken the first steps, of initiating a fresh survey of the
coast, before he had even left London to take up his appointment. It was made by Messrs. Stewart & McDonnell, who were
later appointed by the Secretary of State as both Constructional
and Consulting Engineers, a duality which was to cause a good
deal of trouble. Their survey confirmed that Amanful was the
only place for a harbour at which ships could come alongside,
though the cost was estimated at £3,500,000, which was more
than the Government could contemplate. An interim scheme,

[1] *Events*, p. 95.

which would provide sheltered anchorage for ocean-going ships, with wharves for lighters only, leaving the deep-water wharves until a later stage, was however estimated to cost £1,600,000.

Expenditure of this order was not the commonplace occurrence in 1920 that it is today, and the Unofficial Members of the Legislative Council took some time to absorb the idea. The residue of a 1920 loan would be spent and the accumulated balances heavily committed and, incredibly as it seems today, Guggisberg encountered opposition from all sides. African Members could not overcome their innate parochialism, being more interested in spending money on the railway and bringing it to their own locality, or building schools before the economy could support them, than in this remote national project. Europeans were financially cautious and fearful of the future, for already there were warning signals of the coming slump. Some commercial firms were openly hostile, partly because of their own vested interests in the surf ports and partly because their principals in Britain were worried about the future of the economy and by Guggisberg's 'squandermania'. The Governor never wavered, and it is a remarkable fact that his faith in the country and his economic foresight were greater than those of either the African or the commercial leaders.

In this atmosphere, however, he could not carry Takoradi on his own shoulders, and on 3 February 1921, when Stewart & McDonnell's proposals were fully available, he appointed an Advisory Committee

to investigate the Scheme, more especially in its financial aspects, and to advise Goverment as to the ability of the country to embark on the Scheme forthwith, and as to the manner in which the necessary funds could best be provided.

The Committee included the appropriate technical and administrative officers of Government and the mercantile interests. African opinion was represented by Nana Ofori Atta, E. J. P. Brown and C. J. Bannerman. Faced with the facts, this Committee was forced to agree that the harbour was necessary

not only to cope with future expansion but even to retain existing trade; they were a good deal fortified, incidentally, by the
optimism of an African witness, T. Hutton-Mills. Their Report[1]
was a mixture of enthusiasm and financial caution, but with
reservations about the need for stringent economies in other
directions they reported in favour of the interim harbour
scheme. The Report is dated 11 May 1921, and such was the
Governor's drive that its recommendations were presented by
its Chairman (the Colonial Secretary) to the Legislative Council on 13 May. It met with no opposition, though there was
some controversy, as was to be expected in any West African
situation, about how the land was to be acquired. The Secretary
of State's approval of the expenditure was secured on 20 July.
Work commenced at once—indeed Stewart & McDonnell's
advance parties had been there for some time—so that the
actual building of a deep-water harbour was under way within
less than two years of Guggisberg's arrival in the Colony.

There followed some years of tribulation. Had Guggisberg
not driven the contractors, the Advisory Committee and his
officials as hard as he did during these two years it is doubtful
whether Takoradi would have been built in his lifetime, for
within another year the latent doubts in the minds of the Advisory Committee had been brought to the surface by the slump,
opposition had increased, and pessimism reached its lowest
depths in the Budget Session of 27 February 1922.

Guggisberg rode this particular storm with bland authority.
He started by brushing aside[2] a resolution that the building of
the deep-water harbour should be deferred:

Personally I am all in favour of cutting losses if a false step has been
taken, but to cut a loss of this amount, to abandon a carefully thought
out scheme on which the whole future of the trade and therefore of
the progress of this country depends, is a proposal equivalent to
committing political hari-kari. In view also of the inner history of
the attacks which have from time to time been furiously launched

___

[1] *Sessional Paper* No. 8 of 1920–21.
[2] '. . . I therefore refused to allow a resolution of this nature to take up the time
of the Council. . . .'! (Author's exclamation mark.)

upon the scheme, of which Honourable Members approved last May, any weakening of our attitude would make the Gold Coast the laughing stock of the British Empire.

He was convinced that the proper reaction to an economic slump was to build for the future, when prosperity should have revived, and not to sit supinely under adversity.

This was not popular with Unofficial Members. Caseley-Hayford joined with J. D. McKay, who represented the mining interests, in protesting against such treatment. They admitted, with obvious ruefulness, that the Legislative Council was merely an advisory body and had no power to control the Administration, with its official majority; but that if they were to be treated as serious people they should at least be allowed to say what they thought, without arbitrary restrictions of the kind which the Governor had imposed. Today this would seem a very reasonable view, but whether or not in his heart of hearts Guggisberg may have thought it reasonable he was not proposing to have it for one moment:

I am perfectly within my powers . . . and I still adhere to my decision.

He went on to say that the Government was willing to listen to anything anyone wanted to say, provided—in effect—that he agreed with it.[1]

It would show the most supreme lack of courage if I gave way and allowed the motion to stop the work.

It was to be another forty years before anyone spoke like this in the Ghana Legislature. No democrat could approve of it, but Guggisberg was not a democrat, and the Gold Coast was not a democracy. The scheme went on, and was the economic salvation of the country when the tide turned.

This had been a crisis of the kind which could be met, and was indeed met, by resolute leadership. It had been a near

[1] In spite of his uncompromising attitude he was not being merely dictatorial or obstinate. He had argued in his opening address that the economic position was sounder than the critics believed, and he continued to argue this as criticism mounted throughout the year. He argued it in detail in a Despatch to the Secretary of State on 17 August 1922, in another context. He proved to be right. See Kimble, *Political History*, p. 57.

failure of nerve, and Guggisberg's nerve had remained steady. The other tribulation which he had to suffer over the building of Takoradi Harbour was of a continuous, nagging kind; not a specific crisis, with which he would have dealt, but a constant worry about which nothing could be done, and which played into the hands of those who now bitterly opposed the harbour. The trouble started in 1923, after he had ridden roughshod over the Unofficial Members, and when the contractors started falling behind schedule and asking for an extension of time. At first this was not their fault, as they were held up for materials by strikes in England, and the extension they needed was only a few months. Very soon, however, after an inspection by the firm in their capacity of Consulting Engineers, they put the completion date back by more than another year, so that the original date of December 1924 became June 1926.

Meanwhile, and ironically, opposition had started to fade away as trade revived and indeed the Government was embarrassed by urgent demands from the business and commercial world, and from the Customs and Railway Departments, for *extended* accommodation at Takoradi, and by the request of a representative committee that the original plan for deep-water berths should be no longer delayed; if this were to be met, yet another six months would be added to the time-table. The position, which was made worse by the fact that Stewart & McDonnell were both Consulting Engineers and Contractors, appeared to Guggisberg to be so unsatisfactory that he asked the Secretary of State to appoint an experienced Harbour Engineer to review the whole project, in terms of the original and revised schemes, the estimate of cost and the date of completion.[1] This expert duly arrived in April 1924, and reported in the following July. His report was comforting in that his analysis of shipping facts amply confirmed the urgent need for Takoradi Harbour. It brought the Government little comfort apart from this.

It now appeared that the firm had under-estimated not only the time but the cost; the original £1,600,000 was likely to

---

[1] *Events*, p. 89.

become £2,500,000, and the work would take another three and a half years to four years to complete, though both cost and time could be made to cover an amended plan to provide three deep-water berths. This took the completion date to early 1929. Shortly after this Messrs. Stewart & McDonnell threw up their contract,[1] and were replaced, on 15 September 1924, by the firm of Sir Robert McAlpine; the Government retained their own independent Consulting Engineer in the person of the expert whom the Secretary of State had sent out, Mr. Frederick Palmer, C.I.E., of Messrs. Rudd, Palmer & Tritton.

Nothing could have been more damping to the spirit, or more embarrassing to a governor who had behaved as Guggisberg did, than to have to eat his words to a Legislative Council whose Unofficial Members he had dealt with so peremptorily three years earlier, and he cannot have looked forward to explaining the facts to the Budget Session of 1925. He need not have worried. His frank and factual statement was accepted without debate, and supported unanimously by the Unofficial Members; if any of them felt tempted to say 'I told you so', they resisted the temptation. By now they had got the measure of their Governor, and in any case he had been right and they had been wrong on the economic facts.

From that point onwards, moreover, matters started to improve, at any rate so far as timing was concerned. The new contractors went ahead of schedule, and though they had originally allowed for the end of December 1930 for the complete scheme, modifications were made as the work progressed, and it was possible for the ceremonial opening to take place on 3 April 1928, nearly a year after Guggisberg's final departure from the Colony. It was performed by Mr. J. H. Thomas, the then Secretary of State. In these days of air travel and Independence celebrations one could assume that Guggisberg, the

---

[1] The firm's main justification of the delays and rising costs, and of their own resignation, was that they were not allowed by the Colonial Office to purchase certain materials outside the U.K., a condition imposed by the Secretary of State after they had signed the contract; and that British manufacturers were incapable of supplying the right plant or delivering it on time. The point has a curiously contemporary ring.

driving force behind Takoradi, would have been invited to attend as an honoured guest. Even at that time, since he was unemployed, it would have been courteous to invite him. Possibly some protocol concerning former governors and the scene of their labours may have prevented it; possibly the Colonial Office and colonial governments simply did not think in those terms. It was a great personal disappointment to him that he was not there, but at least he had the satisfaction, on his final departure from the Colony, of anchoring inside the breakwaters.[1]

On the day itself the only tangible reminder of Guggisberg was the new harbour tug *Sir Gordon*; it was followed by the second, *Sir Ransford*. This was wholly fitting, for until he became Governor of Sierra Leone in 1925 Ransford Slater had been the pillar on which Guggisberg leaned. He was Colonial Secretary before Guggisberg's arrival, and succeeded him as Governor. Through the immensely complicated harbour negotiations in particular Slater had worked himself into the ground, and in all aspects of Sir Gordon's administration he was always his right-hand man and complement. He had none of Guggisberg's more characteristic qualities; he was the perfect Secretariat man; but the Guggisbergs of this world need the Slaters, and would be helpless without them.

By the time everything was finished, £1,600,000 had become £3,400,000, but on the other hand Takoradi was finished in time to prevent Sekondi from seizing up finally with congestion and over-work.

Guggisberg did not foresee the industrial development of Accra or, of course, the Volta Dam and hydro-electric scheme, which have given birth to the greater harbour of Tema, the technical possibility of which does not seem to have been understood by any surveyor or engineer in his day. Indeed, he forecast that the development of trade in the Gold Coast would always be concentrated in the west and north, and would be centred entirely on Takoradi. Nevertheless his energy and foresight created the conditions in which the country's overseas

[1] The first ship to do this was the Norwegian *Agnete Naerst* on 8 November 1926.

trade could prosper for another vital decade. He himself claimed no more, for his last word on the subject in *Events* was this:

With the completion of Takoradi there should be no necessity for any serious undertaking by Government in harbour development in the next ten years.

He had made good his bold statement to Lord Milner.

The story of Takoradi, though lightly sketched, has included a little detail because the harbour owed so much to Guggisberg's personal conviction, and because its vicissitudes brought out those personal qualities with which this book is primarily concerned. The other features of his transportation policy do not call for a corresponding narrative, since in the development of railways and roads he was the executive rather than the creative force. All his predecessors, both at Government House and in the Railway and Public Works Departments, had understood the need and had done what they could in the circumstances of their day.

Guggisberg's personal stamp on railway development was made in three ways; by the urgency and drive which he brought to bear upon it; by his attempts at a more coherent policy of coordination between road and rail; and by his revival, which involved a reversal of Clifford's policy, of plans for an extension of the railway into the Northern Territories.

To Guggisberg everything was always urgent, but by the third year of his governorship urgency over railway development was sharpened by fear. Like every thinking person in the country he was worried by its dependence on cocoa, and with the rise of competition in Brazil and in other West African countries he foresaw a glut in the world market which would result in trade going to the country with the cheapest internal transport costs. If this was not going to be the Gold Coast he could see his plans for education—the end to which all other activity was a means—evaporating into thin air. He was aware of a particularly formidable rival in neighbouring Nigeria, with her

good harbour, her inland water transport, her active programme of railway building and her vast increase in cocoa
production. This was one of the main themes of his Annual
Message for 1923.

It is interesting to note in passing how well by now he had
mastered the art of speaking in simple words to people who,
whether sophisticated or not, were disposed to think in terms of
parable or simile:

There is a small cloud on the horizon, a very small storm cloud that
promises to grow steadily and steadily until the whole sky is overcast.
Like wise traders who are compelled to sell their goods in the open,
we must put up awnings against the coming rain. These awnings are
railways.[1]

He looked back to the great world rubber boom, and its
reaction:

I wonder, Honourable Members, if the Legislative Councils of
rubber colonies in their prosperous days ever felt alarmed about
over-production? Did they see it coming, and did they strain every
nerve to improve their communications and cheapen their transport
so as to compete with their rivals?

This speech mounted in controlled intensity. Alarmed himself, he did not hesitate to alarm the cocoa farmers and the
Legislative Council with a picture of what might lie ahead:

Not only are railways required, but they are required now; as soon
as it is possible to build them. Nothing is to be gained, everything is
to be lost, by deferring their construction until competition becomes
intense. This intensity will first begin to be felt by the end of 1926.
By that date therefore we should have more railways. Any post-
ponement will lead to our being beaten in the world's cocoa market.
Should that occur the Gold Coast will inevitably for a period at any
rate be in a bankrupt condition. With more railways we shall be
safe for all time; without them our future is not only imperilled, it is
doomed.

He was not, of course, dependent on the Legislative Council,
in the sense of needing their support to go forward with his plans.
His official majority was assured, and he had made it amply
clear over Takoradi that if he thought it necessary to overrule

[1] *Debates*, 1923–4, p. 45.

the Unofficial Members he would unhesitatingly do so. But by this time the need had disappeared. A new note could be heard in the debates which followed his annual orations. African members would, as always, air their local grievances, and demand that railways, roads, water, or whatever was under discussion, should be brought to their own particular area or Province, for in Gold Coast democratic thinking they were delegates of 'their people' and could do no other; they would also criticize the Government on certain matters that affected them emotionally, particularly those which concerned the appointment of Africans to public office; but they had also begun to think nation-wise under Guggisberg's tutelage and to admire and trust their Governor. When he spoke in this vein about railways or any other aspect of development policy they now listened with a new respect. He had won their confidence. No less had he won the confidence of the professional and technical officers under whose hands the railways had to be built. Firm and informed leadership was eliciting a response in terms of effort, keenness and morale; railway workers had the feeling of being part of a crusade, and not merely a salaried staff.

In his efforts to co-ordinate rail with road Guggisberg was working at an awkward period and in an unknown medium. Motor transport was improving every year, but its costs per ton mile were still so high, and its revolutionary possibilities still so speculative, that he inevitably misjudged the future. It was not, however, for want of trying, and his calculations were valid in the light of existing knowledge.

As early as 1921 he had taken the personal initiative of asking the General Manager of the Railways to conduct an experiment in transport in close consultation with political and agricultural officers in the Western Province. Here the railway passed through a cocoa belt some eighty or ninety miles wide, but even at times of high prices only about a quarter of the crop was reaching the market because of lack of access.

It seems to me that in encouraging the people to plant cocoa and in neglecting to provide them with the means of transport, Government may almost be accused of breaking faith.

He accordingly asked the Railway to peg out routes for feeder
roads, such as could be built by communal labour, but in such
a way that if they proved profitable they could be converted
into Public Works Department roads without re-routing; and
on these roads to provide a service of lorries.

By November 1922, he had produced an exhaustive memorandum, into which he had put a great deal of personal effort.
One of the vital problems was comparative transport costs.
Head-loading could be estimated with some accuracy, and was
about six and threepence per ton mile; lorry transport was
more speculative, as it varied with the state of the roads and the
weight they could bear, but on an average it was about half
the head-loading costs; but rail costs, particularly for any
journey over about fifty miles, were well below a shilling. At the
time this was conclusive, for no one could foresee that all-weather
roads could ever be afforded on a significant scale, or that
lorries would grow to their present size and efficiency. Accordingly policy crystallized round the provision of railways as main
arteries, with roads feeding them to a distance of around
thirty-five to fifty miles. 'Roadrails' or 'light tramways', which
had once been the Governor's hobby-horse, had been pushed
into the background by the improving lorries.

The Governor's own eye was on every calculation; he himself
got down to the arithmetic, and as an engineer, he spoke in the
language of the railwaymen and the Public Works Department.

With regard to the Northern Territories, Guggisberg was an
over-optimist, as indeed he tended to be about the productive
possibilities of the Gold Coast generally. He was accused, and
cheerfully accepted the accusation, of being a fanatic about the
Northern Territories. Clifford, in framing an economic policy,
had recommended virtually abandoning the North for the
foreseeable future, even cutting down administration to a skele-
ton form, in order to concentrate on the high potential areas of
the Colony and Ashanti. In terms of economic development
this was a perfectly respectable policy, but Guggisberg would
have none of it. In one of his first despatches to the Secretary

of State, written within six weeks of his arrival, he proposed to reverse it, and to build a railway from Kumasi to Gambago, in order to open up the Northern Territories for economic development, not to meet any existing need. Nothing came of this, nor has come of it to this day, though economic surveys of a more scientific kind than Guggisberg could have commanded have more than once been made in the intervening years.

But Guggisberg's belief in it was constant, and beginning in 1925, at his direct instigation, three alternative routes to the northern border were reconnoitred, not only by railway engineers and surveyors but by the geological, agricultural and veterinary departments, in order to build up a picture of potential produce and traffic. He was not alone in his belief, for in 1926 the Parliamentary Under-Secretary of State (Mr. Ormesby-Gore) gave it the weight of his authority in a Report which he had made on his visit to West Africa.[1] In this he stated that it was the clear duty of Government to build a northern railway when the finances of the Colony permitted, though he projected this into the unspecified future when the surveys would have been completed and when the effect of Takoradi Harbour on the economy had made itself felt. Guggisberg dealt with the subject at length in his last Message to the Council before his departure, but concluded sadly: 'The whole scheme is one on which the final recommendations will fall to my successor.'

These, then, were Guggisberg's particular interests, but it is probable that, as in other fields, his most important personal contribution was the imponderable one of morale. He took a more active part in details than most governors would have done, because of his own engineering expertise and interest, but even so progress was dependent on the pace and willingness with which the Department went to work under its General Manager, E. W. Cozens-Hardy, who was in charge almost throughout Guggisberg's time. There seems little doubt that the whole staff responded to the Governor's leadership, and that *esprit de corps* was exceptionally high. It was a favourite war-time saying of Guggisberg that 'there are no bad regiments in the

[1] Cmd. 2744.

British Army, only bad commanding officers'; this precept he tried consciously to apply to departments and governors.

Three major projects, under what might be called conventional railway development, had been listed in the Ten Year Programme. First, the main line from Sekondi to Kumasi was to be strengthened, re-equipped and to some extent re-routed, as it was becoming incapable of taking the increasingly heavy traffic; this work was completed by October 1926. Second, the line from Accra to Kumasi, which stopped at Tafo, had to be completed; the first train ran between the two towns in September 1923. Third, the Central Province Railway, linking the two main lines and tapping the rich cocoa areas of the Province, was to commence and be pushed forward as far as possible; a start was made at the end of 1923, and when Guggisberg left eighty-one miles was open to traffic. At the end of 1919 there had been 269 miles of railway in the Gold Coast; by the end of 1926, 475, in addition to 250 miles of the Sekondi–Kumasi line that had been virtually rebuilt.

The building of roads has always exercised a peculiar fascination over the minds of colonial administrators; to make a road where none existed was an achievement which carried almost spiritual overtones, and gave a sense of complete fulfilment. Guggisberg, who had walked, indeed hacked his way, through much of the Colony and Ashanti during the early years of the century, had better cause than most to be in love with roads, but they could not figure very prominently in his Ten Year Programme, at any rate in terms of financial allocation. A road of sorts, good enough to carry a light lorry in the dry season, could be built by communal labour, provided that the local chief and his people were persuaded that it was a good idea; but the step in financial terms from that to an all-weather road of any kind that was then known to the Public Works Department was so colossal, and the needs of the harbour and the railways, which could not be built by amateurs, so overriding, that the road building programme in the Ten Year Programme was bound to be modest. A few main arteries could be improved and pushed forward a mile or two at a time, but the main concern was to see that the so-called 'pioneer' roads followed traces which would allow posterity to build permanently on the same routes.

Accordingly, Guggisberg's road policy for some years was based on encouraging Political Officers, and through them the chiefs and people, to turn out and build feeder roads themselves, though one improvement which could be ascribed to his foresight was that feeder roads were planned in advance of the railway extensions, thus avoiding the anomaly that had been allowed to develop in the Western Province. From about 1924, however, improved techniques in building both roads and lorries called for a more sophisticated policy.

Hitherto, since trade had far outstripped communications, it had been the deliberate intention to sacrifice quality to quantity. Anything, even roads which were a sticky quagmire in the rains and a corrugated, pot-holed hell in the dry season, could be tolerated in order to get the produce moving. But no one was more conscious than the Governor that this was inadequate and impermanent, and he was assiduous in encouraging the Public Works Department to experiment in economical road conversion. By the beginning of 1924 the Department had devised a method by which, provided the foundations of the road were good, a vastly improved and more durable surface could be laid with tar and metal. It cost about £1,000 a mile, but was infinitely cheaper than the concrete or 'tarmac' construction which wealthy countries could afford. It was a sort of compromise with tarmac, and was given the name 'tarmet' to signify this.[1] From now onwards the improvement of the main trunk roads by Government was given a higher allocation, and the services of contractors and of the Governor's old friends the Royal Engineers were enlisted. The beginnings of a trunk road system began to take shape, and would have done so more quickly but for the delays and frustrations of obtaining either plant or personnel.

[1] '. . . a layer of granite or quartzite laid on the old gravelled surface and rolled with a motor roller down to a thickness of 4 inches, then blinded with quarry screenings, tar-sprayed by a pressure spraying machine, and sanded.' (*Debates*, 1927–8, p. 111.)

Simultaneously the Department had enormously improved its techniques in building ordinary laterite roads.

The effect on exports was immediate; no less dramatic was the effect on the Governor's touring:

Thanks to the new roads, I have been the first Governor to enter many important towns in the Colony and Ashanti. From careful enquiries made at these places it was apparent that the prices for cocoa paid to the farmer rose between 50 and 100 per cent after the arrival of the motor road. In many places far distant from the railway, through which I had trudged laboriously on foot during my previous service in this country, I found the streets and roads thronged with motor lorries laden with cocoa and crowded with passengers, very often both.[1]

Nowhere was the road revolution more remarkable than in the Northern Territories:

It is possible to get from Kumasi to Tamale in twelve hours, a distance of 240 miles, and to complete the whole circuit of the Northern Territories in less than a week. . . . In the old days an officer took on the average between thirty and forty days to get from Navorongo to Sekondi when he was going on leave, as against four or five days today. Apart from saving time thus uselessly spent by Government officials, the new motor roads are steadily opening up trade in the Northern Territories. . . .

But progress was bringing its own difficulties, and by 1926 Guggisberg was having to face a problem the existence of which he had previously denied—that of competition between road and rail, which has troubled other Governments in other countries. It took Guggisberg by surprise, as he frankly admitted, and he never really found the answer to it. On the improved roads lorries were now having no difficulty in undercutting the Government railway, and Government was faced with the problem of largely financing its own competitor, while having to maintain unremunerative roads in more distant parts of the Colony. He never reached a positive answer, which would have taken him into fields of socialistic thinking which were alien to his nature. He was still groping for it when he left, and his last statement of policy was a negative one, to the effect that Government could not undertake to improve a road that followed the

[1] *Debates*, 1925–6, p. 45.

same route as the railway. It was, however, a considerable achievement to have created the problem at all, even if he could not solve it. During his governorship 3,338 miles of new motor road were constructed at a cost of £1,233,147, including 260 miles which were tarmetted.

It would not be easy to prove a clear chain of cause and effect between Guggisberg's policy of transportation and the increase in the country's trade, but it is a fact that during the seven and a half years of his governorship the increase in annual earnings averaged out at about £13 million and the increase in annual revenue to the Government at about £2,600,000.

In Guggisberg's imagination the lorries on the feeder roads, the freight trains to the coast and the ships outward bound from Takoradi were carrying an ever-widening variety of products— palm oil, sisal, ground-nuts, shea-butter, cotton, coffee, sugar and tobacco—for he had satisfied, or persuaded, himself that there was no tropical crop that would not thrive in the Gold Coast. The reality was very different; the lorries, trains and ships carried mainly cocoa, and his attempts to diversify the agriculture of the country bore little fruit over the years. One by one they were examined, tried out, and often showed fair experimental results; but one by one they sank into oblivion, or secondary importance, in the face of the conservatism of the farmers, the easy money to be made from cocoa and the reluc- tance of the Department of Agriculture to be taught its own business. Yet something must be said about these experiments for three reasons; first because they illustrate the imaginative kind of planning that was always going on in his mind; second, because he always thought of the infrastructure of communica- tions as a creative thing, designed not only to serve the existing needs of cocoa but to develop a variety of alternatives; and thirdly because, although he had no special agricultural know- ledge, he did not hesitate to take hold of the professional De- partment and stir it up when he was convinced that it was falling short of its responsibilities.

What first set his mind working was the fall in cocoa prices in

the second year of his governorship, following an unprecedented
boom in which the people of the Gold Coast had all but fatally
lost their heads. Eighty-three per cent of the country's exports
was accounted for by a luxury product; it only needed the
women (mainly) of Europe and America to buy fewer choco-
lates, and higher education in the Gold Coast would be set
back again.

He admonished the Legislative Council on these matters in
his Budget Speech of 1921, in which his imagination went to
work in devising more baskets in which the Gold Coast eggs
could be contained. He was principally concerned to revive
the trade in palm oil, which had fallen into decay because of the
greater lure of cocoa and the destruction of trees for palm wine.
It always offended his sense of fitness that the country was so
dependent on a luxury crop, and he would gladly have exchanged it for palm oil, with its industrial uses and its more
stable demand. From year to year his advocacy of it never
flagged, and important improvements were obtained from an
experimental scheme near Takoradi; yet little came of it, and
towards the end of his career he was having to admit that the
best results obtained in the Gold Coast were inconsiderable
compared with those of scientific plantation agriculture in the
Far East and the Congo.

His other great dream, never to be wholly fulfilled, was the
development of the Northern Territories by ground-nuts and
shea-butter, to which in later years he added ambitious plans for
cotton. On this subject his optimism touched exaggerated
heights, and he could say to the Legislative Council:

I repeat now what I said last month in this Chamber that *the whole
future* of the Gold Coast is bound up with the development of the
ground-nut and shea-butter industries of the Northern Territories.[1]

Granted a railway to the North, which he himself was
assuming, his apparent dreams may well have been a serious
possibility, but as the railway was never built we cannot know;
more modest developments along these lines have of course

[1] *Debates*, 1920–1, p. 34.

followed the improvement of the northern roads. But we can appreciate what he was after, in 1921:

Honourable Members, with means of transportation—with a deep-water harbour at Takoradi and a railway from Kumasi to the neigh-bourhood of Tamale—we will assure the safety of the Gold Coast trade. We shall have four baskets of articles greatly in demand—cocoa and palm oil from the south, ground-nuts and shea-butter from the north—together with seven little baskets of rice-copra, sisal, corn, sugar, coffee and tobacco—little baskets, Honourable Members, but good . . .

And with the safety of our trade assured comes assurance of our revenue—the sinews of war for our campaign of education and progress.

To diversify agriculture and experiment with crops was of course the normal work of the Department, which had been pursuing it, though without his turbulent energy, long before his arrival. But one crop was his special and personal concern, and in advocating it he had to overcome the apathy and scepti-cism of the Director of Agriculture. He had a vision—a not un-common occurrence with him—of the whole of the Accra plains being covered with sisal. His personal initiative led to a Govern-ment Sisal Plantation some four miles from the port of Accra which appears to have been remarkably successful. In intention it was no more than a demonstration plot to convince the coastal farmers that sisal was an industry with a future, but from 1924 onwards it operated as a profitable venture in its own right.[1]

Guggisberg is not usually remembered for these things, and indeed he could point to no great success. Cocoa was too easy and too profitable, and in spite of its vicissitudes it kept the country going. With sufficient for his wants the Gold Coast farmer was not a man to be plagued by visions of how much better things might have been or to share the Governor's apprehensions about the future of higher education if the

[1] *Debates*, 1925–6, p. 25. The writer made extensive enquiries in Accra to try to discover what had happened to the sisal industry, but no one in the early 1960s could tell him, though one or two survived who remembered the episode. It apparently lived on the energy and enthusiasm of the Governor and did not survive his departure.

country failed to compete in the world cocoa market. Sufficient
unto the day . . . It must have been a trying atmosphere for a
man of Guggisberg's temperament.

But in appreciating his work as a whole it is important that his
efforts in the realm of agriculture should not be altogether
forgotten. Nor for that matter his limitations, for he was the
victim of a not unfamiliar conflict. On the one hand he saw
that the marketing of primary produce was a highly competitive
business in the world market, in which success depended on
cutting costs, improving quality and determining the optimum
scale of production. His eyes were constantly on the rest of the
tropical world, from Latin America to the Far East, and he
knew of the results which flowed there from the application of
science to plantation agriculture. On the other hand he believed
passionately in the social good, in terms of happiness, character
and independence, which accrued to the family farmer, be-
holden to no one, surrounded by his family, organizing his own
way of life, though mildly spurred by the persuasions of the
local Agricultural Officer. Throughout his time of office he was
concerned, as all Governors of the Gold Coast have been, in
combating the indolent methods of the farmers, and he travelled
widely to exhort them to prevent disease, keep down weeds,
improve fermentation and follow the advice of the Department
of Agriculture. But never did he question the assumption that
farming must rest upon the family unit. On the contrary his
exhortation was 'Make your farms smaller.' It happens that
cocoa, more than most crops, can be made to pay on these lines,
though not at its maximum potential; but Guggisberg saw the
other, and to him unpalatable, side of the picture when he came
to study the comparative facts of palm-oil production in the
Gold Coast and the Far East. It was a matter in which it was
difficult to have it both ways. Meanwhile, and mercifully, the
lorries, trains and ships were offered more than they could carry.

His concern to preserve the natural resources of the country
quickly involved him, as it had involved all previous governors
and adminstrations, in the acutely sensitive question of forest

preservation. It was a matter in which, at the end of his own administration, he believed himself to have failed because he was compelled to introduce legislation to make the chiefs and people behave sensibly, whereas he had pledged himself at the outset to win their co-operation by reason and persuasion. To any informed and detached mind, capable of looking a few generations ahead, the need to set aside very large tracts of forest reserve was transparently clear. Guggisberg himself had been shocked by the change in the appearance of the country between his leaving as a surveyor in 1908 and returning as Governor in 1919, and the facts in the possession of the Forestry Department amply confirmed the increasing urgency of the situation. Wholesale destruction of trees was destroying humidity, drying up water supplies and threatening the whole future of agriculture. It was a situation in which there was, in theory, a strong case for compulsion, since the Government could see clearly what the chiefs (or more often their advisers, since the chiefs were frequently intelligent men) were incapable of seeing, and had a moral obligation to save the people of the Gold Coast and their descendants from the consequences of ignorance and folly.

But compulsion, however justifiable in theory, was no longer practical politics, for in the previous twenty years the matter of forest reserves had become inextricably interwoven with that of land in the wider sense, and of the Government's supposed intention to expropriate it. Some blame attached to previous Administrations for their insensitive handling of the subject (though their good intentions had been unquestionable) but whatever the rights and wrongs of this it would have been impossible for Guggisberg in 1919 to grasp this nettle without risking political disaster. To put it in its lowest terms, to do so would have given him the worst possible start, and would have undermined the trust which he succeeded in winning in such a uniquely short space of time. It would not have been in character had he shirked the problem merely because his popularity would have been at stake—his firm stand over Takoradi suggests the improbability of this—but it happened that his own

preference was for reason and persuasion, and he was confident
both of his ability to persuade and of the chiefs' capacity to follow intelligent reasoning. He based this firmly on his experience
of the chiefs during his surveying days of 1902 to 1908.

In this he over-estimated his own influence and the chiefs'
capacity for logical thinking; or perhaps it would be fairer to
say that he under-estimated the damage done by his predecessors and the Africans' abandonment of reason on any
matter touching the ownership or use of land. At any rate persuasion failed, and his Annual Messages show an increasingly
querulous note at the failure of the chiefs to see reason, or at
least to act upon it. He had thrown the onus on the chiefs of
voluntarily reserving areas of forest land, under the technical
advice and guidance of the Forestry Officers, and was himself
indefatigable in explaining why forest preservation was necessary and in assuring the chiefs that indigenous rights in the land
set aside would be inviolable. At the same time he took Unofficial Members of the Legislative Council and other influential
Africans into his confidence and tried to recruit them as active
colleagues in his campaign. Virtually nothing came of it.[1]
The chiefs and people remained suspicious, and found the
utmost difficulty in following the argument that the felling of
trees would alter the climate, lower the water table and threaten
the cocoa industry. The educated element could follow the
evidence, but found the practical issue too hot to handle.

For some years Guggisberg resisted pressure from the Forestry
Department to legislate, but after a time, baffled and frustrated
by apathy, and by the tendency of the chiefs to agree that the
advice was right and then to do nothing whatever about it, he
began to increase the pressure. In his Annual Message of 1924
he had issued a stern warning, without tying himself to an
actual time limit. A year later—a year in which infinitesimal
progress had been made—he imposed the limit; in March 1926,
legislation would be introduced, unless the chiefs and people in
the meantime had taken significant action. In 1926 he himself

---

[1] By 1926 only 240 square miles of forest had been reserved out of the 6,000 which
the technical advisers thought was the necessary minimum.

was compelled to act. In spite of everything the Government had obtained less than 10 per cent of the reserves which were necessary even to preserve the cocoa industry, on which almost all the trade and prosperity of the country depended. Legislation was prepared, and was enacted in 1927. Immense pains were taken to avoid the deprivation of owners of land, or any appearance of it, and it was still made possible for the chiefs to act voluntarily, if they so desired, instead of being subject to compulsion. Moreover Guggisberg continued most assiduously to oil the wheels by explanation and persuasion, and had the satisfaction of gaining support for the Forestry Ordinance from his own creation the Provincial Councils of Chiefs. Nevertheless, it was one of the only two real disappointments of his governorship—the other being his failure to achieve anything effective in improving municipal government in the large towns.

We have digressed somewhat from the Ten Year Plan in order to discuss Guggisberg's involvement in agriculture and forestry, upon which the whole economy rested. The Plan itself was mainly concerned with transportation, which accounted for about three-quarters of the expenditure under the Ten Year Development Programme; most of the rest—hydro-electric works, drainage, water supplies and posts and telegraphs—would properly be called infrastructure in modern phraseology. A little was allocated to public buildings, including Achimota, which would more properly be called 'suprastructure'. All had to bend to the economic facts of the slump at the end of 1921. As has been said, hydro-electric developments were virtually abandoned, town improvements were drastically curtailed and the railway programme was cut back; on the other hand far more was spent on Takoradi than was originally estimated for.

The Plan had involved two phases—the first four years in which both income and expenditure could be fairly accurately foreseen, the former consisting of a £4 million loan raised on the London Market, and an allocation from revenue of £2½ million; and the last six years, in which the programme would depend on the results achieved in the first period and (though this was not stated) on the condition of the economy. It was therefore reasonably flexible in conception, a point which Guggisberg had some difficulty in getting the literally minded, and financially nervous, Unofficial Members to understand. At the beginning of 1922 he was complaining of 'the extraordinary misconception . . . in the minds of those who are interested in the financial condition of this country':

The Programme has been read as meaning that the Government intends to expend the amounts shown in the table in the next ten years. This is not the case. . . . The object of the Programme is to give as clear an idea as possible of the material development necessary for this country. Without a programme of this nature it is impossible to draw up plans for the carrying out of either loan works or extraordinary works on a systematic and economical basis.[1]

It may be that it fell short of a Plan in the sense in which the word is used by contemporary development planners, using sophisticated techniques of economic forecasting. Guggisberg himself always used the word 'Programme'. It was, in plain terms, the first systematic appreciation of what needed to be done, within the broad limits of possibility; and this was a considerable advance on anything that had gone before.

The slump was a serious, but not a fatal, blow, for at the end of his governorship some £16½ million had been committed out of the original programme of £24½ million. If the Legislative Council had been a deciding, instead of a deliberative, body the result would have been more modest, but, as we have seen, Guggisberg held steadily on course and refused to be infected by the panic of the Unofficial Members. He had naturally to make serious cuts, but over communications, and particularly over Takoradi, he refused to give way to insistent demands to cut back. Indeed, practically the whole of the £6½ million for the first four years was spent as planned. In his final Budget Speech he was able to say:

We declined to withdraw any part of the Programme that affected communications, as we felt strongly that, whatever other economies

[1] *Debates*, 1922-3, p. 46.

we practised, a trade slump was the best time for making communications catch up with trade requirements. . . . Our confidence was eventually justified, for instead of decreasing our revenue rose, and our aggregate balance steadily mounted from £1,612,000 in 1919 to well over £3,000,000 in 1924, and in spite of reductions in taxation.

For an amateur, and a man who 'lacked administrative experience', it was not a bad effort. The figures[1] speak plainly for themselves:

| | Original Plan 1919 | Revised Plan 1922 | Revised Plan 1927 |
|---|---|---|---|
| Harbour | 2,000,000 | 1,840,000 | 3,551,000 |
| Railways | 14,581,000 | 6,076,000 | 5,948,000 |
| Roads | 1,000,000 | 750,000 | 1,619,000 |
| Water Supplies | 1,790,000 | 1,208,000 | 634,000 |
| Town Improvements and Drainage | 1,850,000 | 300,000 | 740,000 |
| Hydraulic and Electric Works | 2,000,000 | 200,000 | 199,000 |
| Public Buildings (including Achimota) | 1,100,000 | 1,000,000 | 2,273,000 |
| Post and Telegraphs | 90,000 | 422,000 | 336,000 |
| Maps and Surveys | 200,000 | 120,000 | 200,000 |
| Agriculture and Forestry | — | — | 252,000 |
| Takoradi Town | — | — | 669,000 |
| Miscellaneous | — | 100,000 | 225,000 |
| | £24,611,000 | £12,016,000 | £16,646,000 |

For an amateur, his financial policy in general was also impressive. In his Budget Speech of 1923, which included his major statement of financial policy, he confessed that he had some difficulty in understanding certain aspects of the accounts[2] (adding characteristically that he had asked his financial advisers to produce something clearer). But he was unwilling to allow finance, the basis of all development planning, to remain the private mystery of his financial advisers, and by application, common sense and above all by a search for *principles*, which could be stated simply and clearly and from which all subsequent action would flow, he mastered the finances of the Colony sufficiently to enunciate a more coherent and systematic policy than had existed under any previous governor.

[1] Compiled by Professor Kimble, *Political History*, p. 56, from the Governor's Annual Addresses.

[2] *Debates*, 1923-4, p. 24.

In his first year funds were plentiful and his principal contribution was to imbue his advisers and his Legislative Council with financial courage and an expansive outlook; Unofficial Members were apprehensive at seeing their unprecedented reserves disappearing in development expenditure on the strength, as it appeared to them, of the Governor's hunches, and the commercial Members in particular thought that the obvious and natural thing to do if the country was well off was to reduce the already light taxation on imports and exports. In his second and third years, with the trade depression, his contribution was to keep his financial nerve while others were in danger of losing theirs, and to insist that the right thing to do in a slump was to spend for future development instead of marking time and retrenching. But by 1923 he was speaking with confidence on a more permanent financial policy.

In tackling any problem he liked to clear the way by stating principles; this was the way his mind worked, and until he had got his principles on paper he was apt to be at sea, for he disliked muddling through or extemporizing. When tackling the problem of education he overwhelmed the Legislative Council (and the Directorate of Education) with fifteen principles, later increased to sixteen. In the realm of finance he restricted himself to three.

The first—a typical example of his liking to get things straight —was that a rational distinction should be made between Recurrent and Extraordinary Expenditure, which had been allowed by imprecise thinking to become blurred, and that annual revenue should cover both; if revenue was falling short, Extraordinary Expenditure, above a certain minimum without which development would altogether stagnate, should be restricted. But revenue was also to allow more providently than in the past for major renewals which would otherwise descend as an intolerable imposition on a future generation and in particular for a Railway Renewals Fund which would replace the haphazard method whereby necessary replacements were voted from year to year. (Otherwise, as he pointed out in 1923, the renewal of the rails laid in the first two years of his governorship would impose an impossible burden on the revenue round about 1956.) He thought in terms of £100,000 a year.

The second principle concerned a General Reserve Fund, which had not hitherto existed, and which was not to be touched without the express permission of the Secretary of State and in the direst emergency. To this he proposed to devote £500,000 of the existing accumulated balance, and to build it up annually by its own interest until it had reached a maximum of £2,000,000, after which the interest might be devoted to general revenue expenditure.[1]

The third principle was that the accumulated balance, after setting aside the Reserve Fund, should be spent on revenue-producing works.

Although these measures may now appear elementary they represented a financial policy which had not previously existed, and were characteristic of Guggisberg's orderly and purposeful mind. In the event his financial optimism was fully justified, and even at the end of the worst financial year of 1922–3, when the Government budgeted for a deficit of £700,000, the surplus balances did not fall below £1,979,000;[2] by 1925–6 they had risen to £3¼ million. Not the least of Guggisberg's achievements in the financial realm was that he stood up with great courage to the Secretary of State's own Committee on West African Trade and Taxation, which reported in 1922 that the revenues of the West African colonies had been abnormal, that they were not collecting sufficient revenue to cover recurrent charges, and that the work of post-war reconstruction had been undertaken on too lavish a scale and with too great rapidity.

On the 1st March, 1923, I informed Honourable Members of this Council of my reasons for disagreeing with the conclusions of the Committee so far as the Gold Coast was concerned, and everything that has occurred since that date has more than justified my opinion.[3]

[1] The Reserve Fund was never touched, even during the depression of the early 1930s, and after the Second World War was transferred to the country's development reserves. Kimble, *Political History*, p. 56.
[2] *Events*, p. 176. On pp. 175–8 Guggisberg traces the story of the revenue and the surplus balances in some detail.
[3] Ibid., p. 177.

To finance the work on Takoradi, Guggisberg had raised a loan of £4 million on the London market at 6 per cent (which incidentally was subscribed in a few hours), and a further loan of £4,628,000 at 4½ per cent in 1925 for later capital expenditure under the Ten Year Programme. For the rest the huge developments of his régime were financed from accumulated balances and from revenue.

These economic matters were first, in point of time, to occupy his attention, and were the subject of his first despatches to the Secretary of State; his preoccupation with them lasted until the day of his departure. All colonial governors had to keep a large number of balls in the air at once—indeed the juggling metaphor is not inappropriate—and there was nothing exceptional in the fact that Guggisberg dealt simultaneously with economics and finance, the constitutional problem, public health and hospitals, native administration and a dozen other important questions besides. This was routine for the occupants of Government Houses, who in any case were well served by their principal officers. What distinguished Guggisberg was the detailed, and often professionally expert, attention he gave to the subject-matter of this chapter; the immense amount of touring that he found time for in the midst of it all, and in which he achieved his unique identification with the chiefs and people of the Gold Coast; and the fact that to the normal burdens of office he added the most personal of all his commitments; this was no less than the conversion of the Gold Coast to a new gospel of education and the building of a temple to his gods at the village of Achimota, near Accra. To this activity we now turn.

# 6

# Education
## and the Vision of Achimota

ALL colonial governors had to concern themselves with education. It was one of their most important responsibilities, a major item in their budgets and the most popular of all topics with the people whom they governed. Most governors returned to the subject for the first time after a lapse of many years since leaving their own Public School and University, where they had in any case learnt little of the problems of primary education in a state system. Accordingly they were content to leave matters very largely to their professional experts. The content of the curricula, the aridities of the examinations, the complexities of junior and senior primary—these were for the Directorate of Education, and governors were content to advise them if they sought advice and to encourage them by their public speeches, in which education was always a happy subject for oratorical rotundities.

This was not Guggisberg's way. He took hold of the Department of Education in the Gold Coast and shook it; at times he appeared to be running it. Psychologists might find it interesting to consider why a man like Guggisberg should have had an obsessive interest in this subject. His upbringing and career are suggestive, but here it is sufficient to repeat that he was a born headmaster and that he thought the people of the Gold Coast deserved the best of everything.

His own views on education suffered from an inexperience which, in his position of authority, was more than compensated by a relentless enthusiasm. Even if he knew little about how children should be taught he had the deepest convictions about *what* they should be taught, and he based these on a knowledge of West African life which had extended over ten years in bush, village, town and headquarters office. Above all he was dedicated to the proposition that they *should* be taught—as many as possible and as quickly as possible—and that their education was the ultimate goal of all other activity. He lacked the ability to formulate his ideas persuasively. Through all his innumerable speeches on the subject a philosophy of education struggles to find expression, and fails narrowly to do so. He expressed himself forcefully and fluently, but not always felicitously, and his original concept of Achimota was, from the viewpoint of a professional educationist, a considerable muddle.

The impression of a man inarticulate in the higher and more abstract realms of thought, yet struggling to express high and abstract truths about education, is nowhere more evident than in his animadversions on character-training. This was to him the essential foundation of all teaching, and it seemed almost retrograde when the number of schools exceeded (as of course it did) the number of teachers of high moral character who were capable of imprinting it upon the children they taught. How a happier state was to be brought about was a constant puzzle to him, which is not surprising, as it has puzzled everyone before and since, in Britain as in Ghana. His first pronouncement on the subject, in a major speech on education of 20 February 1920, was naïve. It amounted to putting all children in boarding schools, since 'moral training is so difficult to carry out in day schools that it may almost be said to be impossible'. Primary and technical, as well as secondary, education must be run on boarding-school lines, and the Government would somehow find the money to make this possible. Apart from the fact that this ran away from the problem, it was a wildly impracticable suggestion financially, unless education was to be confined to the privileged few, which would have been the antithesis of what he wanted.

As the years went by he became more voluble and more earnest on this topic, though not noticeably more enlightening.

He was a little exasperated at his failure to solve the problem as
he would have solved one in logistics, a little strident in his
protestations, a little apt, one must confess, to make pronouncements of the obvious with an air profundity, a little pontifical
in tone. The year 1925 found him in full flood, having retreated
a little from his position on boarding schools, and relying
strongly on the educational precepts of Dr. Jesse Jones.[1] He
spoke of the simple virtues, which were many, and familiar.
He demurred from what he had heard was a widespread view
that character is formed at the mother's knee, believing that
mothers had serious limitations. He held that character is
formed more at school than anywhere else, and he intended
that it should be so formed in the Gold Coast.

The following year, unable to leave the subject alone yet unable to throw very much more light on it, he leaned heavily on
an unnamed writer and went over such ground as love of
country derived from a knowledge of its history and folk-lore,
and the beneficent influence of organized games and handi-
crafts. As always at the end of these harangues he paid tribute
to the influence of religion, without adding appreciably to what
has been said thoughout the centuries on this subject. In the
end his arguments led him, as they have led others, to the
irresistible conclusion that character-training in schools must
stem from the personal character of the teachers, and he seemed
aggrieved that these were not such as to lead to an early fulfilment of his hopes.

Indeed, there is throughout these speeches a sense of grievance
that what was so clear in his own mind could not be put on the
drawing-board and given to contractors to translate into visible
reality. Typical of his impatience, and of his misguided belief
that education could blossom as a result of directives and
memoranda, was his manner of supporting the Boy Scout
movement. This is not an irrelevancy in a chapter concerned
with education, for in Guggisberg's mind Baden-Powell was
perhaps the greatest educationist of all, and few books written
at the time expressed his beliefs more aptly than *Scouting for*

[1] See pp. 285 et seq.

*Boys* and *Rovering to Success*. Guggisberg would have had everyone a Boy Scout. Indeed, he said as much, for one of his less sensible public statements was that 'every schoolboy must be one; every schoolmaster must be a scoutmaster'. It was a point of view that younger members of the Achimota staff were to contemplate a little ruefully in later years, when they found themselves at the Governor's wish, which was apt to be law, partaking in training courses at Gilwell Park during their leave in England.[1] It was all a little elementary.

(In 1927, however, he spoke—ahead of his time for Africa— of the value of the 'union between parent and teacher'. His problem was that he was having to learn while himself adopting the role of teacher.)

What he was really groping for were the ideas which at much the same time were simmering in the mind of the young Kurt Hahn in Germany, from which eventually flowed the Gordonstoun philosophy of education, later expressed in the kind of training associated with the name of 'Outward Bound'. This would have delighted him; regrettably, for him, it took root in England a decade too late. Meanwhile, his conviction that book-learning was dominant in the Gold Coast schools, and that when divorced from character-training and a spirit of patriotic service it could do harm to the country which might outweigh the good, led him to some intemperate expressions of opinion. At times he seemed almost to align himself with the philistines in disliking the 'educated native', when 'education' meant a smattering of knowledge learned by rote or a degree fought for against odds in the unedifying *milieu* of London University, where the character is not trained. Even Achimota never fully satisfied him, and it was not until he visited the Negro Colleges of the Southern States of America that he felt himself among kindred spirits.[2]

To start with, however, he had to get down to the brass tacks of education in the Gold Coast as it was in 1920, and this he did with breath-taking speed and verve.

[1] I owe this anecdote to Mr. Charles Deakin.
[2] See pp. 286–8.

As we have seen[1] his immediate legacy from Clifford was the report of a Special Committee under the chairmanship of Mr. Kingdon, the Director of Education, and to this he applied his mind with such intensity that within four months of his arrival, and in the midst of such other preoccupations as Takoradi, he was ready to make the first of his major policy statements on education to the Legislative Council.[2] In this he did his best to say courteous things about Kingdon's Report, but could not diguise the fact that he thought it poor stuff, wholly unequal to the challenge of the situation and indeed largely irrelevant to the problem at its deeper level. He excused its deficiencies by saying that its terms of reference had been too imprecise and its composition insufficiently representative; he acknowledged that it made few 'useful suggestions'. He then metaphorically dropped it in the waste-paper basket. A new era had begun.

The chief value of the Kingdon Report to Guggisberg had been to open his eyes to the fundamental weakness of the whole system of education in the Gold Coast:

Reading between the lines of the Report, a lamentable state of affairs in our educational system was revealed to me.

I therefore conducted further enquiries, to ascertain the opinion of those educationists who I knew took a deep interest in the subject. The result of these enquiries strengthens my previous conviction . . . that *the educational system of this country is long out-of-date, and that far-reaching reforms are urgently required.*

Far-reaching reforms began forthwith.

So tightly packed were Guggisberg's statements of policy on the multifarious matters which engaged his attention that it is difficult to compromise between quoting them *in extenso*, which would be tedious and misplaced, and commenting on their general purport, which would quite fail to convey their urgency and breadth. He delighted in lists, categories, points and principles, and these descended on the Legislative Council with the steady, relentless drumming of tropical rain. There were no vague or ample generalities. What the Council listened to, in effect, were battle orders.

[1] p. 86.                    [2] *Debates*, 1919–20, p. 159.

On this occasion, the first of many on which he expounded what was wrong with education and how he proposed to put it right, he started with a list of the most important reforms he proposed to make, but since these merely enumerate the basic essentials of a system of education anywhere one can only suppose that what had previously existed was as bad as Guggisberg thought.

He had already, on 5 March 1920, appointed a new, smaller and more professionally expert committee to pick up matters where Clifford had left them, and this time he saw to it that nothing was wanting about their terms of reference, for he told them in precise detail the problems to which they were to address themselves. In our own day we are not unfamiliar with expert commissions on education which aim to produce, some five years hence, recommendations which may be implemented in another twenty. The pace at which the Educationists' Committee, as he called it, was to move was somewhat quicker. He was speaking in mid-February. Their report was to be laid before the Council in May and he himself was to take it 'home'[1] the same month for a conference with the Colonial Office and the 'leaders of the British Educational World'. To make this possible the Committee held forty-two three-hour sessions in eleven weeks.[2] One is inclined to wonder whether a report produced at this break-neck speed could have much permanent validity, but such thoughts did not customarily disturb the Governor. He was determined to get things done, and would have been quite capable of writing the report himself had this been necessary.

To assist the Educationists' Committee in its deliberations, much as a commander in the field might assist his troops by giving them their orders, he had elucidated the Government's education policy in the form of TWELVE POINTS, his first public attempt to formulate a philosophy of education. Since these POINTS ranged somewhat inconsequentially from the Pay of

[1] The odd habit of referring to England as 'home' to an African audience persisted to the end of the imperial story, and was a source of great irritation. Guggisberg was not alone in being guilty of the curiously insensitive slip.

[2] C. Kingsley Williams, *Achimota—The Early Years*, Longmans, 1962, p. 16.

Teachers to Natural History, and from Religion to the Education of Women, they do not read as a very coherent philosophy; but each one dealt with what appeared to him to be major deficiencies in the system as he had found it, and they were matters which the Committee would neglect at their peril. Occasionally his instructions were illuminated by remarks which the African legislators must have heard with surprise—and not always with pleasure, for committed though they were to education they had become so conditioned to the formal and unimaginative concepts of the time that they were deeply conservative in their thinking about its actual processes:

The position of a teacher is far more important in this country than that of a doctor, a lawyer, an engineer or any other profession or trade.

Examinations are necessary evils, and therefore must be cut down to the greatest possible extent.

And a little later, in translating his *points* into a *future system*, he gave a directive which should have been written in letters of gold. In the secondary school system, he said, the first two years would comprise general education supplemented by technical education; in the third year the two would rank equally; in the fourth year *technical education would come first and general education second*. In the long run this precept was to fall by the wayside, and thirty-seven years later the heirs to independent Ghana were to complain bitterly of the fact. In condemning the colonialists for irrelevance in education they should at least have exempted Guggisberg.[1]

Trade schools—Industrial Schools as he called them—were in fact one of his deepest interests, and it is significant that those of his European contemporaries who still survive are unanimous in putting them almost at the head of his achievements. These were of course young men at the time, struggling with the parochial frustrations of their jobs as A.D.Os. In their daily

[1] This kind of condemnation was in general unfair. The files of any African Education Department will show that throughout the century the claims of technical and agricultural education were being pressed. Resistance came from the African people and not from European educationists. Even Guggisberg's powerful voice was of little avail after his own time.

lives the lack of bricklayers, carpenters and mechanics was a far
deeper reality than the lack of a deep-water harbour or a university, and it is natural that they should remember him as the
first Governor who brought a glimmer of hope that they might
build what they desired to build in their districts. Four such
schools were established by the end of 1922, and are remembered with especial gratitude by those who experienced them.
This feature of his educational plans has been underrated, or
perhaps overshadowed by the greater monument of Achimota,[1]
and it was an innovation for which the Governor could claim a
great deal of personal credit.

His mind ranged on from Trade Schools to 'Technical
Schools'. As we have seen, all secondary education was to be
impregnated with technical training, but there were certain
kinds of technical school which 'it is not possible at present,
if ever, to combine with a secondary school'. The word 'technical' strikes a little oddly in relation to some of his plans, for they
included schools which would specialize in surveying, engineering, medicine, law, divinity, geology and forestry. But what
is so striking about this speech of 1920 is its contemporary ring.
Leaving aside divinity, it is almost identical with those made in
the 1960s in one African country after another, after they had
reached independence and found themselves so lacking in
technical and professional skills. Guggisberg was making these
speeches for them, forty years earlier.

But widely though his mind ranged over the general field of
education it returned inevitably to the dominating interest—a
Government Secondary School, around which there were
already revolving in his own mind, though he was not yet
explicit about them, ideas of an embryo university. His 1920
animadversions on the Secondary School were less contemporary, for it was to be run, specifically, on the lines of an English
Public School, and in choosing its site he was disproportionately
concerned to protect its pupils from the temptations of a large

---

[1] In his concern for trade schools, as indeed in the whole field of education,
Guggisberg was greatly inspired and helped by the Ven. Archdeacon G. W.
Morrison of Kumasi.

town, a fear which haunted the European mind until the end of the colonial empire. The equation of the town with vice and the bush with virtue was one of its oddest traits, and resulted in a large number of educational institutions all over Africa being most inconveniently situated. It is interesting, by the way, that Cape Coast, the traditional centre of secondary education, was ruled out on the ground that there was no likelihood in the foreseeable future of providing it with electricity or water.

But this is to anticipate, for the speech of February 1920 was simply a curtain-raiser. Achimota was some way ahead, locked in the Governor's mind. Even so the African members of Legislative Council could scarcely believe their ears, for as Professor Kimble says:

In educational matters Guggisberg was more impatient than the nationalists, having a clearer idea of what was wrong. Certainly nothing quite like this had ever been heard in the Legislative Council before. Caseley Hayford at once rose to congratulate the Governor on his statement, and for taking the educated community into his confidence; the other unofficial members were left speech-less.[1]

Later in the same debate, on quite different matters, other African members did raise their voices. Time after time one notices the strange and touching element of gratitude that a Governor should have taken them into his confidence. It is an illuminating comment on what they had been accustomed to and despite some of his own educational eccentricities, it shows how soundly Guggisberg was building from the start.

The Educationists' Committee had been appointed by Guggisberg on 5 March 1920, and it reported, incredibly, on 22 May, though its Report was not published for more than another year. We say 'incredibly' because the Report[2] was in effect a survey of the past, present and probable future of

[1] *Political History*, p. 111.
[2] Its speed and unanimity were probably made easier by its small size and the fact that its members, being largely drawn from the Churches, were of like mind on fundamentals. Also, of course, the Governor was looking over its shoulder and urging it on.

education at all levels and throughout the country, and was not merely concerned with broad generalizations but grappled with such gritty and technical matters as salary scales and grants-in-aid. It stemmed from two important principles which would be thought commonplace today but which were revolutionary in the context of the time; first, that education was so supremely important that it should be regarded as a first charge upon the revenue and the ultimate purpose of all productive activity; and second that it should be rooted in all that was best in African religion and custom and should strengthen African culture and institutions instead of encouraging those of an alien race. It gave special attention, as might be expected, to a new Government Secondary School, and made itself a small niche in history by recommending as the site 'a waterless, uncultivated hill covered with long grass and scrub, near the village of Achimota, and about eight miles from Accra'.[1]

It is hardly surprising that Guggisberg found himself in full agreement with the Report. What was more significant was that there was considerable common ground between Guggisberg's own views, as embodied, one might almost say, in the findings of his own Educationists' Committee, and the views of a wholly independent and unprejudiced Commission from the other side of the Atlantic. For in the same year that Guggisberg was putting his full weight and authority behind educational reform the Phelps-Stokes Commission was visiting West and Southern Africa.

In 1909 Miss Caroline Phelps-Stokes, an American, had bequeathed her fortune in trust for purposes among which 'the education of Negroes, both in Africa and the United States' was prominent. The Trustees had already conducted valuable research into American Negro education, a field in which very advanced work had been done in the Institutes at Hampton, Virginia, and Tuskegee, Alabama.[2] They were now extending

---

[1] *Events*, p. 141.

[2] Which Guggisberg was to visit after his retirement from the Gold Coast. See pp. 285 et seq.

their investigations, in accordance with the wishes of the bene-
factor, to Africa, under the leadership of Dr. Jesse Jones, who
had himself worked at Hampton. Among the members chosen
for this visit was J. E. Kwegjir Aggrey, a Fanti from Anomabu,
who was teaching at Livingstone College, Salisbury, North
Carolina, having studied and taught in the United States for
over twenty years. His appointment had caused some misgiving,
but in the event he 'stole the show',[1] at any rate so far as the
Gold Coast was concerned; what was more important he
formed a friendship with Guggisberg which was to bring him
back to his native land—a friendship which was to last until
Aggrey's death. They first met in London in August 1920,
where the Commission had paused on its way to West Africa,
and where Guggisberg was on leave with the Educationists'
Report in his pocket. Some weeks later the Commission joined
a ship at Monrovia on which Guggisberg was returning, and
they made the voyage to Cape Coast together.

It was an exhilarating experience for Guggisberg, who had
been pressing his amateur ideas about education on a largely
sceptical audience, including his own experienced officials, to
learn from a team of professional educationists how near to their
own mark he had been. Almost everything he heard about
Hampton and Tuskegee seemed the embodiment of his own
thoughts—of an education rooted in the soil or founded upon a
craft or trade, practised in community, giving pride of place to
character-training and imbued with the Christian religion.
The Commission's subsequent Report, written by Jesse Jones
and published under the title *Education in Africa* gave him the
keenest pleasure and encouragement. Admiration was mutual,
for the Commissioners, having seen much in West Africa that
appalled them, especially of pupils being 'filled like empty jars
with useless learning',[2] were heartened by the Governor's
Report, which they regarded as a document of importance for
the whole of Africa. Guggisberg saw them off to Nigeria with
regret.

[1] Edwin W. Smith, in *Aggrey of Africa* (Ch. X), gives a vivid description of his
triumphal progress through the country.    [2] E. W. Smith, op. cit.

Thus fortified, he continued to forge ahead. The vision of Achimota was sharpening in his mind and he was itching to get it on the drawing board. In May 1922, two years after appointing the Educationists' Committee, he set up a new one in its place. This must surely have been the first committee of comparable importance to have had an African majority in its membership, for the names of Nana Ofori Atta, Hutton-Mills and Dr. Papafio were added to those of the original African member, Spio Garbrah, while Europeans numbered only three —the Director of Education, in the chair, and the two missionaries Wilkie and Fisher. It was to be concerned with secondary education, but specifically with the educational complex— perhaps the only accurate way of describing it—that was to take shape on the waterless, uncultivated hill near the village of Achimota.

Before following the story of Achimota any further it would be fitting to revert for a moment to 1920 and 1921, and to other fields than secondary education. For the process of reforming education comprises matters more tedious and less dramatic than dreaming of a city set on a hill, and it would be misleading to suggest that his vision distracted Guggisberg from the 'nuts and bolts' of primary education.

We have already seen that he initiated Trade Schools— schools at which boys would

continue their education for one-third of their time, the remaining two-thirds being employed in learning an artisan's trade, in growing their own food, and in learning the latest methods of cultivation of one or more commercial agricultural products.[1]

He applied himself no less to improving the sorry pay of teachers and to extending their length of training; infant teaching was reorganized and pupil-teaching abolished; and the Accra Technical School was enlarged. All this was accompanied by a drastic reorganization of the Education Department itself. While attending to these matters he was campaigning

[1] *Debates*, 1920–1, p. 18.

vigorously for the wider education of women and girls, which at that time found only a limited acceptance either among educationists or parents. (One of Aggrey's devices during his visit was to ask the girls in the school to stand up; their infinitely small number would produce roars of laughter and drive his lesson home without the need for words.)

The Governor's searchlight played upon every nook and corner of the system. His planning of Achimota was, in a sense, his relaxation. It was one that was to earn him enemies among both races. It was foreseeable that a large part of the European community would be hostile to his plans though in the early years, judging from his public pronouncements, it would have been difficult to say precisely what these were, for almost every kind of education and training was to be thrown into the Achimota melting-pot. It was reasonably clear, however, that Achimota was intended to bring the preparatory school, the public school and the university, with a dash of Gilwell and an admixture of Tuskegee, to the African's doorstep. It was to offer higher education at its best, or at least according to the Governor's principles. The typical European response to this was one of scepticism. 'These people'—the characteristic European phrase which persisted into the 1950s—were not ready for it. The Governor was a sentimentalist, or, worse, was courting cheap popularity. These castles in the air would come to nothing.

It would have been difficult for Guggisberg to come to terms with this attitude, for it violated his own most sincerely held beliefs, but it would have been better if he had been more sensitive to it, and avoided giving his opponents grounds for justifiable complaint. Unfortunately he fell too easily into the error of favouritism. Although this is to anticipate the narrative, he was later to offer unwisely personal patronage to the Achimota staff. On one occasion he returned from leave with them in the same ship, which was met at Sekondi by the Governor's launch. At such times the more eminent civil servants on board, possibly prompted by their wives, are apt to edge forward unobtrusively hoping for the distinction of accompanying the Governor ashore; Guggisberg regarded them with a glazed look and signalled to the young Achimota staff to get into the launch with him. In the first year that they were recruited it was his custom to invite them to lunch at Christiansborg Castle in order to get to know them better—unexceptionable, but for the fact that others in Government service might have expected a higher precedence for such an honour. In the 1920s, protocol in a British Colony was not to be so lightly disregarded. He would also invite them to his country retreat at Aburi, where he would unbend with them in a manner more appropriate to the subalterns' mess at Woolwich than to Government House. It must of course be hard on governors who occasionally enjoy playing the fool (as Guggisberg, surprisingly, did from time to time) to be almost totally restricted in their opportunities for doing so, but they cannot hope to frolic with the young and escape the criticism of the staid and senior. On one such occasion, at Christmas, a notable romp was interrupted by the unexpected arrival of Decima from England. (It is interesting that she could have turned up in the Gold Coast without his apparently knowing about it.) This did not help the gaiety of the party, for by this time he and his wife were drifting apart, and she herself was no friend of Achimota; she preferred, in spite of a genuine fondness for Africans, to patronize them.[1] This special patronage did the Achimota staff no good, and was a mistaken kindness on the Governor's part. It resulted in an unpopularity with the European community which they had done nothing to deserve— indeed it led to their being deliberately cold-shouldered.

European opposition to Achimota had of course deeper roots than the Governor's favouritism. It could probably be traced to a subconscious fear about their own declining influence and authority, even to the loss of jobs, if Achimota were, impossible though this seemed, to fulfil the Governor's hopes. It stemmed also from the classic European fear that higher education would result in Africans becoming politically conscious, a circumstance akin to blackwater or yellow fever. Guggisberg himself would

---

[1] I am assured by one of Guggisberg's friends that on one occasion, in the house of his sister-in-law Eva Moore, he came across the draft of a letter to *The Times*, written by his wife, which was a venomous attack on his Achimota policy.

hardly have approved of this, except within the ambit of native institutions; he never really worked out the logic of Achimota, in terms of nationalist politics, believing apparently that an English public school would produce the same results in the Gold Coast as in England.

African opposition to Achimota was perhaps less to be expected, though in colonial days it was virtually impossible for a governor to do anything that was not, in some improbable way, open to misconstruction. Opposition did not, of course, come from the Chiefs or from the élite of the Legislative Council, who were by now Guggisberg's whole-hearted disciples. Nor did it come from the 'nationalist' élite outside the Legislative Council, which was beginning to find cohesion through the National Congress of British West Africa. At its first meeting in March 1920, Congress had declared in favour of 'a British West African University', and although the Governor and the nationalists were not always in sympathy, in the sense that neither would willingly have chosen the other as an instrument of enlightenment, their aims were broadly in line. On the one hand, Congress could claim some share of the credit for Achimota; on the other, the Governor's enthusiasm for a university did more than anything else to soften the nationalists' suspicions towards him.

Opposition did come, however, from the *Gold Coast Independent*, which spoke for the lesser élite whose hopes of advancement rested on the status attaching to an English university or an Inn of Court. Mingled with these selfish motives was perhaps a genuine fear that Achimota would cut out educational opportunities for Africans overseas, for Guggisberg was very clear that he intended it to replace these, and he was always less than fair to the University of London or the other institutions to which Africans could gain access. At any rate, the *Independent* saw Achimota as an imperialist plot designed to prevent Gold Coast Africans from going to the United Kingdom. It declared war on the Governor, warning him with delightfully unconscious irony that when the *Independent* struck it struck with 'the jawbone of an ass'.

Opposition also came, more disinterestedly, from the Negro

intelligentsia in the United States. According to Professor Kimble,[1] even the venerable W. E. B. du Bois strongly attacked the Report of the Phelps-Stokes Commission, and by implication Guggisberg's own ideas, on the ground that its emphasis on vocational education and the preservation of native culture formed part of a white man's plot to maintain the African as a willing but more useful servant to the imperial cause. This grievance was taken up by the *Gold Coast Leader*. There was a grain of truth in these attacks. Guggisberg's paternalism led him to wish to protect the African from the impact of western culture in a way which we can now see to be mistaken. He did not perceive that 'ideas know no frontiers', or that western technology is inseparable from other aspects of the western way of life. Nevertheless he was, according to his lights, utterly sincere.

Nor—to revert to his personal characteristics—was Guggisberg able to avoid the very human temptation to act the part of *grand seigneur* to humbler mortals than the Achimota staff. Whenever he had an hour to spare he liked to look in on a primary school, much as other men might drop into a pub or go for a stroll with a gun and a dog. On these occasions he would listen to the headmaster's—or more probably the headmistress's —recital of what was wrong and would unwisely promise to put it right. Lesser men than governors might find it agreeable to assure an attractive headmistress that her grievances would be remedied, but governors must not allow themselves to be lesser men, or to wave the wand of authority in disregard of the proper channels. Indeed it mattered little what one did in British colonies as long as one did it through the proper channels, but to disregard these was to court disaster. Although disaster could hardly encompass a governor, a promise to provide his favourite school of the moment with equipment, when others were ahead of it in the queue, could hardly earn him popularity with a Department of Education.[2]

.          .          .

[1] *Political History*, p. 114.
[2] I owe these glimpses of Guggisberg's foibles to Mr. C. S. Deakin, Lord Hemingford and one of the headmistresses concerned.

To revert to the story of Achimota, the new Educationists' Committee was appointed on 23 May 1922, and its report was published on 22 August 1923.[1] It was specifically concerned to plan, design and phase the building of a Secondary School or College on Achimota hill.

Typically, Guggisberg presented it with a preliminary Memorandum which anticipated much of what might ordinarily be thought to be its proper work, since he advanced, admittedly as a 'basis for discussion', a fairly precise building programme for the first four or five years. He also threw into its lap a set of detailed plans which he had himself commissioned from a Cambridge architect, a Major Skipper. Normally one might suppose that a Committee of this kind would commission plans itself, or consider alternatives. Had any member of this Committee been guilty of such error, his ideas would quickly have been readjusted by the Governor's 'Remarks on Major Skipper's drawings'. For example:

Major Skipper's lay-out is excellent, and will be adhered to.

He allowed it, however, to 'draw up terms of reference for my approval', and these are interesting as being the first precise definition of what Achimota was supposed to be. The Committee was among other things to consider:

. . . how far it is possible to combine in one Institution students applying for
(a) general secondary education
(b) training as teachers
(c) technical education in various trades and professions: and how far it is possible to associate both sexes therein.

The last phrase is not without interest. Guggisberg was always a great advocate of the education of women and girls, but this was a normal and respectable attitude. To advocate co-education was somewhat revolutionary and might seem out of character with the man himself. It brought opposition on his head from the Missions and African leaders alike. At this point he was being tentative in his proposals, but in later years he

[1] *Sessional Paper* No. 1 of 1924–5.

became a strong and open advocate of co-education, and was indeed more adventurous in his thinking than Fraser, to whom he was otherwise usually willing to defer in strictly educational affairs.

The Committee's Report was voluminous and comprehensive, and cannot concern us here. Its work in planning the details of the project was invaluable, but the establishment of Achimota was settled before it began its work, as may be seen from the sudden appearance of the architect's plans, and in addressing the Legislative Council on 6 March 1924, five months before the Report was published, Guggisberg was talking about an accomplished fact. Indeed, matters had already got as far as this:

I hope that honourable Members will assist in laying the foundation stone of this important building before the end of this month. It is difficult, however, to see how construction can be completed before December 1925.[1]

In recollecting the pace of colonial development in 1924, the slowness of communication, and the detailed supervision of the Colonial Office, this rate of progress verges on the incredible. One is tempted to wonder what Guggisberg would have achieved forty years later, with an independent government and the support of the whole world behind African development—but the thought is fruitless, for Guggisberg, a paternalist and authoritarian, could have found no place in this later world.

It is fair to add that Guggisberg was now working in a more favourable climate of opinion in so far as the Colonial Office was concerned, for it was a time of educational stirring in the Colonial Empire, and restrictive or negative attitudes of mind were being abandoned. The International Missionary Council, guided by that arch-intriguer for good, Dr. J. H. Oldham, had set in motion forces which resulted in the appointment by the Secretary of State of a committee of exceptionally high distinction, under the name of the Permanent Advisory Committee on

---

[1] The foundation stone was in fact laid on 24 March. The College opened to students on 28 January 1927.

Native Education in the Tropical African Dependencies. Guggisberg had hailed this development with almost intemperate enthusiasm, and was luxuriating in the feeling that he was no longer a lone pioneer, but that the highest authority in London was behind him, even if he still had to fight his local battles against reaction.

But the speech of March 1924 was more than a report on progress. For the first time he spoke publicly of Achimota as the future University of the Gold Coast:

> In planning the administration I have therefore thought it advisable to consider the prospect of the College eventually becoming a University.

The year was 1924.[1]

This led him on to two propositions, the first of which refuted all contemporary official thinking, the other of which broke with all colonial precedent. He confounded the view, which persisted in British Africa long after the Second World War, that the 'horse' of secondary education must come before the 'cart' of university education. This view is simple enough to explode, but it did not seem so simple in 1924, and Guggisberg was certainly the first governor to explode it. Secondly, and this was an even more difficult proposition to sustain in 1924,[2] a university must be 'endowed and managed by a Board *independent of the Government*'. Since he was determined that the embryo College should become a university as soon as possible he proposed that it should be accorded privileged status forthwith, and that it should form a 'separate and special' Department of Government, using the services of Treasury accounting and audit, but wholly independent of the Education Department in its internal economy and administration.[3]

The Director of Education, D. J. Oman, was a patient and much tried man. From the moment of Guggisberg's arrival in

---

[1] He had already said, in speaking of the more immediate future: 'As I see it, Achimota will be more of the nature of a university college than a secondary school.'

[2] It has again become difficult, for different reasons, in independent Africa.

[3] Here he was influenced by Fraser, with whom this kind of independence was virtually a condition of accepting the 'headmastership'. Fraser actually took office under the more fitting title of Principal.

the Colony he had been harassed, overworked and put upon; he served the Governor faithfully, and his reward was to see his authority and that of his staff constantly eroded by Guggisberg's direct interventions, and finally to have the College taken out of his hands. He is one of the unsung heroes of the Guggisberg revolution, but it casts no slur on his memory to say that these things could not have been achieved under his leadership. He was a good servant and a willing horse, on whom an accident of history had launched a human dynamo. He and his colleagues would have been less than human if they had not occasionally resented it.

[The College's] internal administration and economy will be entirely in the hands of a carefully elected headmaster, who will be directly responsible to the Governor.

Which brings us to the Rev. A. G. Fraser and to Aggrey, whom we have already encountered. This is a biography of Guggisberg and not of them, and their story has been told elsewhere.[1] But some brief reference must be made to that astonishing triumvirate—that 'happy conjunction of three remarkable men', in Mr. Kingsley Williams's phrase. Such 'conjunctions' are never accidental, for men of this calibre attract each other. Guggisberg had angled for them both, and in an odd and complicated way Fraser and Aggrey had each made the other's acceptance a condition of his own.[2] We have already seen how Aggrey entered into Guggisberg's life, and shall see later how he departed from it.[3] Fraser had been known to him only by reputation, but this was a formidable one, based on twenty years' distinguished work as Principal of Trinity College, Kandy. He outlived Guggisberg by thirty-two years, but while they worked briefly in harness he became the Governor's deepest personal friend, to whom in semi-retirement he could speak as to a father in God;[4] this in spite of the fact that as two

---

[1] E.g. in E. W. Smith, *Aggrey of Africa*, op. cit., J. Kingsley Williams, *Achimota—The Early Years*, op. cit., and in *Fraser of Trinity and Achimota*, by W. E. F. Ward (1965).
[2] The story has now been amplified by Mr. Ward (*Fraser*, Ch. 9).
[3] pp. 281-2.                                                                    [4] p. 279.

forceful and self-willed men they occasionally quarrelled, and indeed had one blazing row.[1] It would have been impossible for anyone to quarrel with Aggrey, who was the most disarming of men. He had a unique knack of turning the many insults he received throughout his life, as a black man, into occasions for uproarious laughter, and he accepted patiently the somewhat anomalous position of 'Assistant Vice-Principal'. He could not be made Vice-Principal, for as such he would have had to act as Head of the College in the Principal's absence, and even in the golden age of the triumvirate it was taken for granted that an African could not do this. In fact he would probably not have done it very well, for it was not his *métier*; this was to teach, to inspire and to make his people proud and happy; he was a wonderful orator and an altogether astonishing person.

It is as certain as such things can ever be that Guggisberg, Fraser and Aggrey were, as a team, unique.

Guggisberg was unaccustomed to parsons who were his equal in worldly experience and force of character, and Fraser was a new experience for him. He was puzzled by his personal values, which were simple and unassuming, combined with a determination to get precisely his own way, which was equal to Guggisberg's own. Guggisberg, a respecter of persons and of his own high office, had acquired as Principal of Achimota a man who thought nothing of governors as such. But he knew that he found the man he wanted, and he risked his own popularity in order to build up Fraser's prestige and 'rank' in the Government, and to support him at Achimota even when he had private reservations about what the Principal was doing. He also unbent towards him personally, and as a friendship took root developed the kind of hearty, chaffing relationship that

[1] A sordid affair, arising out of the alleged immorality of the police in the administration of Accra Prison, in which Fraser gave rein to an aggressive and uncompromising nonconformist conscience, while Guggisberg, who disliked the circumstances as much as Fraser, was restrained by the discipline of his office and his loyalty to his subordinates. It took them some time to get over this, but fortunately they managed it in the end. Even less happily (see Ward, op. cit., p. 214) the two men were not on speaking terms when Guggisberg left the country, and did not say 'good-bye'; but this was entirely Fraser's fault.

occurs when men have to unbend from an eminence of their own creation. He also became intensely curious to know what motivated a man like Fraser.

At this time Guggisberg's religion could have been expressed as a belief in God, King and Empire, though he was a good deal clearer about the last than the first. He was a good Church Parade Christian, and rarely failed to pay tribute to the good influence of religion as occasion arose. But he had no basic beliefs and had found no encouragement in the Gold Coast missions, which behaved like rival shop-keepers. His first battle over Achimota, once it was established, was in a dreary controversy with the Bishop, who laid down conditions for Anglican support of Achimota which involved a kind of *apartheid* between Church of England boys and others. Guggisberg wavered a little over this, for the Bishop was an influential person and Guggisberg was not as much at home with religion as with road-building; but Fraser, to whom bishops presented no difficulty at all, stiffened his morale and together they disposed of the intransigent prelate, who retired into a dignified silence.

But despite these experiences religion was beginning to nag at his mind. As he tried to grapple with the elusive problem of character-building he came to realize that the springs of human conduct cannot be taken for granted, but that he must study them as he would have studied any factor in a building specification; that if he was to draw up plans for the godly upbringing of Gold Coast youth he had better start thinking about God. It is not easy for a colonial governor, moving in lonely eminence, to seek instruction in such matters, and Fraser came to him, literally, as a god-send. Behind a bluff and facetious façade Guggisberg started to probe.

A matter which caused him disproportionate unease was Fraser's habit of wearing shorts, which seemed to him improper in the Principal of Achimota; he told him, in his best headmaster's style, that he did not expect it of him, and on seeing him shortly afterwards in the streets of Accra in the offending garments he stopped his car and asked him why he had to do it. Fraser replied that they were useful for gardening, that they

were perfectly respectable, and that it was all the same in the
sight of God. 'I've no religious capacity,' said Guggisberg.
'Religion means nothing to me, nor does God.' There ensued,
with the Governor sitting in his car and the Principal standing
on the pavement—with the chauffeur as sole witness to the
mysterious ways of Providence—the following conversation:

F.  That's not surprising considering the way you live. But every
    man has a need to know God and should give God every chance
    to meet him.
G.  How does anyone get to know God?
F.  Jesus knew and showed us how. One should give God an hour
    every day.
G.  How much time do you give him?
F.  Half an hour, but you could start with ten minutes.
G.  Will it work?
F.  Yes.
G.  Damn it, it's worth it. I'll do it!

There are worse ways of being converted than by having a
sporting flutter, which was the spirit in which Guggisberg
approached the problem of prayer. He was sufficiently resolute,
and sufficiently curious, to take his side of the wager seriously,
and from that day he set aside ten minutes out of every twenty-
four hours to try to discover what Fraser had been talking about.
It is impossible to know whether these moments were just refreshing pools of quiet in a busy life or whether they could be
called a religious experience; but much later he told Fraser that
he had been giving God his ten minutes and that it paid.
'It's damn well worth it,' he added, for he was never exactly
articulate about the inner life.[1]

In his remaining years, which were to be few, he retained the
habit. He never became a religious man, as the phrase is usually
employed, and in the bitterness and disillusionment of his last
illness he thought he had been pursuing an illusion. But from
the time of his friendship with Fraser he became more openly a
religious seeker, and at the end could reiterate that 'it paid', for
he was able to put some thoughts about religion into stilted

[1] This account derives from a conversation which Professor J. D. Fage had with
Fraser before his death.

words, and to affirm that faith had brought him consolation and hope.

Within a week of laying the foundation stone on Achimota Hill Guggisberg went on leave, travelling by the S.S. *Aba*. Most people on these occasions use the voyage to relax in a deck-chair or in the pleasant futilities of deck-games and drinks. Guggisberg, a leading exponent of the busman's holiday, used the time to write a booklet on education, an altogether inhuman effort after the pressures of his tour. 'My only excuse for writing it is that some of my African friends have asked me to do so; they say—with justice—that I have spoken much on the subject in public, but that the spoken words does not reach many literate Africans in the "far, far bush". . . .' It was published later the same year under the title of *The Keystone*. In it he says nothing that he had not already said a dozen times before, and in volume it is insignificant compared with any one of his major speeches, parts of which it incorporates. On the other hand, being written in the peace of a sea voyage, and being a deliberate attempt to simplify and to distil, it is perhaps the most coherent statement that he ever managed to make about his obsession. For the cover of the printed book he drew an arch, with its central keystone, under which he inscribed the words:

Education is the
Keystone of Progress:
mix the materials badly, omit
the most important, and the
character-training from
education, and progress will
stop.

This thought, needless to say, he developed into a central chapter, in which he struggled afresh to define the indefinable. Of more interest is a lucid plea, based on the history of nations, that Britain should work for the self-government of her dependencies. He is forthright about the need to 'cut out Europe' from the educational system and of its failure to offer character-training. Much of the booklet is better expressed than were his speeches on the subject, and it remains a modest but worthy memento of what he was trying to achieve.

Fraser and Aggrey, with an advance party of four members of staff, arrived in the Gold Coast in October, and from that point onwards the story of Achimota belongs primarily to them. Fraser's first act, incidentally, was—with Guggisberg's approval —to widen the already comprehensive field of the College's proposed activity, for at one end of the scale he introduced a kindergarten school, with which the Achimota teaching was actually to begin, and at the other he incorporated the Accra Training College. Achimota accordingly started life as a more capacious compendium of education than even Guggisberg had supposed, but Fraser had made it clear at their first meeting that he believed that the 'School' should begin from the bottom of the educational ladder.

Not that the Governor dropped into the background of College affairs, for this would have been impossible, and for the next two years, while the buildings were going up, he was a constant visitor to the site. Whenever he was in Accra he would as a matter of course go there at least three evenings a week, partly to walk round and see how things were getting on, and partly to assure himself that the contractors and foremen were adopting his own high standards of what constituted a day's work. Achimota, like Takoradi Harbour, suffered from trouble with the contractors, whom Guggisberg held strictly to the letter of their contract and who eventually asked to be released from it. The construction was eventually taken over by the Public Works Department.

In April 1925, the Prince of Wales visited the Gold Coast, and Guggisberg had cause to regret that the foundation stone had been laid the previous year. However, His Royal Highness was persuaded to authorize the use of his name for the College, which now took the shape that it was to retain until the University of Ghana began to diminish its importance some thirty years later. It was to comprise, when teaching started, the Prince of Wales School, with a kindergarten, a lower primary school for boys and girls and an upper primary school for girls; and the Prince of Wales College, with an upper primary school for boys, a secondary school and a 'university college'. It was now estimated that the College would open on 1 January 1927. It opened on the 28th.

Meanwhile, with Achimota at least launched and in capable hands, the Governor turned his attention once more to wider fields of education throughout the country. As if he had not already said enough, he collected his thoughts, took stock of the position, and resumed his investigations, his sermons and his plans with an enthusiasm unabated since he first arrived in 1919.

While the Achimota plans had been going ahead with unusual speed, comparatively little had been happening as a result of the earlier (1920) Committee's work. Even Guggisberg had been somewhat dismayed by the cost of their proposals, and the primary school building programme had had to be cut back to finance Achimota at a time when trade expansion was slowing down. Moreover the appointment of the Secretary of State's Advisory Committee had caused him to hesitate, for though he was not usually diffident about using his own judgement he was deeply impressed by the wealth of knowledge and experience now available through this Committee and wanted to check the Educationists' proposals against it. Accordingly the time available since 1920 had been consumed first in costing and financial cogitation and later in gathering experience, through the Secretary of State's Committee, from other countries. There was little to show for it in the way of new developments (though swift action had been taken by 1921 to right some of the worst of the existing wrongs) and African members of Legislative Council were beginning to be restive. Guggisberg used the Budget Session of 1925 to resume where he had left off in 1920. He explained what had been happening and started on one of his familiar analyses, but before doing so he charmingly took some blame upon himself:

No blame can be attached to the Director of Education, for the delay is far more due to my personal attitude towards the subject. I take such deep interest in our educational problem that I have ventured (*sic*) to take up personally a question which really belongs to my technical advisers.

It must have been agreeable for Mr. Oman to listen to these words, though his pleasure may have been modified when in the next moment he heard that the trouble with education in the country was that the system was 'rotten to the core'. Having again described, with gusto, why this was so, Guggisberg, fortified by five years' experience and by the wisdom of the Secretary of State's Committee, went on to put Government's objectives in final form. Some years earlier he had summed up his views in TWELVE POINTS; these he now elaborated into FIFTEEN PRINCIPLES, which remained his stand-by, and his criteria in reporting progress for the two remaining years of his governship.[1] They are a little difficult to discuss in the space available, partly because their recital required twenty-two pages of his printed speech and partly because they were not in the ordinary sense 'principles'. They could more properly be called a programme.[2]

Under these fifteen heads, remorselessly repeated at his two final Budget Speeches of 1926 and 1927, he was able to report improvements in such basic matters as the reduction in the size of classes, the increase in the number of places for girls and the building of new training colleges; and in those other matters dear to his heart, such as instruction in local history and native folk-lore, teaching in the vernacular, organized games and character-building activities. One important 'principle' involved a phased retrenchment of 'bush' schools in the hands of unqualified teachers, an unpopular move from which he did not shrink. In 1920 he had commissioned a revolution in education; from then until 1925 he had studied its strategy; from then onwards the revolution slowly gathered momentum. Impatient though he was, he did not rush these particular fences.

[1] Except that in 1927 he found that he had inadvertently left one out, so that they became SIXTEEN; but since this related to Trade Schools, and since these were his earliest concrete achievement as far back as 1922, the omission can be ascribed to a mere slip of the pen.
[2] They are described in *Debates*, 1925–6, p. 70 onwards, and must rest there so far as this book is concerned.

He made one final contribution, which has a topical interest today, for the impulse behind it died away after his departure and it has been left to Dr. Nkrumah's Government to revive his intention and extend his work. He brought the neglected Northern Territories, whose champion he had always been, into the general educational advance. Nothing gave him comparable satisfaction in his last two years, for not only had he a strong emotional attachment to their open plains and wide skies, and a paternal fondness for their simple inhabitants; he also had the fascinating prospect of painting on a blank canvas, for apart from the work of the White Fathers in the extreme north there was little that could be called education,[1] though a demand for it was growing as a result of migratory labour to the south. Guggisberg saw a glorious opportunity for avoiding the mistakes which had been made in the Colony and Ashanti. No longer need his eager steps be hampered by a clutter of useless schools, by irrelevant syllabuses and by worship of the white man's book. Here the Fifteen Principles could be applied in all their idealism and rigour. A model school would be built at Tamale which from its very inception would extol the dignity of manual labour, teach the useful arts and trades and instil the healthy disciplines. From this centre 'the whole system of primary education will radiate throughout the Northern Territories'. In 1926 he secured the agreement of the Secretary of State to establish a separate Department of Education for the North.

This was by no means the beginning of his interest, for in 1922 the first of all his Trade Schools had been built at Yendi, to the delight of the Chief Commissioner, who called it 'the biggest thing done in all the 20 years since I have been out';[2] and the foundations for the advance of 1926 had been laid at a Conference he had called in December 1924, on 'Steps to Co-ordinate the Advancement of Christianity and Education in the Northern Territories'. But by 1926, with Achimota under way and the Fifteen Principles established to his satisfaction, he was

[1] There were five Government primary schools in the whole region.
[2] Quoted by Kimble, *Political History*, p. 117, from the Chief Commissioner's confidential diary.

able to give fuller attention to the part of the country where his heart had always lain. He was fortunate in his principal lieutenant, for the Rev. A. H. Candler, whom he appointed Superintendent of Education, was one of those men whose work and name outlive their departure and demise. To this day the name of Candler ranks almost with the triumvirate among the surviving few who knew him.

In Guggisberg's last Budget Speech of 1927 he was able to report the acquisition of a site for the new school near Tamale, the approval of building plans which roused his enthusiasm, and the transfer of the Trade School from Yendi to Tamale. One imagines—though this is speculation—that plans for an Achimota of the North were shaping in that fertile mind. But nothing could have come from this, for by now his final passage home was booked.

Guggisberg's personal experience over Takoradi Harbour had been bitter and his treatment by the Colonial Office ungracious. Not only was he not invited to the opening ceremony, but the Secretary of State, J. H. Thomas, had failed in his official speech even to mention his name. This appears to be incredible, but people who were there confirm that it was so, and it is substantiated by Fraser, in a tribute at Guggisberg's Memorial Service.[1] Fraser added that 'Mr. Thomas admitted afterwards that whilst he had come here prejudiced against Sir Gordon [why, one wonders?] by the things he had heard, the Gold Coast had opened his eyes to see what great work he had done there, and he had found Sir Gordon's name writ large across all its prosperity.'

But the farewell to Achimota, whose opening preceded that of Takoradi Harbour by almost exactly a year, was altogether fitting. It took place on 27 January 1927, three months before Guggisberg went away, so that it could hardly have been better timed; and it was a typically Gold Coast occasion.[2] That is to

[1] Kingsley Williams, op. cit., p. 7.

[2] I base this description, aided by a little imagination, on Mr. Kingsley Williams's account. I have also borrowed from him the final paragraph of this chapter which has a very special aptitude today.

say there was noise and colour, the beating of drums and the blowing of horns and that indefinable sense of *bien-être* that the West cannot hope to emulate. There were not enough seats or standing places; many people arrived six hours ahead of time; mammy-lorries hooted and blared. Brilliant cloths, among them that of the Asantahene, who had returned three years earlier from twenty-four years' exile in the Seychelles, mingled with the frock-coats and wing-collars of the legal profession. The dust rose; the sweat poured; the shouts and laughter rang.

The ceremony itself, for such as could penetrate so far, was in the Main Hall, into which some 2,000 people were officially squeezed; about the same number had to stay outside. In his speech the Governor used the opportunity to make public the policy he had already declared to the Legislative Council some three years earlier—the Fraser-Guggisberg policy it should properly be called[1]—that Achimota should go forward to its destiny free of Government control:

I am fully aware that in uttering these views I am adopting a revolutionary attitude that would terrify the majority of Governments, but nevertheless it is my firm conviction that, *if* Achimota is to be a complete success here, *if* its influence is to extend throughout Africa, *if* it is to fulfil the expectations it has aroused in many thoughtful minds, *if* it is to be a pride to the African, it must develop a free, inspired and natural life. This will be its greatest possible contribution to the education of the Empire.

Rebellion and pride were mingled in these words, and Nana Ofori Atta and Caseley-Hayford, who replied, were deeply affected. 'Your name will be immortalized in the history of Achimota and the Gold Coast. . . . The hearts and souls of the people are with Achimota . . . the greatest day in the history of the Gold Coast . . . here we have a triumph of co-operation.'

When all was ended the bells rang out for the first time in the College Tower; the clock, whose cost had so distressed an official in the Colonial Office, ticked on unemotionally. As

---

[1] Fraser actually prompted this speech, which was based on an article which he had written for the *Manchester Guardian*. Guggisberg was at first unwilling to make it, as it was revolutionary in the context of the time. However he deliberately decided to have a final fling.

dusk fell the crowds streamed back on the six-mile walk to Accra. This was on the evening of the twenty-seventh:

Early on the morning of the 28th a long line of students numbering 120, a certain Nkrumah among them, could be seen approaching from Accra, every man with a bundle on his head. . . . The students of the Training College were coming to Achimota for the first time.

# 7

## The Nationalists and the Constitution

THE African nationalists came to understand Guggisberg too late, when the time had passed for what might have been an immeasurably fruitful partnership. For his part Guggisberg never fully understood them; the most that can be said is that he realized his failure to do so, without being able to account for it. They accepted him at first with watchful respect, which turned to doubt and suspicion as he unfolded plans to spend the country's treasured surpluses, for they differed from their later successors—*inter multa alia*—in being cautious and conservative in matters of finance. It was an unaccustomed luxury for the public purse to be full, and the prospect of emptying it into Takoradi Harbour gave them no pleasure, but roused the suspicions which were always latent in the relationship between educated native and colonial ruler, even in those far-off, relatively placid days. As they listened and observed, their doubts retreated somewhat, and when the proposal for a government secondary school developed into the vision of a university college they suppressed their doubts and gave him their support. They could hardly have done otherwise, for a West African University was one of their own declared aims, and they could not reasonably have resented a vigorous drive by the Governor to fulfil it.

But colonial relationships were never governed by reason. It was somewhat embarrassing to nationalist pride that a British Governor should steal their thunder; and a natural suspicion, which was never far below the surface, caused them to be aloof, sensitive and vigilant. They never wholly accepted him while he was among them, and although warmth began to colour their admiration as the years passed the gap of misunderstanding and suspicion was never bridged. They could not believe that their real business could lie with the Governor, or that they could have regarded him as any sort of ally in their battle with the enemy in London. In their admonitions and petitions to the Secretary of State they passed him by, thus wounding him and harming their own cause. Any chance there might have been of understanding between nationalists and the Administration was made more remote by a split between themselves and the weightier conservative chiefs, as represented particularly by Nana Ofori Atta, Paramount Chief of Akim Abuakwa. Faced with a choice of allies Guggisberg found himself, through temperament, instinct and belief, in Ofori Atta's camp, so that having almost touched hands he and the nationalists drifted away from each other again. It was only in retrospect that they accepted unreservedly that Guggisberg was a great man and a true friend of the Gold Coast.

The irony of the position was that Guggisberg and the nationalists wanted very nearly the same things, and that there was so much in common between the causes which the Governor pleaded in his official despatches and those which the nationalists pressed in their petitions. A colonial governor's dilemma was that he had to remain aloof from those whom he would have liked to take into his confidence, inhibited from private discussion of Colonial Office policy, which he had to represent always as the fount of unquestionable wisdom. This seems unavoidable, but the price of such official rectitude is often very high, and it is exasperating to see how Guggisberg and the nationalists pulled against each other unnecessarily.

Not that they could ever have reached complete accord, for on the most sensitive topic of all—elective representation in the legislature—Guggisberg would almost certainly have remained entrenched in his own conservative belief that the people were truly represented by their chiefs. But although disposed to be dogmatic he was not a wholly obstinate man, and a human contact between them might have altered the course of Gold Coast history. The gulf need not have been unbridgeable, for the nationalists of the 1920s were not strident or stubborn, nor could they remotely have been called revolutionary. Their proceedings showed an odd respect for British authority, and their petitions to the Colonial Office were wont to conclude with declarations of almost embarrassing loyalty to the King-Emperor and affirmations of belief in the beneficence of his Empire. They were asking, with due respect, for more responsibility and more assistance from the Mother Country, and even on the subject of elective representation they would have been as shocked as Guggisberg by the notion of 'one man one vote'. They merely thought that they—the intelligentsia—deserved more responsibility than the chiefs, that they should find some way of voting for each other, and that they should have an equal share in government with the colonial officials. Responsible self-government was not then in their thoughts.

A later generation would hardly recognize this as nationalism, but such indeed was the spirit of the demands advanced by those who included men of ability, integrity and balance. Inevitably one is led to speculate what would have happened throughout the Colonial Empire if self-determination and a measure of self-government had been extended to the Gold Coast in the early 1920s to men of this temper and calibre; and whether this might indeed have been possible but for a foolish and unnecessary suspicion of a Governor who would certainly not have been their enemy, even if he could not have gone the whole way with them. A quarrel with Ofori Atta, an improper and discourteous attempt to circumvent the Governor—and one of the opportunities of history was lost.

Although Guggisberg was not technically at fault in any official action that he took, his failure to come closer to these men haunted him for the brief remainder of his life, and he never succeeded in throwing off a sense of personal guilt. Sir Leslie M'Carthy, lunching with Guggisberg at the latter's London club after his final retirement from British Guiana,[1]

[1] Conversation with the author. Sir Leslie was Joint Secretary of the National Congress of British West Africa in Guggisberg's day, and later a judge of the Gold

was embarrassed to be asked why he had been unpopular with educated Gold Coast Africans, and wherein he had failed. Sir Leslie's revealing reply was that the African 'Establishment' had been brought up to emulate Europeans, and that Guggisberg was not sufficiently European for them; as for the nationalists, whom he did not identify with the Establishment, he admitted that they were suspicious of Guggisberg to start with but that they had come right round to him before he left, and were in fact the first people to form a bridge between the Governor and the 'upper crust'. But Guggisberg was not consoled by this answer, and went on to confess to a sense of failure not only in his relations with educated Africans but in his 'Africanization' policy, for which in fact he had little to reproach himself.

Sir Arku Korsah[1] describes the attitude of the nationalists to Guggisberg as 'ambivalent'. They treated him badly by shunning—or not seeking—his confidence, but by and large they supported him, which was a considerable compliment since they were bound by the solidarity of their beliefs to regard him as the agent of the Colonial Office and thus officially committed to the support of the chiefs. Indeed, one considerable section of the nationalist camp, the Aborigines Rights Protection Society, split quite openly, and more or less evenly, pro- and con- the Governor.

So near and yet so far. In his surveying days Guggisberg had built many bridges in the Gold Coast. As Governor he just failed to build an enduring bridge between himself and those Africans whose aims were so close to his own, but who were outside his former experience of the Colony, and whose education in the Inns of Court was so alien to the kind in which he believed. Suspicion was mutual, and was overcome too late. Guggisberg himself never overcame it as completely as the nationalists, for it was Caseley-Hayford, their leader, who spoke the moving words from Achimota hill.

·            ·            ·

Coast Supreme Court. I think his recollection must have been slightly at fault; it seems more likely that this conversation took place after Guggisberg's retirement from the Gold Coast but before he went to British Guiana.

[1] Conversation with the author. Sir Arku, as a young barrister, was one of the first municipal members of the Legislative Council; later Chief Justice of Ghana.

The word 'nationalists', which has been employed loosely, must be defined with more precision. Guggisberg arrived in the Gold Coast as Governor at a time when the first 'nationalist' movement, which was based on preserving tradition against the encroachments of the twentieth century, was giving way to a more positive and militant one which accepted the twentieth century and wished to establish the natives as equal partners with the British in developing West Africa and, more distantly, to establish the British West African Colonies as twentieth-century nations.

The Aborigines Rights Protection Society[1] had been founded in 1897 as a movement of protest, and arose from mutual ignorance and misunderstanding on the part of the black and white communities. The colonial government was insensitive to the working of African minds and imperfectly informed as to African assumptions about land and community. This led it to promote legislation (on mining and timber concessions and on forest reserves) which was well-intentioned and even enlightened on the basis of its own assumptions, but was anathema to the chiefs and educated natives whose thinking proceeded from different premises, and whose minds were clouded by the suspicion that it was the British intention to alienate their land and thus destroy the very basis of their society. The A.R.P.S. was not hostile to British rule or indifferent to the material benefits of colonial government, but at that time and place the land on which people lived was thought of in much the same sense as the air they breathed, and the process of regulating it for public purposes required more knowledge and finesse than the British possessed. Accordingly their benevolent intentions aroused deep hostility, which became manifest in the A.R.P.S. It was not a nationalist movement in the contemporary sense.

In the first place it was local, being confined largely to the Western Province and specifically to Cape Coast; secondly it

[1] It seems strange to modern ears that the Gold Coast intelligentsia should voluntarily have described themselves as 'aborigines', but the name derived from the Aborigines Protection Society in London, which espoused causes similar to the ones they had at heart.

was not a mass movement but an élite, in which the coastal intelligentsia, mainly lawyers, acted as a 'front' for the Western Chiefs; and thirdly, although it purported to act as a bridge between Government and people in all matters, and to promote Gold Coast unity, it was primarily concerned to preserve ancestral lands, ancient customs and 'inalienable rights'. Within the limits of such purposes it had achieved some success. By petitioning the Colonial Office and sending delegations to London it had secured amendments to the more obnoxious clauses of the Lands Bill of 1897 and the Forestry Bill of 1910, and had later come to regard itself as the Government's indispensable consultant—an idea which had no basis in law and very little in convention—and as a potential electoral college for African representation in the legislature.

But the Society committed the unforgivable sin of not keeping up with the times:

. . . [it] failed to adapt its structure and tactics to the changed circumstances of the twentieth century; and its leaders hardly realized that power was slipping away from them, in favour of those who were more concerned with a fundamental change in the colonial relationship than with the preservation of traditional rights.[1]

The 1914–18 war gave nationalism a sharper edge. During this time, with Clifford at Government House, the greatest of the early nationalists, J. E. Caseley-Hayford, was extricating himself from the embrace of the A.R.P.S. and was starting to 'voyage on strange seas of thought, alone'. The parochial affairs of the Gold Coast chiefs and the preservation of their inalienable rights was beginning to interest him less than West African unity, West African representation at the Peace Conference (the disposal of the German colonies was, he thought, an African concern) and West African independence. The vocabulary of nationalism which was to become so familiar in another thirty years was beginning to emerge. It was not yet angry or over-

[1] Kimble, *Political History*, p. 358. Ch. X—'The A.R.P.S. and the National Congress'—tells the whole story. This part of the chapter is not concerned to repeat or summarize it, but merely to set the stage for Guggisberg's entry.

demanding. The nationalists of those days were solidly behind the Allies in the prosecution of the war,[1] and continued to protest their loyalty to the British Crown and their desire to remain within the Empire. But they were also formulating demands for increased opportunities for Africans, especially in law, medicine and the public service; for rational economic development; and for a greater share in the process of government, with a limited franchise. And although they were not even thinking of self-government they wanted 'self-determination' for West Africa to the extent of a share in the post-war settlement. To further these ends Caseley-Hayford was determined upon a joint meeting of kindred spirits from all the British West African colonies.

At first he set about his mission with good sense and propriety. He tried, but failed, to win the A.R.P.S. to more positive and spacious thinking. He also approached Clifford, as was proper, in order to inform him of what was afoot and to ask for his co-operation in forwarding their representations to the Secretary of State and the Allied Powers. Clifford was cautious, but not unfriendly or obstructive; in any case the matter could not concern him for very long as he was only a few months away from the end of his term of office, and the full weight of the negotiations would inevitably fall upon his successor. Unfortunately Caseley-Hayford soon began to act with less circumspection and discretion, and as a result alienated two powerful men, one being Ofori Atta and the other, a little later on, Guggisberg himself. In both cases he went behind their backs when he would have lost nothing by trying to carry them with him as far as they would go. He had offended Ofori Atta by his direct approach to Clifford, and he later offended Guggisberg by presenting him with a *fait accompli* over a deputation to the Secretary of State and a proposed petition to the King. The dissensions which were set afoot by these two acts had wide repercussions, and seriously prejudiced the success of the nationalists' demands, which were in themselves reasonable.

---

[1] Caseley-Hayford himself was responsible for initiating a successful 'Imperial War Fund'. Ibid., p. 376.

He divided Guggisberg's own loyalty, when he could probably have had a measure of support from him for the asking.

When Guggisberg arrived as Governor in October 1919, Caseley-Hayford and his friends had been working for over a year on the West African Conference, and six months had passed since they had officially approached Clifford. In less than another six months the Conference was actually meeting in Accra.

Guggisberg was therefore present, and in control, when the new nationalism was born. He apparently arrived with no inkling of what was happening (one supposes that his handing-over conversations with Clifford had been perfunctory) and in his immediate absorption with development he appears to have underrated its importance. Later[1] he was to say:

We have arrived . . . at a very critical period in the history of the Gold Coast. How critical it was I did not know when I landed here in October 1919. I recognize it now.

In later years governors arrived at their posts primed above all in the politics of the colonies they were to govern, expecting to spend most of their energies in persuading, negotiating and reconciling. These were the inevitable accompaniments of constitution-making. Guggisberg in his innocence had primed himself in the facts of trade and transport, and hoped to spend most of his energy on nation-building in a material, and not in a political or constitutional, sense. It was perhaps fortunate for the country that he did not get absorbed at once with the nationalists, for even his phenomenal energy could scarcely have achieved what he did in his first six months, and encompassed also the mentally exhausting task of 'playing politics'. Alternatively, of course, it could be argued that in the Gold Coast at that time politics were ultimately more important than harbours, and that had he spent more of his time with politicians and less with engineers the Gold Coast might have been better prepared for the tidal wave of politics which was to engulf it

[1] April 1921, at the end of an immense debate in which Ofori Atta and Caseley-Hayford fought one another tooth and nail, and at formidable length.

after the Second World War. But he could not do everything, and what he wanted to do above all was to 'build a deep-water harbour at Takoradi'. He was less familiar with the deeper waters of nationalism.

He had no animus against the nationalists as such, provided they carried the support of the chiefs, and no prejudice against their original proposals when he came to study them. He was interested in what they had to say and approved of most of it.

I was interested to see that amongst the most important of these Resolutions there was scarcely one in which I had not, since my arrival in the country, invited the co-operation and confidence of the African members of the Council and other leading citizens of the Gold Coast.[1]

Had he realized that the Resolutions were central and not marginal to the future of the Gold Coast he would probably have been careful not to be away from Accra when the Conference was actually meeting.

Had I not been away on tour at the time, I should personally have attended every meeting of the Conference and should have taken the greatest interest in what was said.

In the light of hindsight, no engagement could have been as important as this one, even if, as is probable in West African circumstances, the notice was short and would have involved disappointment and inconvenience elsewhere.[2]

The Conference was duly held in March 1920, with six representatives from Nigeria, three from Sierra Leone, one from the Gambia and a contingent of over forty from the Gold Coast.[3] Eminently restrained and respectable though it was, it none the less sharpened further its demands for constitutional reform and elected representation in the legislature (though not in the executive), and for increased opportunities for Africans in public life. This was perfectly acceptable to Guggisberg, as was its formal resolution to establish itself as a 'National Congress

[1] Speech of April 1921, op. cit.
[2] Apparently the Conference was not a closed or secret affair. Any reputable person of either race could have attended if he wished.
[3] Kimble, *Political History*, p. 381.

of British West Africa'. What was not acceptable were the tactics which the National Congress now proceeded to employ.

In short, they rushed their fences. It had been decided by Congress to bring their grievances and proposals to the attention of the British Government and the world at large by sending a deputation to London, a procedure for which there was now ample precedent, and which had earned the A.R.P.S. a fair measure of success. Guggisberg must have known of this, for there was nothing clandestine about the Congress proceedings, and there is no reason to suppose that he would have been obstructive about it. Indeed, all the evidence points to the fact that he was anxious to co-operate with any intelligent group, and that he was sensible enough to realize the importance of the educated professional community, even if his conservatism made him cling to the tenuous hope that they would be willing to take second place to the chiefs. At this stage, unfortunately, they were not in a mood to give to him their complete confidence, and the actual fulfilment of their plan to go to London was hurried and secret. They were there, in September 1920, before he was aware of their going, for they had failed to appraise him of their departure or of their plans on arrival. He learnt of their intention to petition the King some time after the petition (a massive one) had been drafted.

Within a year of his arrival, therefore, he was placed in a position which no governor could relish. Apart from the discourtesy and disregard of established procedures, it was made to appear that in his absorption with communications and education he had underrated a political movement of the utmost importance, so much so that its leaders did not trust him sufficiently to keep him informed of what was going on; and the fact that there was an element of truth in both these suppositions could hardly have assuaged his pride or abated his annoyance. The Colonial Office, understandably, did not look kindly on governors to whom this kind of thing happened. In point of fact Guggisberg was badly let down by the Congress, for at its Conference in March they had resolved to proceed towards their objectives by constitutional means only, and Guggisberg had so informed the Colonial Office. However, in his general benevolence towards the Gold Coast and all its people he might have accepted the position more in sorrow than in anger had it not been for the activities of Ofori Atta, who certainly viewed it more in anger than in sorrow.

In London, as in Accra, the representatives of Congress abrogated to themselves the right to speak for their country by reason of their education and superior understanding, the opening shot in a war which culminated thirty years later in the virtual extinction of the chiefs as a political force under the Government of Dr. Nkrumah. But in these early days the chiefs, or most of them, were not disposed to take the claims Congress lying down. For Congress was preaching a revolution-ary doctrine, and as its implications began to sink in, the chiefs regarded it with incredulity and horror. Nana Ofori Atta, who had now been twice slighted by the Congress leaders, counter-attacked vigorously. His *tour de force* was to come a little later, in December 1920, when he denounced the activities of the deputation, in the Legislative Council, and condemned their calculated treachery to heritage and birthright, in a speech of sustained force and passion. Meanwhile, however, knowing that the petition was complete and might shortly be presented, he got to work both on his fellow paramount chiefs and on the Governor.

Distracted from what he regarded as his proper work, Guggisberg was caught between several fires. Ofori Atta was at his elbow, pressing him to put the deputation in its place; Con-gress, whose importance he was beginning to realize, was put-ting forward proposals to which he was not wholly sympathetic and which he would have preferred to advance himself, in his own way and at a time which fitted in with his master plan; the Secretary of State was demanding explanations. The situ-ation was infinitely exasperating and he was only half prepared for it.

On 23 October he sent the Secretary of State a telegram which, for two reasons, is worth a moment's consideration.

Firstly, it must have had some influence on Milner's reception of the petition, which was presented exactly a week later; secondly, it hit the nationalists hard, and the incident stays sharply in the minds of their survivors to this day, when recollection of other events has become fragmentary and confused. For in this telegram Guggisberg rejected their pretensions and came down unambiguously on the side of ancient tradition and indirect rule. His fair and moderate words about the West African Conference's aspirations, spoken a few months earlier, seem to have been forgotten, or to have been overwhelmed by Ofori Atta's eloquent pleadings and his own ill-treatment by the deputation. He told the Colonial Office what it wanted to be told

The general purport of the telegram was depressingly familiar. The Congress delegates did not represent anyone but themselves; the Colony was not ready for the proposed reforms; the institutions which it was British policy to uphold would be undermined; evil influences were at work, as was instanced by the fact that a trade union was being formed. Clifford was saying much the same thing, in even less inhibited language, of the Nigerian delegates, so that the two enemies made common cause. The Colonial Office had no difficulty in accepting their arguments, and in advising His Majesty accordingly.

We can only speculate as to what went on in the Governor's mind. That he was justifiably angry is unquestionable, and anger is not conducive to objectivity; that he suffered from the occupational disease of reformers, in wanting to do the reforming himself, is probable; that he was over-persuaded is likely.

Dr. J. W. de Graft Johnson, whose memory of the affair is vivid, is convinced that Guggisberg was guilty of an error of judgement, and that he allowed himself to be persuaded into sending the telegram.[1] On the other hand there can be no doubt that its terms did reflect the Governor's personal beliefs, for he was saying the same kind of thing as late as the summer of 1927, when he had retired from the Gold Coast and was completely free to speak his mind. He was certainly not a man to be

[1] Conversation with the author.

persuaded against his better judgement in any matter which he thoroughly understood, as was soon to be shown by his uncompromising attitude to the critics of Takoradi Harbour.

This telegram was followed later (2 January 1921) by another, in which he summarized Ofori Atta's denunciation of the Congress in the Legislative Council on 30 December, and in which his approval was implicit. He also made it clear that the A.R.P.S., representing the chiefs of the Central and Western Provinces, had refused to join the Congress movement, which had no claim to be representative of the people. An additional offence, in the eyes of Congress, was that he asked the Secretary of State to publish his summary in *West Africa*, in which journal Caseley-Hayford had recently published some remarks derogatory of the Gold Coast Government.

The deputation's chances of success must always have been slight. On the Coast, ideas liberated by World War I might seem urgent, even irresistible; the passionate arguments of serious men demanding a share in shaping their own destiny might seem formidable; the clashes, intrigues and denunciations might suggest that something of moment was afoot. But in the course of time this ferment was congealed in official papers, to be placed upon a desk in a calm, well-ordered office in Whitehall, there to be studied by an official fresh from a calm, well-ordered country-house in Surrey. In this *milieu* passion was distasteful and urgency incomprehensible. The emotional outpourings of the African heart were examined with academic distaste, and reflected upon in acceptable prose. It would be wrong to say that minutes must reflect policy, for this had yet to be revealed, but they must not violate principle, as embodied in the words *festina lente*. First Milner, then Churchill, and later Thomas and Amery, advised by their officials, advanced majestically to the conclusion that the time was not ripe. Due weight was, of course, always given to the opinion of the man on the spot; but the most influential man on the spot at this time was Clifford, Governor of Nigeria, who by now was becoming somewhat intemperate in his official observations on the West African scene, and whose despatches were acquiring a characteristically Nigerian ebullience, as well as gubernatorial omniscience.

In these circumstances it would be exaggerated to suppose that the views of the Governor of the Gold Coast, had they been radical or progressive, would have greatly affected the course of events. But they were neither. On the contrary his two telegrams on the subject must have made Milner doubly sure that Clifford and his own officials had judged the political situation correctly, and that Caseley-Hayford and his men were mountebanks. The principles of indirect rule, and of the gradual evolution of indigenous institutions, were vindicated. Milner advised the King in this sense, and refused to see the deputation himself.

This was not the end of Congress, which survived, though with dwindling political effectiveness, until its founder's death in 1930. So far as Guggisberg was concerned, its activities had offered him the chance of a first-class political education. He does not appear to have been sufficiently supple, intellectually, to have made the best use of it. When the heat of the battle was over he returned to a reasonable and friendly attitude to the deputation, and assured them that he understood—indeed welcomed—the claims of the educated community to share in the government of the country. But nothing could budge him from the conviction that they should play their part within the traditional framework,[1] or that the ballot box in African conditions was a potential source of evil. He presided, in April 1921, over the marathon debate in the legislature in which Caseley-Hayford and Ofori Atta attacked each other's point of view with vigour and tenacity, and in the course of which, incidentally, the former was able to show that by no means all the chiefs of the Gold Coast were unalterably opposed to the Congress aims. But in his speech at the end of this debate Guggisberg had nothing to say that he had not already said before.

His summary of events was cool and fair; his defence of the Government's attitude to Congress, based largely on the point

[1] Later he was to modify this view. He came to believe that the proper channel for the direct representation of the educated community was through the municipal councils. But this, as we shall see, was not by any means easy, and in any case there were only three of them.

that no individual governor of a Colony could take official cognizance of resolutions affecting three others, was reasonable; his justification of his second telegram, and of its appearance in *West Africa*, was convincing. Though clearly shaken by the recent attitude of the Gold Coast press, which under the influence of Congress was giving the public a foretaste of the uninhibited journalism of later years, he pleaded in moderate terms for racial co-operation and restraint. Finally he put his finger on the only point that really mattered—'Was the Congress representative or was it not?'

Unfortunately he did not attempt to formulate a reasoned answer to this vital question, which was to bedevil politics in British Africa for another twenty years. It was one to which extraordinarily little logical thought was ever given. The weakness of the typical British position was illustrated in Guggisberg's own later despatches on the reform of the Constitution, in which, without apparently realizing it, he sought to maintain two conflicting arguments:

(a) that chieftainship was a democratic institution, which represented the will of the people;
(b) that if people were given the vote chieftainship would be destroyed.

Making all allowances for the advantage of hindsight, it seems odd that so many intelligent men in the British Empire could have advanced both propositions simultaneously for as long as they did, and to have held that illiterate peasants could only be represented either by other illiterate peasants, which would have been absurd, or by chiefs, who would be overthrown if those same peasants were given the vote.

What Guggisberg did learn, however, as far as one can judge from the public record, was that he had underrated the political importance of constitutional reform, and from that point onwards he gave it, within the context of his own inflexible views, a fuller share of his attention.

The National Congress had been launched on a wide programme of reform, with much of which Guggisberg was in full agreement; for example, economic development and African-ization were the causes dearest to his own heart. Inevitably, however, Congress began to give priority to the increased participation of Africans in government. This also had his support, but as to their method of achieving it, by some kind of extension of the franchise, he remained adamantly conservative. What the Africans were asking for at that time, in terms of a franchise, was neither precisely elaborated, nor unanimously supported.[1] The A.R.P.S. desired that they themselves should be an electoral college to the Legislative Council, which, had the idea ever been taken seriously, would have opened the door either to the chiefs or to the educated commoners who were their spokesmen. The Congress, on the other hand, wanted by whatever means to give the educated community the represen-tative voice, and were disposed to regard the chiefs as largely irrelevant to the twentieth century.

Universal franchise was not at that time in anybody's mind. But the minds of the Governor and of all the senior Europeans in Native Affairs and Provincial Administration were domin-ated by the belief that the true representatives and spokesmen of the people were the chiefs, and that constitutional represen-tation must grow naturally from the indigenous political systems of the country. As for the ballot box, Guggisberg never spoke of it without a shudder. These were the days when the Labour Party was emerging in Britain as a possible alternative Govern-ment, and Guggisberg, in common with most of his colleagues in the colonies, supposed that if they came to power they would lay waste the work of generations by greeting Africans pre-maturely as equal citizens in the Commonwealth and giving them the vote. 'We are safe', he wrote unofficially to a friend in the Colonial Office in 1921, 'as long as you can keep the Labour Party out of power.'[2]

---

[1] It was common ground between the A.R.P.S. and the Congress that they wanted equal representation in the legislature, and also a device, borrowed from the West Indies, which would give Africans control in financial matters. But they were vague as to who should vote, and how.

[2] Professor Kimble (p. 439) quotes an extraordinary speech he made in Man-chester in which he warned his audience that if the 'idealists' gained power in

The belief that a few educated men, largely from the legal profession, could not represent the aspirations of a mass of illiterate peasants was, as we have seen, held in the teeth of a good deal of evidence into the 1950s. One cannot therefore blame Guggisberg unduly for holding it in the 1920s, or allow it to detract from his reputation for being a progressive Governor. At least he did not maintain, as did some of his contemporaries and successors, that the peasant's point of view was best represented by an expatriate Government or District Commissioner. He genuinely wanted the people of the Gold Coast to speak for themselves through their own representatives. But he was, quite simply, over-impressed by the potentialities of chieftainship in a developing country; he gave an odour of sanctity to an institution which, whatever its virtues, was as prone to intrigue, self-interest and chicanery as any in the world; and he was, more surprisingly, short-sighted in supposing that the educated community who wore (in those days) European suits and stiff collars could be kept away from the conduct of government affairs once they were determined to take part in them. But it has to be remembered that officially he worked in a Service committed to indirect rule, and that privately he was disposed to glamorize an institution which appealed variously to his liking for the exotic, the paternal, the traditional and the aristocratic. It should also be remembered that apart from Aggrey (who, incidentally, thought that Guggisberg was not reading the times aright) his greatest African friend was Ofori Atta, a paramount chief of towering stature.

Although Caseley-Hayford and his friends had taken the political initiative out of the Governor's hands, and put him in a position where, not having chosen the time or the weapons, he was on the defensive, he was by no means a political obscurantist. Left to himself, he would have got round to reforming the Constitution in his own good time. Indeed, one of his first acts as Governor had been to meet the A.R.P.S. on a friendly footing

Britain they might want to give the colonies self-government. If this happened 'within the next hundred years' Manchester businessmen would be well advised to invest elsewhere.

and to canvass their views, and it was not his fault that he did not have equally frank and free discussions with the National Congress. If he was at fault, it was in allowing himself, as has been stressed elsewhere, to become immersed in development at the expense of politics, but this again was an error that persisted until African independence. The typical British point of view, to the end, was that what 'mattered' in Africa was economic development and not politics or the vote; the simple question 'Mattered to whom?' was never asked, let alone answered.

With the crisis of the deputation behind him, and its lessons at any rate partly learnt, he promoted constitutional affairs in his order of priorities. His inheritance from Clifford[1] had been a Legislative Council which contained the germ of representative government in that three paramount chiefs were nominated to represent the main ethnic groups in the Colony. Guggisberg had realized from the first that nomination was now insufficient and that, provided it was done within the indigenous framework, the elective principle must somehow be introduced. He canvassed views, still notably from the A.R.P.S., and by early in 1922 he was ready to address Churchill in constructive terms, in a despatch which enclosed the current A.R.P.S. proposals.

He had now moved sufficiently far to propose a Committee of Inquiry into the elective principle, in order to bring it down from the level of slogan and rhetoric to that of practical politics; but this did not find favour with Churchill, who preferred the established method of informal consultation and strictly moderate reform. It was thought that an open inquiry would by its very existence commit the Colonial Office further than they wished to go. Action in the field of constitution-making was slower than in civil engineering, and while the roads, the railway and the harbour were extending visibly under the Governor's energizing touch it was another two years before he was able to put a draft constitution on the drawing board.

[1] p. 93.

During these two years he had faithfully carried out his orders
to consult. He had discussed reform with his Provincial Commissioners, the Paramount Chiefs, the A.R.P.S., the unofficial
members of the Legislative Council and his private African
friends; and while on leave he had discussed it at the Colonial
Office. From this welter of talk emerged the Constitution of
1925, with which Guggisberg's name came to be associated.

In essence, the three Paramount Chiefs of Clifford's Constitution were to be increased to six, and were to be elected by
their own kind instead of being nominated by the Governor;
while the three 'educated natives', instead of being nominated
at his discretion, were to be elected, on a restricted ratepayers'
franchise, by the three leading municipalities of Accra, Cape
Coast and Sekondi, once these had come within the terms of the
Municipal Corporations Act of 1924. There was still to be an
official majority. Looked at from the vantage point of Ghana,
1966, it seems incredible that it needed two years of argument
to frame such modest proposals, or that they should have been
regarded as forward-looking and even adventurous; but they
were the first in which the elective principle was accepted for
the purpose of choosing a Legislative Council, and they represented a watershed in Gold Coast politics.

The feature of the proposals which attracted most attention,
and which gave Guggisberg the greatest satisfaction, was the
device by which the chiefs were to be chosen. In each of the
three Provinces of the Gold Coast Colony[1] there would be
established a Provincial Council of Head Chiefs, i.e. chiefs
who did not come under the jurisdiction of any superior chief;
these would elect six members to the Legislative Council in
the proportions (based on population) of one from the Western
Province, two from the Central and three from the Eastern.
Informal councils of this kind had some roots in history, at any
rate in the Eastern Province, and once the new proposals were
made, industrious amateur historians in the Administration
delved into the past and produced evidence of ancient sanc-

---

[1] Ashanti and the Northern Territories were still excluded from the representative process.

tions; for it was always gratifying to exponents of indirect rule to show that the organs of colonial government were no more than indigenous institutions in modern constitutional clothes. The hopes which Guggisberg placed upon them were high, and as events proved exaggerated. He saw them as great bulwarks against the rising tide of alien modernity, clasping the mass of simple people firmly to the bosom of their native institutions and safeguarding the country from the disintegrating influence of semi-educated and politically conscious young men. His enthusiasm carried him further, for he thought of them as the future basis for rural local government, matching the municipal councils of the larger towns and relieving the 'political officers' of many of their responsibilities for development and welfare. Beyond this again he saw them as unifying forces in the building of a Gold Coast nation.

A speech of 1925 shows how he regarded them, and incidentally how comparatively little he seems to have learnt from his experience of Caseley-Hayford and the Congress.

I have never concealed my conviction that it is on the native institutions of this country—with the exception of the necessity of giving certain populous municipalities a voice—that the gradual development of the Constitution must be founded. It was at the preservation of native institutions that I aimed when devising what is the outstanding feature of the new Constitution—the Provincial Councils. These Provincial Councils are really the *breakwaters defending our native constitutions and customs against the disintegrating waves of western civilization*.[1] They are the chief means by which the nationality of the Africans of the Gold Coast will be built out of the many scattered tribes; for it must be remembered that, although each Council functions for its own Province, yet arrangements have been made by which these Councils can meet and discuss common problems.

The reality was less encouraging. There was difficulty in getting the Western and Central Councils to meet at all, or to elect their representatives, and thereafter and until he left the country Guggisberg was constantly having to meet criticism

[1] Author's italics.

from Africans of the very institutions that he claimed the Africans desired. Because they refused to see what was good for them, from time to time a familiar querulous note affects his utterances and in the last month of his governorship he was compelled to go through the familiar routine of forwarding to the Secretary of State a petition from the A.R.P.S. against the whole Constitution. In making this protest the A.R.P.S. was hardly impartial, as the Provincial Councils had undermined their own position, but they drew attention also to some inherent contradictions in them to which Guggisberg appears to have been insensitive throughout. The position of a chief elected to public office was in many ways ambivalent, and was certainly not in conformity with native custom. It was even debatable in some cases whether, by custom, he should travel to meetings and speak in public; while to engage in the rough-and-tumble of politics and to be open to the humiliation of defeat made nonsense of the 'royal' element in his office. Head Chiefs found themselves in an invidious position both as regards lesser chiefs and their own State Councils. But although the Provincial Councils never justified Guggisberg's high hopes they helped to launch a Constitution which was to serve the Gold Coast for another twenty years.

The other 'elective' element in the Legislative Council was to consist of three members elected by the main municipalities. The election here would have been an altogether more 'democratic' proceeding, as the word is commonly understood, since it was to have been based on a reasonable ratepayers' franchise. Unfortunately resistance was absolute—not to the process of election as such, but the acceptance of the Municipal Corporations Ordinance which was its necessary pre-condition. In those days the Gold Coast people could always be relied upon to present a solid and united front against any proposal that they should be taxed or rated, and as property rating was an integral part of the Ordinance there arose a spontaneous and unanimous howl of protest. In the end, as a stop-gap measure, the three municipal members had to be nominated, which was arranged with some difficulty, and which could hardly be said to have accorded with the spirit and intention of the new Constitution.[1]

Apart from these difficulties of persuading the people that his brand of democracy was what they wanted, Guggisberg in the course of his negotiations (principally with the A.R.P.S.) had to deal with three contentious matters of some importance, in each of which he took a line which would now be regarded as unduly cautious, or even, if the word has not become so abused as to be meaningless, 'reactionary'.

The first, which was crucial, turned on whether the Head Chiefs in Provincial Council would be obliged to elect one of their own number, or whether they could elect an educated man or commoner to represent them, for the conditions imposed on the Head Chiefs themselves amounted to little more than reasonable facility in the English language. Had Guggisberg, and of course the Colonial Office, given way on this the fangs of the A.R.P.S. and the educated community might have been drawn, and it is interesting that he was advised by one of his own officials[2] that this might be a proper course to take. But Guggisberg would have none of it, as he believed it would undermine the chiefs' authority, and that the commoners would have been too slick for them. (It is clear, as it happens, that the Colonial Office would not have sanctioned the suggestion either.)

The second arose from a claim by the A.R.P.S. that Africans should be represented by election in the Executive as well as the Legislative Council.[3] It is interesting that although Churchill, the current Secretary of State, rejected this claim he was prepared to contemplate one or two Africans being nominated, and it was Guggisberg himself who opposed this.

The third concerned an unofficial African majority. To this Guggisberg, without any prompting from the Colonial Office, was consistently opposed. He said on one occasion that no

---

[1] Municipal government is discussed in a little more detail in the next chapter.

[2] John Maxwell, Acting Colonial Secretary.

[3] In this matter, as in the matter of an unofficial majority, the proposals of the A.R.P.S. varied from time to time. These variations are summarized in Kimble, *Political History*, pp. 436–7.

reasonable white man in the Gold Coast could deny that Africans must govern their own country in the foreseeable future, but for the time being he stood solidly with those who believed that the time was not yet ripe. He took the puritanical, and no doubt proper, view that hard work and practical accomplishment must precede such constitutional achievement.

It is on the work done by the Chiefs in their Provincial Councils, and by the Municipal Councillors in their towns, that future changes will depend.[1]

He went on to place the onus very largely on the latter, since he was now beginning to think that the extension of municipal government, and of the municipal franchise, was a condition precedent for future constitutional progress. In spite of his devotion to the chiefs, and his high hopes of their Provincial Councils, he was always realistic in appreciating the growing importance of modern urban government, and the increasing emphasis which he placed on the future role of town councils was perhaps the biggest concession he made during his governorship to western political modernity. It was also to be his biggest disappointment.

They [the Municipal Councillors] will, by honesty of purpose, firmness of character and appreciable self-sacrifice, have to bring Municipal Government to a state of efficiency that will justify further powers being conferred on them. With the advance of higher education, with the spirit of high endeavour, and with the guidance of Divine Providence they should succeed in the end, although there may be many a fall by the way.

He clearly knew his municipal councillors, who were conspicuously lacking in the qualities he adumbrated, and have so continued; and there has indeed been many a fall by the way. Divine Providence has withheld its guidance. But it is interesting that, by inference, he did not consider the chiefs to be in need of this particular homily.

The purpose of this chapter is not to tell the story of the birth

---

[1] *Debates*, 1926–7, p. 36.

of the Guggisberg Constitution, which was long and complicated,[1] but to portray the Governor's reaction to nationalism
and his behaviour in a political situation—the first of its kind in
colonial Africa. We must therefore curtail the narrative, and
state simply that in spite of these vicissitudes, and others which
have not been mentioned, the Constitution was published on
10 December 1925, and the new Legislative Council met for the
first time on 26 August 1926. It was set on its course with some
success, if without unanimous enthusiasm, and with some
regrettable gaps in its proper membership. It served the Gold
Coast until it was replaced by the last 'colonial-type'[2] Constitution launched by Sir Alan Burns in 1946.

In considering Guggisberg's stature as a Governor in the
political field it is more than usually necessary to rid oneself of
the advantages of hindsight. In recent years every former British
colony in Africa has assumed full responsibility for its own
affairs with a suddenness that has been breath-taking and
occasionally catastrophic. On the credit side African governments have displayed more energy, imagination and financial
courage than their colonial rulers ever did, and have tackled
tasks which were once assumed to be impossible. On the debit
side there have been breakdowns in administration and the
surrender of standards in public life, all of which can be traced
to the grave inadequacy of trained and experienced men at the
time of independence. It is a truism that the new States would
have had a better start in life if preparation had been more
thorough and if responsibility had been transferred earlier and
more gradually.

Knowing what has happened, it is natural that we should
judge the rulers of the 1920s by their capacity to see what we
now know was going to happen, and by the steps they took to

---

[1] It is told in summary in F. M. Bourret, Ghana, *The Road to Independence*, and
in detail in Kimble, *Political History*, Ch. XI.

[2] A pioneer Constitution none the less, as it was the first in Africa to provide for
an unofficial majority, and drew Ashanti into the process of representative government. It soon had to face the criticism of the formidable new Convention Peoples'
Party, but at the time it was the occasion of great rejoicing.

prepare for it. If we adopt this almost impossibly high standard we must admit that in the field of politics—but only in that field—Guggisberg was short-sighted and insensitive. It is only fair to add that so was everybody else.

To a degree far exceeding other colonial administrators of his day he believed in the potentialities of the people he governed, and was convinced that once the barriers to education were removed they would surprise the world by their achievements. He made it his life's work to remove them. But he appears to have been so prejudiced against the political institutions of his own country that he could only think of them as disintegrating influences from which the Gold Coast people must be safeguarded. In this, of course, he was merely emulating Canute, and it was his intellectual limitation that he was unable to see it.

Since none of his contemporaries could see into the future with any greater perception than himself—indeed his successors were largely unable to do so in the early 1950s—he cannot be criticized on this ground alone. On the other hand he cannot wholly escape criticism, for he was in charge of Britain's most advanced African tropical colony, and was dealing with an intelligentsia whose attainments should surely have suggested that the future—or a large part of it—lay with them. It is strange that he should have thought that men of their calibre could fulfil their personal destinies behind the façade of chieftainship, *once they had decided otherwise for themselves*. His fault, as a politician, lay in a paternalism nourished by egotism. He knew what was best for his people and was utterly devoted to the task of achieving it for them; when they failed to see this he was saddened by their limitations, not his own.

In his advocacy of the natural rulers and the indigenous forms of government he was surprisingly insensitive to the working of minds trained at the Inns of Court or in overseas universities, and to the effect on them of western institutions. In his insistence on sound municipal government as a prerequisite of further political progress he was equally insensitive to the pressures which played upon the unfortunate councillors.

Having for four years listened to the nationalist case, presented with different emphases by the A.R.P.S. and the West African National Congress, he devised a constitution which doubled the representation of the Head Chiefs while leaving that of the educated community where it was before. Furthermore, he seemed genuinely surprised when they didn't like it. In his efforts to energize a recalcitrant Western and an apathetic Central Provincial Council, and to secure the adoption of the Municipal Corporations Ordinance by the principal towns, in order that the Constitution should go forward as he had planned, he was reminiscent of the father who takes his small boy out to enjoy himself, determined that he should be happy, even if he had to beat him to achieve his purpose. Having presented disappointed people with a kind of democracy they didn't want, he could hardly have expected them to leap joyfully to the task of making it work. The delight and pride which consumed him once the Provincial Councils were in some kind of working order was his rather than theirs.

The nationalists, of whatever hue, were never bitter towards him (once they had recovered from his telegrams of 1920 and 1921), for they respected his unfolding work in economic development and education, with which he was vigorously occupied throughout the constitutional argument. He for his part was never less than courteous towards them, and he managed to restrain his own justifiable bitterness towards them when they slighted him, as an individual and as Governor. But the gulf between them was temperamental and philosophical. Caseley-Hayford, the African, approached the political problem as a liberal Englishman of the professional middle-class. Guggisberg, the Briton, did so as an African romantically attached to his heritage and tradition. But Guggisberg had the advantage of authority and the consciousness of authority.

It can perhaps be expected of a statesman that he should adapt his views to changing circumstances. When Guggisberg became Governor he was largely unaware that the old colonial world was beginning to slip away, and that Africans were seizing on novel ideas about liberty and equality. It is neither surprising nor blameworthy that he should have relied intellectually on the doctrine of indirect rule and should have been determined to support traditional authority. On the other hand, it is sad that a man so friendly to all Africans, and so interested in every facet of African life, should have associated so long with the nationalists of the time only to understand so little of their point of view that he dismissed it as insignificant. Unfortunately propinquity never developed into intimacy, and at the end of seven years or more his views seem to have become more rigid rather than more flexible.

As late as 1926, on the related subject of Native Administration, he spoke in unqualified terms of increasing the prestige of Native Rulers and supporting their authority. The whole tenor of this speech was one of extreme quietism, which would leave native institutions to develop on their own lines and on their own initiative.[1] This was in striking contrast to Clifford, who ten years earlier, as quoted on page 92, was advocating the appointment of educated or wealthy young men to the State Councils, because unless their growing influence was recognized and harnessed it would destroy the old system. The two men had the same end in view—the preservation of the traditional councils—but Clifford's mind brought more imagination to bear on the problem, and a finer cutting edge.

By contrast, Guggisberg's was a self-satisfied approach. He was as always an indefatigable lecturer, on this subject as on others, and the theme of his discourses was what African attitudes *ought to be*. He was convinced that he knew, and when the A.R.P.S. or the Congress disagreed with him he could only put it down to their lack of comprehension.

He took his prejudices with him into retirement, for on 25 June 1927 he addressed a non-party Committee of the House of Commons in terms which are worth reproducing in full, since they presumably represented his mature and considered view. The Gold Coast Commercial Intelligence Bureau in London thought similarly, for they had his address printed as a pamphlet; for what reason is obscure:

[1] *Debates*, 1926–7, para. 18, p. 16.

With the steady progress of the Gold Coast towards a higher state of civilization, there has naturally come from the better educated community (chiefly lawyers) an increasing demand for a greater share in the goverment of the country. If this small but very noisy minority had its way they would be the elected representatives of all the peoples of the Gold Coast in the Legislative Council, and, as the next step, have an unofficial majority on the Council. For this last-named step they are by no means ready; to give it to them would plunge the Gold Coast into tribal, financial and mercantile chaos.

Their first named demand, that they should be the elected members of all the peoples, would entirely destroy the system of Native Constitutions at present existing, and on which we base the whole system of indirect rule. As for more than $2\frac{1}{4}$ out of the $2\frac{1}{2}$ million inhabitants—they are devotedly attached to their native constitutions and institutions.

We are averse to the use of the ballot box generally, as the country is by no means ripe for it, and moreover it is not a native institution.

For while the permanent retention of all native customs must be a deterrent to progress, too rapid a change, or a change forced on the people by an alien Goverment, would inevitably destroy the national character of the local race without replacing it by something suitable to it and its conditions of life.

Our new constitution is, I believe, far more solidly based on the institutions which the people of the Gold Coast have found best suited to them, and far more likely to develop into something better and wider, than any mushroom constitution based on the ballot box, and the eloquence of European-trained African politicians, over whom the people would have no control except at election time.

In carrying out this task we must, while being fair, not be too fast. And may I suggest that the task is yours, as well as the Governor's? For we are being, and will always be, urged to move quicker by the intelligentsia than would be wise; and when satisfaction cannot be obtained in this respect from 'the man on the spot', deputations of highly prepossessing and apparently reasonable African citizens will visit this country, with the object of soliciting the aid of the members of the Mother of Parliaments.

In all earnestness I ask that they will not be encouraged to run before they can walk—in all earnestness, and for the sake of a race which has immense possibilities, for I place the African of the West Coast on a higher plane, as regards potentiality, than any other native race. He is far finer material, rugged as he is at present, out of which to build a nation.

There were regrets in his mind that he had been unable to

come to terms with the people against whom he now warned Members of Parliament; yet if his mind retained regrets, it clearly harboured no doubts. Today the answer to Guggisberg's rather pathetic question to Sir Leslie M'Carthy[1] seems clear. People who tell you what is good for you, and how good they are to you, are never unreservedly popular.

[1] p. 162.

# 8

# Native Administration and
# Local Government

In Guggisberg's day the expression 'local government' would
have been unfamiliar. If it had meant anything at all it would
have meant the government of Accra, Sekondi and Cape Coast,
for the British had an odd habit of distinguishing between
'municipal' affairs in towns and 'native' affairs outside them, so
that 'Departments of Native Affairs' existed in colonies where
*all* permanent inhabitants were 'natives', and where one would
have supposed that all affairs were native ones. This is partly
explained by the fact that chiefs and their councils were
primarily engaged in dispensing traditional justice, and that
administrative responsibilities were only slowly and incidentally
added to this function.[1] Accordingly as time went by, native
authorities were doing rather more than the law would have led
one to suppose, until the Local Government Ordinances of the
1950s gave their successors the right to do an enormous number
of things, after which they did much less than it would have led
one to expect. In 1919, however, local government outside the
three towns of the Colony was conducted in the French rather
than the British manner, by District Commissioners, while the
chiefs and their councils were in effect judicial tribunals.
Municipal government was something different, for a situation
in which drains, electricity cables, refuse disposal and street

[1] There was a parallel to this in Britain, where the Justices of the Peace were involved in local government in the towns until 1835 and in the rural areas until 1888.
In the Gold Coast, however, this evolutionary process of 500 years was compressed
into a comparable fifty.

cleansing had become essential to daily living, had clearly
ceased to be a native situation and had become a western one.
For the purposes of this chapter, however, it seems fitting to deal
jointly with native jurisdiction, native administration and municipal government, in the light of the Governor's attitudes and
actions.

*Native Jurisdiction and Native Administration*

As time went by, indirect rule in the British African colonies
began to disintegrate because of its internal contradictions,
which were various and confusing. In an age of rapid change the
authority of chiefs in the Gold Coast Colony ceased to be a
simple matter and became one for sophisticated legal argument,
as it was not clear whether it derived from their own people or
from the British Crown. Nor in day-to-day practical affairs was
it easy for a chief to be the agent of his rulers and the leader of
his people simultaneously, for these did not always see eye to eye.
The greatest difficulty arose from the emergence of an educated
class, for chiefs were mostly simple men and the intelligentsia
did not take kindly to having to accept them as repositories of
power and agents of administration; though educated men
differed among themselves as to this, the elder ones often being
torn between intellect and tradition, and disposed to support
the status of the chiefs while aspiring to usurp their authority;
the younger being more openly rebellious and recalcitrant. The
chiefs for their part were as ill-equipped to deal with communications and sanitation as the English country squires to master
the social consequences of the industrial revolution.

Indirect rule was not the avowed policy of the Gold Coast
Government until after Guggisberg's day, when the chiefs,
whose authority had on balance been declining, enjoyed a brief
Indian summer; but it had, of course, been the practice for some
time and the tensions and paradoxes which we have mentioned
had become apparent in the sphere of what was called native
jurisdiction, as well as in the ambivalences of the A.R.P.S.

In the Colony[1] they had been manifest in a long and incon-

---

[1] Different considerations applied in Ashanti and the Northern Territories.

clusive struggle to amend that Native Jurisdiction Ordinance of 1883 in such a way as to satisfy the Government, the chiefs and the educated community against the background of social change in the first quarter of the century. It is not surprising that the protagonists failed to reach agreement between each other, since they were not even unanimous among themselves. There was dissatisfaction and confusion about the legal position of chiefs *vis-à-vis* the Government, about the customary position of the Head or Paramount Chiefs and the minor chiefs *vis-à-vis* each other, and about the *de facto* position of the educated élite, with its self-appointed responsibility to assume leadership, *vis-à-vis* any of them. Successive Governors, notably Rodger and Clifford, had taken the line that native institutions must be strengthened, while at the same time the ultimate power of the colonial Government must not be weakened, an attitude which sums up the dilemma of indirect rule.

But this was the orthodox view of the period, and it is difficult to imagine any British Governor holding another. In what might well be called his Inaugural Lecture—his introductory address to Council on 13 October 1919, Guggisberg had stated it thus:

As the land belongs to the people, its administration must be carried out by the people's representatives—the Chiefs and their Councillors, the Chiefs duly elected by the people in accordance with recognized native custom. It is the aim of the Government to support the Chiefs and Tribal Authorities in the proper exercise of their powers, to preserve native customs and institutions, while keeping in view the necessity, in the interests of all, of fostering the development of the country's resources without prejudicing the people's rights to the land.

The fallacy of this viewpoint, as we now know, is that it does not in the long run commend itself to the natives, who prefer 'one man one vote' and party politics. But apart from the occasional genius or eccentric, men can only work in the intellectual context of their time, and Guggisberg was nothing if not orthodox in his intellectual equipment. He ended in the Gold Coast as he had begun, a convinced indirect ruler. His experience of the nationalists (the same small stage army that was to

join issue with him over national constitution and native administration alike) disturbed and puzzled him, but did not
fundamentally shake his beliefs. He did not begin to question
these until he found himself in the more rootless, cosmopolitan
society of British Guiana, by which time, however, he was beyond
the mental effort of self-examination, except of his own spiritual
life. Meanwhile it must be remembered that even the educated
natives of the Gold Coast were not, in the 1920s, thinking in
terms of ballot-box democracy outside the seaport towns.

Guggisberg's inheritance from Clifford was a piece of unfinished legislation. Clifford's own inheritance has been well
described in the following words:

. . . official attempts to strengthen and systematize the institution of
chieftaincy were bound to identify the Chiefs more and more with an
alien system of rule. The Government was attacked for interfering
with native institutions, and the Chiefs for usurping greater powers
than were traditionally theirs, although they themselves believed
that the main problem was to restore their declining authority. The
resulting clash of opinions and interests, inside and outside the
Legislative Council, continued to obstruct successive well-meaning
attempts to draft legislation that would please everybody.[1]

Guggisberg therefore found this sensitive and complicated
problem awaiting him on arrival. In the background the storm
was blowing up over the wider issue of the Constitution, the
force of which, as we have seen,[2] he tended to underrate. Meanwhile he was primarily intent on his plans for Takoradi and for
the Ten Year Development Plan. It is interesting to recall the
immense pressures which bore simultaneously on a Colonial
Governor in those days, and to recall how much Guggisberg
took upon himself. He had advisers, of course, but more than
most governors he kept his own hand on the tiller.

It was some months before he took the first official steps about
native jurisdiction (by calling a conference of unofficial members of the Legislature in February 1920), but as early as

---

[1] Kimble, *Political History*, p. 473. Professor Kimble goes on to describe in detail
the nature of the opposition which caused Clifford to be disappointed of his hopes
of achieving a settlement of this problem, which he was compelled to hand to his
successor.                                                              [2] p. 167.

November 1919, he had revealed, in a despatch to Milner, the direction in which his own thoughts were moving. Coming from the Founder of Achimota they were a little unexpected, for in effect he was lamenting the fact that the over-rapid spread of education in the Colony had disrupted the indigenous family and tribal structure, and created a new and unprecedented division of people into antagonistic classes. Admittedly the phrase he used was not 'education' but 'western ideas', for he thought then, as he thought to the end, that these could be kept apart. It was perhaps the most serious misapprehension of his governorship. He had hopes that Ashanti would avoid the pitfalls of the Colony, since education there was proceeding more slowly, and the family basis of the nation being preserved. Meanwhile it had become his ambition, and was the key to his policy in this particular sphere, to reunite the tribal leaders and the educated classes. He accordingly set his hand to a task in which, as we can see from the perspective of nearly half a century, he had little hope of lasting success.

Clifford's Bill had been an attempt to bring the 1883 Ordinance into accord with the facts of the twentieth century and to strengthen the control of the Administration over the chiefs' tribunals. It roused a storm of opposition, instinctive, emotional, often contradictory, but of a violence which made the navigation of the Bill impossible. The storm continued to rumble in the background while Guggisberg conscientiously applied his mind to weighing the opinions which pressed in on him from every side. Eventually, as we shall see, he manoeuvred his way to success by throwing the onus on the chiefs themselves to make constructive proposals, realizing that proposals emanating from the Government were, in their minds, little more than an invitation to destructive criticism. Meanwhile he continued patiently to seek an acceptable solution, in circumstances that were somewhat strange; for while he steadfastly maintained that his purpose was to strengthen native institutions the chiefs themselves protested vigorously that his proposed reforms were encroaching on these institutions and would eventually encompass their ruin.

Eventually, in 1922, a revised Bill was presented, of which Guggisberg said later that it rectified 'the most serious fault in the 1920 Ordinance, [namely] the omission of any mention of the "State Councils" '.[1] But this was not a principal issue at the time, and the Bill foundered because it retained the two features most objectionable to African members, namely the appellate jurisdiction of Provincial Commissioners in land cases, and the proposed distinction between Head Chiefs and Chiefs. The debate on this Bill, which began on 28 September 1922, and continued for several days, was of an extraordinarily high order. Even today, when the subject under discussion can hardly appear to be of much importance, it is a pleasure to read the skilled, forceful and lucid advocacy of Thomas Hutton-Mills, who was allowed to speak as counsel for the A.R.P.S., of Peter Awoonor Renner, for the Bar Association, and of Caseley-Hayford and Ofori Atta; not to mention the brilliant and *ex tempore* refutations of the Attorney-General, which drew a tribute in the most urbane traditions of Westminster, even from his African opponents. Time after time the debate, which would indeed have done credit to the House of Commons, returned to the bedrock question of whether, in Caseley-Hayford's words, 'ultimate authority, ministerially and judicially' rested in the Crown or the people, and the more immediate issues were debated within this wider constitutional setting.

Guggisberg's concluding speech, in which he withdrew the Bill, was not of the same order of brilliance or lucidity, but in an unobtrusive way it was notable for its statesmanlike moderation. It will have emerged from these pages that he was not a patient man, and that in getting practical things done he was often autocratic. But on this occasion, handling a sensitive political issue, his behaviour was immaculate. Not only did he bow with ready grace to what he recognized was a sincere and deeply serious concern of chiefs and lawyers alike, but he deliberately refrained from scoring points which would have been legitimate even in his capacity as Governor and impartial President of the Council. For, on two main issues, it was apparent that the Head

[1] *Events*, p. 241.

Chiefs had changed their minds, or had been converted by their legal friends.[1] and gone back on assurances they had freely given him. In one case, concerning the differentiation between the status of chiefs, they had themselves introduced the clause that they were now opposing. But far from chiding them or using the occasion for irony he mildly said:

So opinion appears to have changed, and it is Goverment's duty to recognize that change, and consider it.

In the other case, they had joined in criticism of the Provincial Commissioners' jurisdiction, with which they had previously expressed their satisfaction. 'It is therefore very necessary', he said, 'that further and very close enquiries should be made into this subject.'[2]

It was a creditable attitude in a man of his temperament, at the end of a debate which was to see the end of three years' patient negotiation in which he had tried his best to reconcile conflicting interests. He appears to have taken some pride in the closing remarks of his speech, for he reproduces them five years later in *Events* (p. 241):

The declared policy of Government is the progress of the native races of this country; that being so, measures which are necessary from time to time to harmonize native institutions and law in the natural course of historical development, the harmonizing in fact of the old and the new, must be the special charge of any Government that is responsible for guiding the country in its advancement.

The battle was lost but the struggle continued, as indeed it had continued almost from the time of the original Ordinance of 1883. But by now the Head Chiefs were beginning to feel increasingly isolated and insecure, sensing, possibly, that history was no longer on their side. The A.R.P.S., which had once, in an ambivalent sort of way, been their allies, was drifting away from them and Caseley-Hayford had left them all for the world of

[1] The leading lawyers of the time, quite apart from their *rapport* with the chiefs (which later diminished), had a personal interest in the Bill, as it would have excluded professional advocates from the Provincial Commissioner's hearing of appeals.
[2] *Debates*, 1922–3, pp. 587–8.

modern nationalism; the minor chiefs also were beginning to
desert them, and the dissatisfaction of their subjects was shown
in increasingly frequent destoolments. Guggisberg understood
this very well—indeed, in writing to Amery after the withdrawal
of the 1922 Ordinance he went so far as to remark that the
Government 'would have to do something to strengthen the
power of the chiefs and to prevent their rule becoming a farce'.
A disturbing remark, for if the position was as bad as that the
right course would have been to examine the institution itself
before thinking out new ways of strengthening it; Clifford, one
supposes, with his more analytical mind, would have done this
in spite of his equal devotion to native institutions.

But if Guggisberg's intellectual approach to his problem was
uncritical his skill and diplomacy in planning the next move
were praiseworthy. Viewing the dreary and involved conflict
which had lasted since the turn of the century, he realized that
an entirely fresh approach was necessary and came to the conclusion that any new initiative must now come from the chiefs
themselves and not from the Government. (As is so often the
case, this conclusion seems, from the vantage point of the 1960s,
a reasonably simple one to have reached, but it was original,
almost daring, in the context of the time.) Moreover he had the
foresight to link this problem with the wider constitutional one
that was engaging him. The 1925 Constitution was now being
discussed with his advisers and, as we have seen,[1] the idea of
Provincial Councils of Chiefs was taking shape in his mind.
These could be made to serve a dual purpose—to strengthen the
position of the Head Chiefs nationally, by making them political representatives of their States, and also by making them
supreme authorities judicially within their States against the in-
roads being made on their authority both by the educated
classes and by the minor chiefs (whose defection, incidentally,
was often prompted by the A.R.P.S.).

For a long time, therefore, he held his hand, waiting for the
moment when his two purposes could be fused. Then, early in
1925, he took the unconventional step of inviting the chiefs

[1] p. 178.

themselves to draft a new Native Jurisdiction Ordinance which eventually emerged as the Native Administration Ordinance of 1927. In inviting them to do this, he said:[1]

I shall not propose any definite rules, for I consider that those should be brought forward by the Chiefs and their Oman Councils after careful consideration. . . . My object is dual.[2] First, to suggest the causes which may exist for this suspected (*sic*) weakening of Native Administration[3] and thereby assist them in considering for themselves the best remedies. And second, to impress on the Chiefs and their Oman Councils that they will be supported by the full force of the Central Government in introducing any reforms which are in accordance with the recognized Constitution.

He could hardly have committed himself more explicitly to support of the Natural Rulers, nor indeed could he have given a more open challenge to the A.R.P.S. and the intelligentsia; for by now it was an unambiguous choice between the two.

The Bill was in fact prepared by Ofori Atta, in conference with the chiefs of the Eastern and Central Provinces, for the Secretary of Native Affairs and the Attorney-General gave no more than technical advice when the main work had been done. There was by now, it must be confessed, a certain element of artificiality about the procedure, since the chiefs also were faced by an unambiguous choice—between throwing in their lot with the colonial Government, which had promised them unqualified support, or with the A.R.P.S., under whom their power was likely to be more ceremonial than real. Knowing well what the Government desired, the chiefs produced something very much like it, and the Bill provided the substance of what Guggisberg had been seeking in vain in 1922. This was in large measure to the chiefs' own advantage, since the Bill gave recognition to the State and Oman Councils and extended their jurisdiction, and—of especial importance to the Head Chiefs— gave the Provincial Councils a judicial and administrative

[1] Quoted in *Events*, p. 242.
[2] This was true, but not quite in the way he put it.
[3] Round about this time the expressions 'Native Administration' and 'Native Authority' seem to be superseding 'Native Jurisdiction' and 'Native Tribunals', thus foreshadowing the concept of local government.

function, and made them arbiter over the tribunals of the other chiefs in cases of dispute. But behind all this the supreme power of the Crown—i.e. of the Governor—was firmly entrenched, and the long argument as to whether authority lay with the people or the Crown was settled in favour of the Crown.

This is not to suggest that the Governor had been disingenuous in devising the procedure, or that the chiefs were his mere puppets in the matter. Previous legislation had been bitterly opposed by the chiefs, and there had been no reservation in his promise to support them, whatever they proposed. But the tide of history was bringing the chiefs into alignment with the Government, and in effect they did Guggisberg's work for him. It follows that what they offered in the Bill was deeply unpopular elsewhere, so much so that Caseley-Hayford and Glover-Addo, invited by Guggisberg to become Extraordinary Members of the Council for the purposes of the debate on this Bill, specifically in order to criticize it and to give the viewpoint of the A.R.P.S., coolly declined to have anything to do with the affair.

It was left to A. W. Kojo Thompson, the Municipal Member for Accra, to voice their opposition. He stigmatized the Bill as a Government Bill introduced by a back door, complained that the public had been given no opportunity to make its voice heard, and forcefully presented the objections of the other side; notably that it took away customary safeguards against the autocracy of Paramount Chiefs, conferred upon them rights far in excess of custom and tradition, reduced sub-chiefs, who had traditional authority within their own areas, to mere subordinates, and irresponsibly reduced the jurisdiction of the Supreme Court without substituting any satisfactory alternative.

The debate on the second reading has a particular interest from the point of view of this narrative, since it was Guggisberg's last appearance at the Legislative Council, which took place on 19 April 1927. He sailed the same week on retirement leave, and by chance the business immediately preceding the debate was a motion of appreciation and good wishes, moved by Nana Ayirebi Acquah III and seconded by Nana Ofori Atta. The motion took him by surprise, causing him to say, 'I did not know that I was going to have an opportunity of saying these words and I have not prepared them carefully. . . .' What he had to say was not in fact strictly within the bounds of propriety, for with the coming debate weighing heavily on his mind he went beyond the expected formal thanks and addressed himself to its subject-matter, thus taking part in the debate himself before it had begun. Since it was his last appearance in the centre of the stage the occasion deserves a brief digression.

He appeared at first to be making an *ex parte* statement, which in the circumstances would have been improper. He spoke of the unique degree of co-operation which native constitutions and customs embodied, and pleaded against change:

I feel that the native states of this country are going through a very dangerous phase, a phase in which your native institutions are threatened by more modern ones from Europe; and it gives me very great happiness indeed to feel that I am leaving this country with the Chiefs united in guarding those institutions. . . .[1]

But he modified this by saying that the day might arrive when changed conditions of life would cause the ancient institutions to be altered, and at one point he had 'a little parting word' to say about them. This was to the effect that the Paramount Chiefs should use their permissive power under the Bill to appoint educated commoners to their State Councils, since it was his abiding wish to see the traditional and educated elements reconciled. Had he stopped there all would have been well, but he added an extraordinarily revealing sentence. Should the Paramount Chiefs do this he would watch with interest to

see how far the members of the great professions in this country are going to throw in their lot with the real (*sic*) people, that is the people who are ruled by the Natural Rulers of the country with their State Councils.

Words uttered *ex tempore* on an occasion of great emotion should perhaps not be used in serious assessment, yet on the other hand they may disclose the truth more accurately than

[1] *Debates*, 1927–8, pp. 455–6.

many a considered statement. British administrators before World War II were always disposed to think of a family farmer as a real person and a university graduate an anomaly and a nuisance, though whether at home they regarded themselves as being less 'real' than their gardeners is not clear.

Guggisberg, a more unprejudiced man than most, nevertheless could not escape the habits of thought of the English class which he had adopted. No more than he could feel really warmly towards most of the 'educated natives' that he knew. This is said by way of comment and not criticism, for any possible criticism of this nature is disarmed by the fact that his name lives on in Ghana today when most others are forgotten, and some reviled. In any case, his reverence for Booker T. Washington and his warm personal feeling for Aggrey absolve him from any suspicion of race prejudice as such. He merely, like the English squire he secretly aspired to be, romanticized the peasant. Nowadays it is commonly thought among progressive white people that the *sine qua non* of good relations between themselves and those less privileged, particularly among the coloured race, is 'identification', with a tendency towards overdeference of white to black. Guggisberg's record and reputation show that there are larger considerations than this. The qualities which have enabled Africans to forget those foibles which have irritated them in lesser men were his compassion, his faith in their destiny and his unremitting toil in their service. Armed with these, a self-conscious egalitarianism was unnecessary.

Thus a problem that was the first to greet him on arrival was the last to occupy him on departure. Given his own premises about the future of chieftainship he handled it with unusual diplomatic skill and foresight, and perhaps the only jarring note in his performance, viewed objectively, was that his closing remarks about the A.R.P.S., whom he had in a sense defeated, were of a somewhat patronizing kind:

The passing of the Native Administration Ordinance puts the Aborigines Rights Protection Society in its proper place, and a very useful place, in this country; that is to say a society interested in public affairs but a society of a private nature.

Admittedly the A.R.P.S., as such, had not now much of a future, but the point of view for which it stood was eventually to sweep Guggisberg's political ideas away for ever.

But fortunately, and most fittingly, his final words of all in Legislative Council were an admonition to the chiefs themselves. He reminded them that the sharpest criticism of their opponents had been directed at their alleged lack of integrity:

I would be a false counsellor if I did not point out the danger which the native tribunals run if they are not kept on the very highest peaks of honesty and integrity.

The Colonial Office were delighted by the whole affair. Their minutes purred with pleasure that the chiefs should have behaved in such a textbook manner. The A.R.P.S. and all that it stood for could, they thought, be forgotten, or remain an unpleasant memory in the files. Righteousness had triumphed over evil, which happens all too rarely in this life.

The negotiations which we have been describing concerned the Gold Coast Colony only. In those days Ashanti was curiously separate and remote, being outside the jurisdiction of the Legislative Council and by no means easy even to get to before the growth of motor roads and the completion of the railway.[1] 'Native affairs' were simpler in one very important aspect, since Ashanti, unlike the Colony, was a conquered country and there was accordingly no question of the chiefs having inherent authority in the legal and constitutional sense; whatever powers they possessed were derived unquestionably from the Government. Not that this made life any easier for them, for when Guggisberg had said that the slower growth of education in Ashanti was resulting in the family and tribal structure being preserved the wish had been father to the thought. In fact, the extension of the railway, the growth of the cocoa industry and the irresistible contagion of western ideas were stimulating education very

---

[1] In a debate in 1919 the Hon. E. J. P. Brown, an Akan, mentioned with some pride that he had once visited Ashanti, in 1910, as he was curious to see what the place and people were like.

rapidly. The usual disintegration of customary society was following in the wake of this progress and the chiefs' authority was being very widely questioned; as in the Colony the wiser heads among the educated community would have liked to have it both ways—to preserve the façade of chieftainship in all its former glory whilst quietly taking power into their own hands— whilst the more volatile elements would have preferred a clean sweep with the past. But from the Government's point of view the situation was well under control and their relations with the chiefs were good; moreover there was no argumentative Legis- lative Council to block or question the reforms which seemed to Government to be appropriate. Accordingly it was possible in 1924 to enact an Ashanti Native Jurisdiction Ordinance which gave the Government the powers in Ashanti that they had sought without success in the Colony in 1922. But the principal architect of this legislation was the Chief Commissioner for Ashanti, C. H. Harper, and it did not make any abnormal demands on Guggisberg himself. His own diplomatic skill and political judgement were to be tested in Ashanti by a rather different kind of problem, namely the return of King Prempeh from exile in the Seychelle Islands.

Since the banishment of the King of Ashanti in 1896 it had been the Government's policy to complete and maintain the dissolution of his power by a deliberate policy of 'divide and rule', and this they achieved by building up the powers of the divisional chiefs and treating the Asantahene as no more than the Head Chief (*in absentia*) of the Coomassie tribe. In practice they were somewhat half-hearted even about this, for the rebellion had left behind it a legacy of political apprehension, so that while nominally building up the divisional chiefs' position in order to destroy the Kingdom they kept a very tight rein on their courts and tended constantly to diminish their day-to-day powers, thus assisting those other influences— material prosperity and education—that were tending in the same direction. The pre-war policy in the administration of Ashanti had in fact been a contradictory one, and had resulted in the chiefs' position becoming ambiguous and their authority indeterminate. The purpose of the 1924 Ordinance was to restore their authority as well as to define that of the Government.

In 1918, a number of Ashanti chiefs had petitioned the Secretary of State to allow Prempeh to return, but had received no satisfaction, and the death of the King's mother and brother, and the possibility that he himself might die in exile, was the cause of much concern when Guggisberg arrived in the country in October 1919. Here was another urgent problem which greeted him almost as soon as he stepped ashore, and one in which his heart and his head were again in serious conflict. For on the one hand he was a humane man, who understood the anguish of an African growing old away from his homeland and family, and who thought privately that Prempeh's punishment, as representative of the Ashanti nation, had been sufficient; on the other hand, he was tied by the solemn undertakings of the British Government and of his own immediate predecessor, who in giving an amnesty to others who had taken part in the insurrection had said in effect, 'Thus far and no farther.' Moreover he was himself apprehensive about the possible effects of Prempeh's return, for the last thing he wanted was for his programme of development to be vitiated by political disturbance. But the Africans of the Gold Coast placed great hopes in the new Governor, and at his second Legislative Council meeting, in November 1919, he had to consider an awkward Resolution:

That in the opinion of this Council, the time has arrived when the question of the release of ex-King Prempeh from his exile in the Seychelle Islands should receive the favourable consideration of His Majesty's Government, and we most respectfully and humbly pray that Royal clemency may be exercised in his favour.

The Resolution was eloquently moved and seconded by Nana Ofori Atta and E. J. P. Brown and supported by all African members, none of them Ashantis, a fact which impressed Guggisberg very deeply. Their arguments rested on the peace and prosperity of the country, the loyal services of the Ashanti nation in the War and the reformed character of

Prempeh himself, now converted to Christianity and 'a civilized man'. The European members remained silent.

Guggisberg's reply was brief and clearly embarrassed. He acknowledged the 'pitiful' nature of the circumstances and expressed the 'utmost sympathy'. 'One would only too gladly recommend as a recognition of [Ashanti] loyalty the return of Prempeh, but . . .' For he was bound, in all the circumstances, to temporize, and he made as his principal excuse the impending retirement of the then Chief Commissioner Ashanti, the greatly respected Sir Arthur Fuller, whose departure made immediate consideration 'inopportune'. He promised, however, to bring the arguments in the debate to the special notice of the Secretary of State. He had been in the country little more than a month, and his paramount wish was to be popular with Africans, both from genuine personal regard and in order to win them over to his development schemes. It was therefore a difficult occasion for him and he handled it with some skill.

Although he fulfilled his promise to keep the Secretary of State fully informed of national sentiment and concern, he held the situation in abeyance, so far as any forward move was concerned, for another two years, and it was not until a year after that, in February 1923, that he started to clear the decks for action with the Colonial Office—not that their minds were closed on this subject, for the British Government also was embarrassed by a Prempeh lobby and by Questions in the House, but they would naturally not move easily from the established position. Guggisberg reviewed the history of the insurrection, of the exile, of the policy resulting from the exile and the unsatisfactory results of that policy. This led him on to Harper's work on the proposed Native Jurisdiction for Ashanti, the intention of which, as we have seen, was to clarify the powers and authority of both Government and divisional chiefs. This, he thought, would provide the vital safeguard against future political trouble, for once the divisional chiefs were firmly entrenched Prempeh could return as a private citizen, or at most as Head Chief of the Coomassie.

In 1924 the risk was taken, and the King returned as a private citizen after twenty-eight years in exile.[1] In retrospect the Governor's long delaying action may seem unduly cautious and his fears of disturbances exaggerated. But he was not a free agent, and his task in essence was to persuade the Colonial Office that the time was ripe for a calculated risk while counselling patience to Ofori Atta and his friends. This he accomplished without the slightest breach on either side. It was a matter in which it would have been extremely easy to put a foot wrong, especially with his African colleagues on whose good opinion his success as a Governor depended.

There is another point worth mentioning about the Ashanti Native Jurisdiction Ordinance, namely that it was the first example of colonial legislation to be based on anthropological research, and that Guggisberg was the first British Governor, at least in tropical Africa, to regard such research as an essential forerunner of sound administration. Towards the end of 1920 he had proposed to Milner that Capt. R. S. Rattray, later to become famous as Government Anthropologist, should be appointed Special Commissioner for Ashanti to conduct research into native law and custom as a preliminary to the Native Jurisdiction Bill; in the event he became Head of the Anthropological Department in Ashanti in 1921. There was a happy conjunction of circumstances in this matter. On the one hand a Governor, imbued with the principle of ruling through the chiefs, who happened also to be an engineer, trained to an accurate understanding of the properties of the materials with which he built; on the other, an administrative officer who, though not trained in a scientific school of social anthropology (for these did not then exist), possessed both flair and competence. Rattray appears to have been one of these tiresome people who afflicted colonial governments from time to time—an official whose main interest lay in anthropology. These were normally a thorn in the flesh of Secretariats, for their administration, though able, was apt to be peculiar, and they were

[1] In 1926 Guggisberg received and then sponsored a petition from the Kumasi chiefs asking to be allowed to re-elect Prempeh as their Omanhene. The Secretary of State approved and Nana Prempeh was installed as Kumashiene on 11 November 1926, on the second anniversary of his return.

disposed to develop ideas which cut across official policy or to engage in practices which did not accord with established bureaucratic procedures. A civil servant who is by temperament an artist and scholar should live his private and public lives separately, but for a field political officer in the colonies the raw materials of his public work and his private hobby were inseparable.

These observations are prompted by the fact that there is reason to suppose that Rattray was unacceptable as a Deputy Provincial Commissioner or senior Secretariat Officer, as would have been his normal right, and that the post of Government Anthropologist provided a happy solution to a problem in personnel. This may well have been true, but it is to Guggisberg's credit that he found a constructive channel for a peculiar talent instead of bemoaning the fact that it was peculiar. That Rattray's work was constructive, and that it resulted in better relations between the political service and the chiefs, appears not to be in doubt. Nor is there any doubt that his appointment by Guggisberg at a time when anthropology was only beginning to establish itself as a respectable science, subsequently earned him a personal reputation of considerable magnitude.

The scientific study of social institutions, as a basis for modern administration, has fallen into some disfavour in Africa, for contemporary ideologies are impatient of it. Guggisberg, a military engineer, believed in it wholeheartedly, thus anticipating the cause for which academic anthropologists subsequently 'fought for thirty or more years, generally in the teeth of opposition from educated Africans, although nationalists now declare that they were prevented by British teachers from studying their own cultures'.[1]

Native affairs in the Northern Territories were not necessarily simpler than elsewhere, as Rattray's later researches were to show, but from the Governor's point of view they were at least less contentious. A paternalistic administration had developed excellent personal relations with the chiefs, and Guggisberg's régime was marked by unaccustomed peace and steady, though

[1] Audrey I. Richards, Review article in *Minerva*, Spring 1965.

modest, material progress. His final reference to them in *Events* (p. 232) was characteristically warm and affectionate, for this remote part of his kingdom had always tugged at his heart.

## Municipal Government

British colonial administrators of Guggisberg's day were not usually enamoured of towns, for they had not chosen a career in Africa in order to engage in the mundane affairs of city management. Their interests were rural, their outlook was paternalistic and their emotional attachment was to the wide open spaces or the bush. Quite apart from this, urban administration involved technical knowledge that they did not possess and funds which their governments did not command, for one of the casualties of the British Treasury doctrine of colonial self-sufficiency in finance was that town improvements, which are expensive, could not be paid for on any significant scale. Britain's urban legacy to Africa has therefore been less impressive than that of the French, the Germans or the Belgians, and only since independence have the urban areas begun to acquire some degree of urbanity. The towns presented themselves to earlier proconsuls as problems in politics and administration rather than in physical planning; for here were communities which could not by any stretch of the imagination be fitted into the philosophical framework of indirect rule, and for whom special arrangements had to be made.

Guggisberg was in fact, because of his profession, more interested in town improvements than most governors, for he had been trained to understand such things as surface water drainage, piped supplies, sewage, building costs, sanitation and surveys. But in his day town councils could not comprehend these matters, except in relatively small and incidental ways, and although his concept of municipal government involved their gradual transfer to the councils he, like his colleagues, saw the problem in his own day as an adminstrative rather than an engineering one. Town improvements certainly featured prominently in his Annual Messages, but under the vote of the Public

Works Department. It may be added that it was an aspect of government which attracted his warm support and careful scrutiny, and he was especially concerned with the building of what was virtually a new town at Takoradi to serve the Harbour.

But in the theory of municipal government as such he was forward-looking, and his views on the subject read acceptably today. Municipal government in the Gold Coast had had a long, though hardly a successful, history, and on Guggisberg's arrival was ordered by a Town Councils Ordinance of 1894. This, as so often with colonial legislation, had been enacted from unexceptionable motives, but since it had been designed *for* the inhabitants of towns rather than with their understanding and co-operation it had met with little but resistance, or at best apathetic acquiescence.[1] It was a colonial-type measure, with an official majority secured by the chairmanship of the District Commissioner, and this displeased the élite; it involved municipal magistrates' courts, and this displeased the chiefs; it rested firmly on the imposition of local rates, and this displeased everybody, a circumstance for which the Government could not be blamed, for until independence all Gold Coast Governments were faced with a demand for development coupled with a steadfast refusal to contribute to it through personal taxation, and this was unreasonable; though it was perhaps not so unreasonable to object to the imposition of rates on property by a majority of government officials who were not paying rates themselves.

Nevertheless, the Ordinance was applied to Accra in 1898, to Sekondi in 1904 and to Cape Coast in 1906, with results that Guggisberg encountered in 1919. He found them displeasing. The town councils had no responsible executive officers of their own, being run, as far as they were run at all, by government officials; their revenues were wholly inadequate, since their

[1] Earlier in the century, in 1869 and again in 1887, the educated townspeople of Accra and Cape Coast had themselves proposed a form of municipal government, but the response of the Gold Coast Government and the Colonial Office had been so preposterously discouraging that interest evaporated. (Kimble, *Political History*, pp. 418 ff., Ch. XI, at various stages, gives the full history of the subject.)

rating powers were limited to five per cent of the rateable value of property; they survived at all largely because of government grants; above all they commanded no local loyalty and inspired no local pride. Guggisberg described them forthrightly, in an early despatch to Lord Milner in November 1919, as 'mere inconvenient appanages of the central government and their technical departments'.

In January 1921, he set up a Committee of Inquiry comprising that indefatigable stage army of the political intelligentsia, Caseley-Hayford, Hutton-Mills, Brown and Glover-Addo, under the chairmanship of John Maxwell, to consider the working of the three town councils and to say how they could be improved as 'educational establishments in administrative responsibility'. The phrase is interesting, for in this particular matter Guggisberg was fully prepared to accept the 'British model', which was usually anathema to him. He supposed, no doubt, that there was no other model of any account. But like others who followed him in the 1950s, when local government burst upon the African bush, he did not take the point that the British model had been devised pragmatically simply in order to get urgent social services organized, and that it was only later that an 'educational' philosophy was constructed round it.

This Committee's Report[1] is an interesting essay on the changes in urban life in the thirty years since the Town Councils Ordinance had been drafted, but this cannot detain us here. It adumbrated a new Municipal Corporations Ordinance which would provide for an elected majority, with minority representation for the Government and Chambers of Commerce, but with an elected Mayor; it proposed more spacious powers, including rating powers, though the poorer properties would be exempted altogether and government grants would continue. Inevitably, it also followed the English model. (The chairman, Maxwell, must have been one of the first of a very large army to study English local government while on leave, and to be attached to a local authority for the purpose of extending his professional knowledge.)

[1] Published as *Sessional Paper* No. 17 of 1922–3.

Guggisberg, in despatching this document to London, in October 1923, remarked:

I am personally very anxious, in furtherance of my general policy of the Progress of the People of the Gold Coast, to develop municipal institutions and to place them in a position in which they can form a real training ground in responsible government. They form, in fact, a strong educative factor.

The idea was Joseph Chamberlain's rather than his own, for that great architect of Birmingham's municipal administration, shortly after becoming Colonial Secretary, had issued a circular Despatch, in 1895, on the subject of Municipal Government in the Crown Colonies, in which he had expressed himself somewhat more felicitously on the subject of the municipal spirit and the virtues of a quasi-independence from governments. But Guggisberg's reference to 'responsible government'—if indeed it referred to anything wider than local government—was unusual in the context of the time, and this must be one of the earliest occasions on which a Governor used it so categorically.[1]

The Colonial Office approved the general policy and the Bill, though perhaps with less enthusiasm than Chamberlain, or Guggisberg, would have wished. It was proposed to apply it in the first instance, and as an experiment, only to Accra.

Guggisberg now ran into what he was later to describe as the greatest disappointment of his Governorship. Municipal reform had a prosaic sound, and the phrase is not one to quicken the pulse, but he was now thoroughly seized of it, and was as keen on promoting representative government in the seaport towns as he was on preserving government through the chiefs elsewhere; though how he could have supposed that such an increasingly artificial distinction could endure for very long, it is

[1] But not the earliest. Professor Kimble (*Political History*, p. 185) describes the activities of Sir Benjamin Pine, who came to the Gold Coast as Governor in 1857. He established an elected Corporation, for Accra, with a Mayor, in *1858*, and expressed himself on the subject of municipal government in these terms: 'The best government is that which teaches people to govern themselves, and certainly the object of this Government is not to clean out dirty towns, but to direct the people to that and other objects by controlling and modifying their own Government.' This has a curiously contemporary ring, and he must have been an interesting man.

now difficult to see. It will be recalled, moreoever,[1] that in shaping the 1925 national Constitution, on which he was concurrently engaged, he had allowed for direct elective representation from the three coastal municipalities, provided that they first adopted the new Municipal Ordinance, a provision which had been included partly to allay criticism of the unpopular aspect of municipal self-government, i.e. the rates. Accordingly in addressing the Legislative Council for the first time on the new Ordinance,[2] a certain portentousness overlaid his enthusiasm. (These were in fact two somewhat usual characteristics in his speeches. The habit of saying important things in a colloquial way was not then in fashion, so that many of Guggisberg's utterances seem today rather pompous. On the other hand, when addressing simpler folk, he had the gift of parable, based on the everyday happenings of humble lives.)

I regard this as the biggest step in political advancement ever taken by the inhabitants of this country. . . . Government's policy will be to give full responsibility to the Town Councils while at the same time supporting and guiding them in those complicated technicalities that form a part of modern town administration. Africans elected as Councillors will, I feel sure, approach their task with seriousness and determination, for on their success depends, to a very great extent, the justifications of their race for political advancement.

The first task, however, was to get Africans elected as Councillors at all, since no one in the towns appeared to share the Governor's dedicated enthusiasm. Opposition—to the revision of rates—became vocal as soon as the terms of the Bill were known, and none of the advantages proposed, not even the advantage of electing representatives by ballot to the Legislature, carried any weight in comparison with this grievous affliction. So serious was the outcry that the application of the Ordinance had to be suspended while an official Inquiry was held, and Guggisberg was forced to bow before the storm and withdraw the condition that the towns must adopt the Ordinance before they could be represented in the Council.

[1] p. 180.        [2] Annual Address, 6 March 1924.

Government nomination was substituted, and this in turn proved equally difficult and contentious.[1]

The last Annual Message that he was to give in the Gold Coast, therefore, at the Budget Session on 3 March 1927, was marred by a confession of failure and disappointment:

The failure to make municipal self-government a stepping-stone . . . to elective representation on this Council has been the only real disappointment which I have had as your Governor. . . . Perhaps the time is not yet ripe. Anyway, seeing that the citizens of our seaport towns think as they do, it would not be ripe at the present moment to force the responsibility of municipal self-government on them. Until they feel that they can resist popular outcry, and can help their townspeople to think on more progressive lines, until, in fact, they feel themselves better fitted to bear the responsibility of responsible self-government, the application of the Ordinance should be deferred.

He went on to say that as a temporary measure—or so he hoped—the old 1894 Town Councils Ordinance would continue, with a few amendments, and that the Government, with its official majority on the town councils, would themselves have to take the responsibility of raising the rates.

We have said earlier that one of Guggisberg's greatest gifts was a penchant for public relations and an ability to carry people with him in what he was proposing to do, by taking them into his confidence. This unhappy story seems not to accord with the statement. The blame, however, did not rest with him entirely, for he was misled by the apparent enthusiasm of the members who represented Accra, Cape Coast and Sekondi on the Legislative Council; they for their part, being persuaded of the good sense of what was being proposed, seem to have underrated the unpopularity of the proposed rating revision, though one would have supposed that they ought to have known better, since African representatives are normally in closer touch with their constituents than is the case in Britain. He and they alike were victims of the massive determination of the citizens of Accra never, in any circumstances, to be taxed.

[1] The facts are fully described in Kimble (*Political History*), pp. 447–8.

We have said also that it is difficult to understand why Guggisberg should have supposed that the sharp distinction between indirect rule in the country at large and ballot-box elections in the towns could be preserved for very long. For how, after all, does one define a town? How does one provide for increasing mobility between town and country, or for the spread of sophistication from one to the other? If ideas know no frontiers between one continent and another, how can they exist between neighbouring communities which are increasingly interdependent? It is true that he had not thought these problems out, but on the other hand he did not, in his mind's eye, see a kind of iron curtain between Accra, Cape Coast and Sekondi on the one hand and the rest of the Colony on the other; for in addressing the Council on 26 February 1926, he used these words:

It is probable that the next step will be the extension of the franchise now given, either by adding to the number of towns, or by increasing the number of municipal members.

This took him a further step along the road to admitting that government through native institutions was no permanent solution. The truth is that like others of his generation he was torn, in this as in so many other matters, between the promptings of head and heart. He lived at that awkward moment in time when customary rule appeared to be immutable, and when the great mass of people appeared to want nothing else; moreover, its apparent permanence and propriety were reinforced by his own emotional attachment to it. On the other hand he could not have been blind to the plain facts of urban living and of the growth of towns, nor, even more certainly, could he have been deaf to the extremely articulate élite, who unceasingly assailed him with the view that the future belonged to those who had been educated in the western tradition. He never succeeded in achieving harmony within himself over this intractable problem, so that his utterances seem occasionally to contradict one another. For example, the speech to a meeting in the House of Commons shortly after his retirement[1] has a strangely reactionary flavour compared with the passage quoted above.

[1] p. 187.

But in this he was not alone. Indeed, many of his successors in the Administration of the Gold Coast had not achieved a comparable flexibility of mind a generation later.

Nevertheless, it was a matter on which he never really succeeded in making up his mind.

# 9

## The Public Service

ALTHOUGH Guggisberg had spent most of his career in West Africa as a member of a technical department, and although as we have seen he had writhed under the implied inferiority of engineers and agriculturalists to those who were strangely called 'political officers',[1] he nevertheless, as Governor, upheld the superiority of the political service to all others:

I turn now to that branch of the Government which is chiefly concerned with progress, the Political Service. . . .

. . . I adhere firmly to my opinion that Political Officers come first and foremost.

These two sentences from a speech delivered to the Legislative Council fourteen months after his arrival,[2] although admittedly taken out of context, leave no doubt that he had come to share the traditional colonial service view of the 'heaven-born'. The words were not uttered thoughtlessly, for he was deliberately comparing officers of the Administration with those of the Departments of Education, Agriculture and Medicine, and stating in reasoned terms why he thought them more important. Nor was he turning his back on his former technical associations, or kicking away the ladder up which he himself had climbed. He was simply affirming his belief in indirect rule, and in doing so was expressing views which later became anathema to Africans

---

[1] The words 'political' and 'administrative' seem to have been used indiscriminately in those days. With the growth of national politics 'administrative' became more usual. Today the political and administrative functions have again become indistinguishable.

[2] *Debates*, 21 January 1921.

—that they must walk before they could run, that material prosperity and education were overtaking the people too rapidly, and that the pace threatened to overwhelm 'our native constitutions',[1] and that soundly based progress could only be achieved through the chiefs and their councillors.

The paramount importance of the political officer, as Guggisberg saw it, was based on the fact that he alone stood at the chief's elbow and guided him through the hazards of the new world in which he moved so unsurely.

. . . it is on the steadying, supporting hand of the Political Service that we must chiefly rely for the progress of the people.

I have heard a certain amount of loose talk—I have read a great deal of loose writing—about 'grandmotherly administration'. Well, if it is grandmotherly administration to prevent a child running before it can walk, then I think grandmotherly administration is not so bad as it is painted if it can save the child's face from a severe fall.

In 1921 these words caused no offence, and even E. J. P. Brown, in the subsequent debate, appears to have accepted the Governor's general thesis, though Caseley-Hayford, who might have taken exception to it, was not present. It would not have been accepted so meekly away from Guggisberg's presence or in the conclaves of the A.R.P.S., but he was in a position to say what he liked in Legislative Council, since by now no one could doubt his commitment to higher education and African advancement; nevertheless he was perhaps the last Governor of the Gold Coast who could have put things in quite this way without arousing hostility.

The Political Service was of course British, and Guggisberg himself excluded the idea that this most important branch of Government should ever be open to Africans. It is perhaps unnecessary to add that this view did not arise from an attitude of racial discrimination, or from doubts about African capacity, but was part of the logic of indirect rule. Africans of the necessary calibre had immediate 'opportunities of serving their country in the Oman Councils of the Stools to which they

[1] Over-identification with Africans, even by Guggisberg, was not always acceptable to the intelligentsia.

belong';[1] in the longer term, if indeed his mind reached so far, political officers worked for their own elimination. It was not a view for which any apology need be made; it is simply a different view from the one which ultimately prevailed.

Since this chapter is chiefly concerned with Guggisberg's efforts to advance Africans in the public service, it is perhaps appropriate to start by mentioning this exception to his general rule, and to recall that one of the most serious responsibilities that fell to him, as to any Governor, was to lead and inspire an expatriate administrative service of Provincial and District Commissioners on whom the good government of the country did in fact so largely depend. Leadership and inspiration are qualities which are perhaps less highly regarded today than then, but in the Colonial Service of the 1920s they were important, and meant perhaps more than anything else to a disciplined body of men, educated in the prefectorial tradition and working at strange tasks in isolation from their homeland and their families. Indeed they continued to be important for a long time, as became clear after World War II, when governors were increasingly absorbed with African politicians and the intricacies of party politics. To be a father figure alike to nationalist politicians and to expatriate colonial servants was generally beyond them, so that expatriates, at a crucial moment in their careers, were liable to find themselves leaderless, for no father can delegate his responsibility to another. Guggisberg lived in less complicated times, for although he dealt continuously with politicians he did not do so as *primus inter pares* but as Governor to precocious subjects; nor did he have to negotiate with political parties whose importance locally was equal to that of His Majesty's Government.

It is impossible to say at this distance of time how the administrative service as a whole regarded him, as most of its present survivors were junior officers at the time, and their judgement is apt to be clouded by the awed respect given to a somewhat remote figure. But those who were then senior enough to have official dealings with him testify unanimously to his

[1] This was said as late as 1926. *Debates*, 1926-7, p. 17.

invigorating and quickening touch. He was a leader of men in that he deepened their sense of purpose and made them want to work harder. An administrative officer in a British African colony could feel variously about his job—that it sufficed until his next leave; that it offered an agreeable and adventurous alternative to other available occupations; or that it gave him an opportunity to fulfil himself in serving a people and creating a country. Guggisberg had the knack of making his political officers feel the last, for this was how he felt himself, and his sincerity and enthusiasm were infectious.

The situation which he found, in terms of organization and management, was depressingly similar to that which existed in British West Africa after World War II. He solved it in his own day, but only temporarily, for economic stringency and staff shortages undermined his work, and a generation later various successors propounded very similar solutions, assisted by the new air travel. These in turn were difficult to maintain, and in any case the question soon ceased to matter. But Guggisberg was the first Governor to deal successfully with the absurd situation whereby District Commissioners played an unending game of general post, moving from one station to another, or from station to provincial secretariat, in order to relieve colleagues who were on leave or on the sick list. This resulted in inefficiency, waste of local knowledge and general unsettlement. The value of a District Commissioner's work depended on his staying long enough in one place to exercise pastoral care (for his work had much in common with that of a priest) and to see his schemes through to completion, for administration in Africa was then, as now, intensely personal. Chiefs and people would give their unreserved allegiance to a man whom they had come to know and trust, but regarded the white stranger with reserve, and the itinerant carpet-bagger gave little satisfaction to himself or anyone else; except perhaps to his master in the Secretariat who, moving his men across the map like pawns, had the dubious satisfaction of knowing that each of his stations was occupied by an officer of the correct seniority. A later generation of European wives were driven to distraction, or out of the country, by the interminable shifting of their households from one place to another, and although the administrative officers of Guggisberg's day did not for the most part suffer this domestic complication, it was a rootless, transient existence which served no serious purpose.

I have known of cases where District Commissioners, though for several years nominally remaining in their districts, were for nine-tenths of their time in reality either on leave or acting at provincial headquarters.[1]

Others were not even nominally in one district, but moved constantly from one to another, their household belongings and books rapidly deteriorating from innumerable rough rides in packing-cases.

The root of the difficulty was that the service was below strength as a result of the War—it always seems to have been below strength for one reason or another—so that there was no reserve pool from which temporary replacements could be drawn. Given some reserve, the solution of the problem required no more than common sense and resolution, and these Guggisberg possessed. On his first leave, in the summer of 1919, he tackled Milner squarely on the subject, and won his point; the increase in staff which he persuaded the Secretary of State to sanction, combined with a judicious reduction in the number of provinces, enabled him to achieve continuity of staffing in the districts, and to design for the first time in the history of the service what we should now call a career structure:

The number of officers at our disposal will now result in the normal history of the political officer being as follows:

For his first two or three years he will be employed practically as a relieving officer. He will then as a vacancy occurs become a permanent Assistant District Commissioner in a sub-District and will relieve the District Commissioner of his District when the latter goes on leave. In due course he will receive a district of his own and there he will remain under ordinary circumstances until he receives any further promotion that may come to him. Speaking generally, the political officer will probably remain from eight to ten years in one district.

[1] *Debates*, 1920–1, p. 14.

Rules for promotion were stiffened and fluency in the vernacular was made a condition of any promotion at all. The
service was reorganized on this basis from 1 January 1921.
(Thirty years later Governors in West Africa tried once again to
solve it, this time by abolishing the concept of 'leave' altogether
and substituting two months' annual 'holiday', to be taken by
air.)

Guggisberg was above all a man who liked to get things
straight on paper, and it would have been out of character if he
had not at some time attempted to define the qualities that he
looked for in his political officers. This he did, towards the end
of his career, in these words:[1]

. . . the first essential is a keenness on, and sympathy with, the task of
assisting native races through the present period of development;
firmness of character combined with patience, tact and a strong
sense of justice; initiative in devising ways and means; and finally,
great modesty.

What he perhaps failed to do was to examine, with a sufficiently imaginative and critical eye, the work which District
Commissioners were in fact doing, which consisted in far too
large measure of adjudicating in disputes, in and out of their
courts, on subjects which could have little bearing on the
'present period of development'. Certainly it did not justify his
observation, quoted earlier, that they were the officers who were
'chiefly concerned with progress'. The horizons of District
Commissioners, like those of the rest of us, tended to shrink as
they became occupied with their parochial affairs, so that less
than minor matters, such as deciding which of two illiterate
chiefs was telling the less plausible lies, appeared to become
matters of world-shaking importance. No one can supply his
own corrective in this situation, but it could be considered a
proper function of a Governor to keep horizons spacious and to
relate effort to result.

The Annual Message of 1924[2] does indeed include a vivid
description of the life of District Commissioners, clearly given
for the benefit of Honourable Members who considered them

[1] *Debates*, 1926–7, p. 164.                    [2] *Debates*, 1924–5, p. 115.

expendable. These versatile 'jacks-of-all-trades' are faithfully described, and their road-making, building and other protean activities fully recorded; but Guggisberg apparently saw nothing wrong with the admission that the major part of their work was concerned with chieftaincy disputes and, above all, boundary and land disputes, which had assumed such gigantic proportions that they occupied not only a large part of the District Commissioner's time but practically the whole time of a Deputy Provincial Commissioner, appointed mainly for that purpose. It now seems an odd way for the flower of the British public schools and universities to have spent its time in a situation which cried aloud for elemental welfare, but it was not until the Governorship of Sir Alan Burns that the then Chief Secretary, Henry Gurney,[1] attempted what would now be called a systematic job analysis; this revealed, rather startlingly, that the devotion which District Commissioners gave to their work was equalled only by the irrelevance of much of it to the twentieth century.

Meanwhile, however, Guggisberg stiffened the morale and increased the efficiency of a service which had been almost intolerably over-strained during the War, which had suffered material hardship and under-payment, and many of whose members had suffered also the peculiar frustration of continuing with what had come to seem, in comparison with the struggle in Europe, a parochial task in a remote part of the world, when their hearts were with their compatriots and contemporaries in Flanders and elsewhere. This Guggisberg understood very well indeed, and they drew strength from his sympathy and insight.

It is however for the advancement of Africans in the public service of the Gold Coast that Guggisberg is now remembered in Ghana.

Today it is difficult to realize how deep-seated was the conviction among Europeans that Africans were necessarily incompetent and untrustworthy, an attitude reflected in Colonial

---

[1] Later assassinated in an ambush in Malaya, to the great loss of the Colonial Service and the nation.

Office minutes of fifty years ago.[1] It was an attitude that had profoundly shocked Clifford, who, as we have seen,[2] was quite unprejudiced about Africans on grounds of either race or competence, and who was remarkably courageous in his attempts to right their undoubted wrongs. Resentment of their restriction to subordinate positions was exacerbated by the war-time rise in the cost of living, which made existence barely tolerable on the pitiful salaries which were thought appropriate to them, and both Clifford and Guggisberg were immersed in efforts to contain the flood of demands for salary increases and cost-of-living bonuses within the bounds of what was financially possible and of what the Colonial Office would accept. Both men were equally sympathetic and humane. The difference between them was that whereas Clifford was able to do little more than bring some measure of justice into the situation as it was (apart from a limited success on behalf of medical practitioners) Guggisberg was determined to alter the situation itself, and to base his plans not only on better pay and conditions for those already employed, but on a comprehensive programme of Africanization[3] of all government posts, other than those in the political service.

He did not at first fully reveal his thoughts on the subject, for although he introduced it at his second meeting of the Legislative Council on 17 November 1919, he did so briefly and in a somewhat oblique manner, making it appear as much a matter of present economy as of future policy. He referred to the great increase in the Estimates for the salaries of European officials, especially in the technical departments, arising from their re-employment when the war Was over. But in fact he made himself plain to those with ears to hear, for in a few sentences he adumbrated the shape of things to come:

From every point of view—continuity, cost of passages and progress—I should like to see 50% of the present European staff in technical departments replaced by natives.

[1] See Kimble, *Political History*, at a great many points when quoting from the records which are now open. [2] p. 89.
[3] This ugly word was not then coined; it is unfortunately an extraordinarily convenient one.

He admitted that for the immediate future, progress depended on employing Europeans because of the inadequacy of secondary and technical education, but:

Our policy is to employ every suitably qualified native that we can and to assist the (at present) inadequate technical schools by training them within the departments. We want natives for higher appointments than artisans.

It was the opening shot of a long campaign, in which the majority of Europeans, including most of the technical officers themselves, were out of sympathy with him, and in which he was also handicapped by the fact that the hopes he raised could not be fulfilled as quickly as his words led Africans to believe; for the results of education and training do not become apparent, in terms of higher appointments, until at least a decade has passed, and although he was always careful to point this out, people who have been shown a glimpse of the promised land are not patient about earning their right to enter it.

In July of the following year (1920) he appointed a committee of three Europeans and two Africans (one of them the ubiquitous Caseley-Hayford) to draw up a detailed scheme for an African civil service,[1] and on the basis of its report he later (May 1921) addressed a despatch to Churchill requesting approval for the principle that every appointment in the Gold Coast Civil Service (other than the political service) should be open to Africans, provided they were 'duly qualified in respect of character, education, technical attainments and experience'. The provisos were of a kind familiar in other African colonies in later years, as independence drew near, and were frequently the object of criticism on the ground that Africans could always be rejected because of the nebulous criterion of 'character'. This criterion had been agreeable, however, to the African members of the Native Civil Service Committee, which was unanimous in believing that Africanization should not take place at all if

[1] The Native Civil Service Committee, whose Report was published as a *Sessional Paper*, No. 7 of 1920–1. Earlier, in 1918, Clifford had appointed a Committee to inquire into the 'Conditions of Service of Native Officials'. The difference in title is indicative of a difference in approach.

it resulted in any lowering of standards.[1] This again was a familiar theme elsewhere in Africa in the 1950s. It was an impossible condition to impose, and after reflection it was generally modified; indeed, Guggisberg himself retreated from it somewhat before he left the country. The point of interest is that these matters were being argued in the Gold Coast, under Guggisberg's direction, some thirty years earlier than anywhere else in British Africa.

The despatch to Churchill was followed a month later by a plan for reorganizing the entire Government Service, the object being 'to afford a definite path of promotion from the lowest to the highest service and to carry out the Government policy for the steady replacement of Europeans by Africans'.[2] The proposal was to divide the Service into three—a Senior, a Junior and a Subordinate Service, with Africans gradually eroding the European tenure of the first and replacing the lower-paid Europeans altogether in the second.

The attitude of African members of the Legislative Council to these measures was one of wary acceptance—that curious mixture of gratitude and suspicion which so often characterized their relationship with Guggisberg; gratitude, because they had not known a Governor like him before and because his devotion to their advancement was so apparent; suspicion, because this was the hall-mark of all relationships between white rulers and educated Africans during the colonial twilight, which was already beginning to fall in the Gold Coast. Frequently in debates over the following years the African members had a lot to say by way of objections, protests and grievances. But these, on the whole, concerned the application of Guggisberg's plans, and arose mainly out of specific cases of alleged discrimination or the passing over of individual Africans for selection or promotion. The adequacy and justice of the Governor's main strategic plan does not seem to have been seriously questioned.

Meanwhile, in his first full year of office (1920) he had pushed ahead with African appointments to posts which had normally

---

[1] Though the African members signed a minority report on salary scales and other matters.      [2] *Debates*, 1922–3, p. 41.

been considered 'European', without waiting for the report of his committee of 1920 or later, or for the reply of the Secretary of State to his formal proposals in 1921. At the January 1921 meeting of the Council he was able to report on what had already been achieved, as well as what was contemplated. This was less than he had hoped, and there is a hint of early disillusionment in his remarks as he surveyed the field of candidates. With the exception of doctors and barristers, who formed a separate and highly educated élite, it was startlingly thin, and he looked in vain for candidates for senior posts in the departments which interested him most—such as Engineering, Railways, Geology and Mining. Whenever a vacancy or a new appointment had occurred in any department of Government he had 'conferred long and seriously' with the (Gold Coast) Colonial Secretary and the head of the department concerned, but had to confess that he had often shared the reluctance of the latter to 'try an experiment of this nature' with the human material that was available. Nevertheless, he was able to announce the provision for seventeen appointments previously held by Europeans in the 1921 Estimates, though admittedly they included five medical officers and four magistrates, while the rest were relatively junior administrators, accountants or office assistants, so that progress in the technical field was *nil*. A further twenty 'Special Class' appointments (created instead of asking for more Europeans) included three superintendents in agriculture and a surveyor, but the rest were mainly chief clerks or customs collectors. The exercise brought home with painful clarity the appalling inadequacy of secondary schools and technical colleges from which a wider range of candidates might have been expected to emerge.

In spite of this sharp brush with reality, Guggisberg was not deterred, but went on to propound his aims for the future. These, it seemed, would have to depend in detail on the Secretary of State's approval of the recommendations of the Committee on the Native Civil Service. One is constantly surprised in reading about British colonial administration to recall how recent and how detailed was the supervision of the Colonial

Office in matters which one would have supposed would lie within the competence and discretion of the local government. Had the pockets of the British taxpayer been directly involved this would have been proper, but the tentacles of the Office reached out into aspects of colonial government in which only local money, local knowledge and local interests were involved, and men of Guggisberg's apostolic fervour had to risk their schemes being emasculated by officials in London whose grasp of them was, to say the least, partial; especially in those days when the officials rarely travelled to the countries whose problems they contemplated in the files. The defence of the system was that in the geographical department of the Office there was an immense accumulation of knowledge, which was true; and that more impartial and considered judgement could be reached in Whitehall than in the heat, literal and metaphorical, of tropical Africa, which was more open to question; and that in any case the Secretary of State paid great deference to the opinion of the 'man on the spot'; as to this, it depended on the man and on his opinions. Guggisberg, at any rate, in his physical decline, was to yearn wistfully for what he could have done, had he retained his health, 'away from the trammels of the Colonial Office'.

To return, Guggisberg told the Legislative Council that he proposed a 'progressive programme for the gradual replacement of at least 50 per cent of the present European Staff', which was no more than he had said a year earlier. He acknowledged, by implication, that he had underrated the difficulties; and went on to state a modest, and greatly modified, personal ambition:

Although I should like to see 20% of the European personnel replaced by Africans by the end of my period as Governor, I am afraid this estimate is too optimistic. In view of the state which our education has reached I should be content . . . if we have replaced 10% by that time.

The normal end of his period as Governor, to which he was presumably referring, would have been the end of 1924. By that time, however, comparatively little had been achieved in terms of practical results. Achimota was launched, but it would be some years before teaching started, and another decade before it showed results; the progress of the Accra Technical School, which was bursting its walls, was closely tied to that of Achimota, to which it was to be moved; and although four Junior Trade Schools had been started there had been growing pains, nor in any case would dividends from these schools be paid for several years to come. The result of this lack of progress in Africanization was made very much more severe by the effects of the economic recession which began in 1922, and which caused retrenchment; though this was not the main cause of the growing staff crisis, since it was proving more and more difficult to recruit Europeans even for the diminished number of technical posts available.

At the beginning of 1925, the Governor was reporting that 'the year which is just ending has certainly been the worst that we have experienced', adding plaintively:

There has been a serious amount of unemployment in the United Kingdom, but apparently the unemployed do not contain the type or class of men we require in our service, for the supply of suitable people has been accompanied by most aggravating delays which have impaired the efficiency of practically every Department.[1]

There could have been no clearer demonstration of the value to the future development of the Gold Coast of a planned policy of Africanization, had it been possible to launch it a decade earlier. In this desperate situation the Governor gave instructions that a drive was to be made in the training of Africans in the Junior and Subordinate Service, which could be undertaken within departments, or through *ad hoc* schemes which might show quick results. In the modern argot it would have been called, presumably, a 'crash programme'. The following was typical:

1. I want the Director of Education to confer with Director of Public Works, Postmaster-General and Chief Mechanical Transport Officer on their requirements in Electrical Fitters and on the course and instruments required at the Technical School.
2. Also to consider whether the Technical School is the best place.[2]

[1] *Debates*, 1925–6, p. 159.  [2] *Sessional Paper* No. 5 of 1924–5.

In the event, no room could be found in the Technical School, and Guggisberg instructed that various makeshifts should be adopted and that every effort should be made to apprentice artificers to local firms, as well as developing 'in-service' training in the three departments concerned.

Directives of this kind extended to the training of sub-treasurers, railway locomotive apprentices, post office engineering assistants and telegraphists, veterinary assistants, agricultural and forestry inspectors and P.W.D. overseers and artisans. It is significant that the Department which led the field in Africanization was 'his own', if one may so call it—the Survey Department:

> The Survey Department is one which should be of particular interest to all Africans as it will probably be the first one in which 75% of the *Senior* Service appointments will be filled by their countrymen, thanks to the personal interest and sympathy in the question taken by the Surveyor-General and his officers.

The Surveyor-General, Lieut.-Colonel R. H. Rowe of the Royal Artillery, and inevitably Guggisberg's personal friend, no doubt deserved credit for his work, but the lead which this Department established can surely be traced back to Guggisberg's earliest days on the Coast and to his unceasing professional interest in Gold Coast maps and surveys. It is arguable, if no more, that if the country had enjoyed the services of men of his outlook in other technical departments in the first decade of the century the poverty of African talent would have been less catastrophic in the second.

In 1925, as though to demonstrate his faith in the future in the teeth of immediate set-backs, Guggisberg issued to heads of departments a 'Programme of African Appointments' which was to cover the next twenty years (of which he himself would be present in the country for two). This was an early, and perhaps amateurish,[1] attempt at the kind of man-power survey which later became fashionable in the independent African states, using statistical techniques which were in their infancy

[1] For example, his forecast was that Government expenditure would have reached its final peak by 1936.

in the 1920s; though the variables and uncertainties in the African situation are such that even today the most sophisticated projections are apt to be little more than intelligent guesses, and Guggisberg's crystal-gazing was perhaps not more speculative than these.

By this time the number of Africans holding European appointments had risen to twenty-seven. The programme he laid down, and which he instructed his departmental heads to follow, was, in summary:

|  |  | Europeans | Africans |
|---|---|---|---|
| Number of appointments provided in the Estimates | 1925–26 | 481 | 28 |
| Proposed appointments | 1926–27 | 496 | 31 |
| Proposed appointments by | 1930–31 | 467 | 76 |
| Proposed appointments by | 1935–36 | 396 | 148 |
| Proposed appointments by | 1945–46 | 319 | 229 |

Whether this was realistic or not would depend on whether, by 1935–36, Achimota, the Technical School and the secondary schools were 'delivering the goods'. But the programme's realism, or lack of it, was perhaps not the paramount consideration. What mattered was that everybody now had his battle orders; the time for fair words and academic discussion was past, and the Governor now required his departmental heads to act on his instructions, or to be accountable to him if they failed to do so.

In his Annual Message of 1926 he made the fullest of all his pronouncements on the employment of Africans in the public service. By this time the Secretary of State had accepted his general policy with only one reservation, namely that he had added the Bench of Judges to the Political Service as a reserved occupation for Europeans; otherwise there was to be no limit to African opportunity, and even in the political service itself a number of senior secretariat posts were to be made open. But on this particular occasion the Governor appeared to be more preoccupied with financial economy than with principle— though it would be truer to say that he took the argument from principle for granted, assuming that everybody else did the same, and wished to support it with the financial argument, which, as a result of some long-term financial forecasting in which his advisers had been engaged, appeared to be of growing urgency.

Differences in salaries and pensions,[1] housing benefits, leave passages and other 'fringe benefits' as between Europeans and Africans meant that an African in a senior post would eventually cost the Government an average of £500 a year less than a European, and by the money values of 1926 this was a considerable sum. Moreover, an African was absent from his post on leave for approximately two and two-thirds months every two years as against a European's six. The total sum involved was a formidable one, especially in view of the continual increase in the bill for emoluments arising from increments and accumulating pension rights. Guggisberg therefore supported his basic belief that Africanization was right with a powerful subsidiary argument that it was an urgent and attainable economy.

He emphasized this aspect of Africanization because he thought that Honourable Members (meaning, presumably, European ones) 'did not sufficiently realize the pressing necessity for the adoption of the policy in the interests of economy'.[2] As to the principal argument, that the policy was 'dictated by the spirit of justice', he assumed, perhaps optimistically, that European members would agree that 'British ideas of justice can do nothing but lead to the approval of a policy of fair-play.'

Optimistically, because in this speech he also openly faced his European critics. These had not been lacking since the day when he had first made his policies plain, and they varied from simple, though possibly sincere, reactionaries, who could not contemplate the idea that black men could ever take charge of their own countries, to those with a vested interest in the continuance of the white man's livelihood. Neither were disposed, except perhaps in private, to be quite open about their reasons for opposing Guggisberg's views, but between them they had rationalized their arguments effectively, and the Governor clearly thought the time had come to meet their challenge.

---

[1] European salaries were one-sixth in excess of African, by way of overseas allowance.　　　　　　　　　　　　　　[2] *Debates*, 1926–7, p. 18.

Their first argument rested upon the supposed inevitable loss of efficiency, which Guggisberg countered by saying that a well-organized department, which arranged for good supervision, ought to be able to avoid it, and that it would only have itself to blame if it failed to do so.[1] Their second concerned the even more serious loss of efficiency, dangerous to the national welfare, when the time came for Africans to be promoted to 'Staff' Appointments, i.e. the most senior of all; his reply to this was that, as they well knew, such appointments were made on merit exclusively, and that it was no part of his plan that their attainment should be any easier for an African than for a European:

The African cannot expect to be specially favoured because he is an African, nor do I believe that his solid-thinking countrymen *in twenty years' time* would support him if he did.[2]

This was also his reply to their third, and somewhat disingenuous argument, that racial feeling would be created if and when the senior African in any department was passed over for promotion to a Staff Appointment.

One cannot avoid the suspicion that these were not the real objections of the critics, which, even in those days, it would hardly have been respectable to deploy. However, a year later on the eve of his own departure, he was able to say:

Heads of Departments have accepted the programme loyally, as is proved by the fact that the number of European appointments held by Africans has grown from 3 in 1919 to 38 in this financial year.[3]

But although these were European appointments they were not, with some exceptions,[4] particularly high-grade ones, which would have needed advanced educational or professional qualifications. Real progress in filling these would still have to

---

[1] Here, however, Guggisberg did yield a point, for he added: 'Even if there is a slight loss of efficiency to begin with, I see no reason why full efficiency should not be restored in due course.'

[2] Author's italics. Guggisberg did not envisage Africans reaching Staff Appointments in the foreseeable future.

[3] *Debates*, 1927–8, p. 257. The figure of 38 was in fact 9 ahead of the quota.

[4] They included two doctors, two magistrates, a Crown Counsel, two surveyors, two inspectors of schools, a headmaster and a headmistress. The remaining 27 were not of the same level of responsibility.

wait 'until Achimota and the new Education Ordinance begin
to take effect'. It was with a very special reluctance that he
accepted this, for the words were spoken during his last Annual
Message, a month before he was due to go. He had underrated
the difficulties of the crusade on which he had embarked some
eight years before, and was to some extent disillusioned. Were
he to have lived longer than he did, and to have kept in touch
with Gold Coast affairs, he would have been more disillusioned
still, for his convictions about Africanization were not shared
by his immediate successors, the pressure eased, and the 'programme' fell away. Nevertheless, what he had done in his own
time was unique.

### The Lawyers and the Doctors

These men stood out so strikingly from the mass of their contemporaries that they appeared almost to belong to a different
species. They had two things in common. First, they could earn
much larger incomes outside the public service than within it,
which gave them a unique independence among the educated
classes. Second, they were the only Africans who could claim
to be as well qualified professionally as their European counter-
parts. Between them they have provided the nationalist leadership throughout colonial Africa.

In Guggisberg's day the lawyers were not, for the most part,
interested in the public service, and only a few accepted
appointments as Police Magistrates or Crown Counsel, and
these not among the more able or better known. Strictly speaking there is therefore little to be said about the lawyers in a
chapter on the public service; on the other hand the part they
played in politics was decisive, and certainly affected the public
service indirectly; while the frequency with which they accepted
public duties on Committees or Commissions of Inquiry
seemed to make them public servants in all but name. Hardly
any public investigation in Guggisberg's time was complete unless it included the astringent presence of J. E. Caseley-Hayford.
Furthermore they were an important influence in Guggisberg's
career as Governor.

Throughout his time debates in the Legislative Council were dominated, on the 'unofficial' side, by Caseley-Hayford and E. J. P. Brown; among the non-lawyers only Nana Ofori Atta was of comparable stature,[1] and only J. D. McKay among the Europeans[2] had half as much to say. T. Hutton-Mills had left the Council before Guggisberg arrived, though he continued active in public affairs, but J. Glover Addo and A. W. Kojo Thompson were becoming prominent in the 1920s and C. J. Bannerman and E. C. Quist attended as 'extraordinary' members on occasion. The day of Korsah and Danquah was yet to come. These men were the most articulate prophets of the Gold Coast Revolution which reached its climax in 1948, and what they had to say was extraordinarily important. Although nominated by virtue of their ability to represent the educated community, whose point of view they were expected to express in a strictly non-party Administration, they became in practice an 'Opposition', and almost all the criticism of the Government came in the 1920s, from Caseley-Hayford and Brown (though McKay also was a persistent critic of the Governor's policies, but from a completely different point of view). No Governor in those days could have realized how important his handling of such men might be for the future. In the eyes of the European Administration, from the Governor downwards, they were still the 'awkward squad', who could not be disregarded and indeed must be listened to with a sort of reluctant respect, but who could not seriously be regarded as the future masters of their country. Still less could Guggisberg's Administration have foreseen that in the course of time the British Government would hand over the country not to men like these, who were staunch upholders of the British Empire and admirers of British rule (and revolutionaries only within this accepted framework), but to men of such radical temper that they were disposed to reject all things British.

Guggisberg in his dealings with them was to some extent

---

[1] Fraser believed that Ofori Atta was, in an all-round sense, the most able African of his time.

[2] He represented the mining interests.

blinded by his romantic preference for the chiefs and their native institutions, and failed to assess their true importance. Nevertheless, he never underrated them as individuals, he was unfailing in his courtesy towards them, and was at bottom in sympathy with their aspirations for their country. His fault was the fault of all his compatriots, that he could only see them as 'municipal' representatives, and could not conceive that they represented the mass of people with whom they seemed on the face of it to have so little in common. A little thought might have suggested to this generation of British proconsuls that at home their own social class was not unwilling to represent, on local councils and in Parliament, the working man and farm labourer.

But this is to digress. Within the ranks of the public service proper Clifford had appointed the young lawyer E. C. Quist as the first African Crown Counsel in 1914, and had followed this by appointing C. E. Woolhouse-Bannerman as a Police Magistrate in 1919; Guggisberg in turn appointed another Police Magistrate (W. A. Renner) and another Crown Counsel (L. E. V. M'Carthy). These appointments failed to satisfy the Gold Coast legal profession (though it is doubtful whether the wealthier lawyers would have sacrificed their own substantial earnings for salaried Government employment), but at least a breach had been made in the stultifying tradition of the previous twenty years.

The doctors presented Clifford and Guggisberg with an altogether more intractable problem. First, because their services were desperately needed in the public service, whereas neither Governor would have felt that the community was under-privileged through lack of lawyers. Second, because their work was personal and intimate, and roused the deepest feelings of racial prejudice among the European community; for it was a time when few European men and fewer women were able to contemplate being treated by a 'native'. Indeed, we have already seen that until the First World War African doctors were excluded from the West African Medical Service altogether by their European professional colleagues, and confined to subordinate duties. The A.R.P.S. had protested, and Clifford on this issue had joined forces with them; the result was the concession by the Secretary of State and the appointment in 1919 of Dr. C. E. Reindorf as a *Temporary* Medical Officer within the Service.[1]

But although Guggisberg in his early days was responsible for two more appointments to the Medical Service (Drs. A. F. Renner-Dove and G. J. D. Hammond, neither, incidentally, a native of the Gold Coast), it soon became clear to him that the problem was no longer simply one of overcoming racial prejudice. So far as the European doctors in the Department of Public Health were concerned, this was rapidly ceasing to be a problem, for any personal reservations or prejudices they may have had as individuals were disappearing in the light of their knowledge of the appalling shortage of doctors in the major stations, and of the sheer impossibility of ever staffing an adequate Gold Coast Medical Service with expatriates. During 1920 the Principal Medical Officer had himself designed a scheme of reorganization which would very quickly have employed twenty or thirty African doctors in the Service had they been available.

The real trouble was more deep-seated, and unfortunately for Guggisberg it was of a kind which was bound to raise protests about discrimination when stated openly, and when plans were announced to overcome it. For young Africans, newly qualified in the United Kingdom, were not in the circumstances of the time able to get clinical experience in British hospitals after qualifying, nor was such experience available in the two or three relatively primitive hospitals in the Gold Coast. Accordingly African doctors were *not*, at the beginning of their careers, as good as Europeans, which was a difficult thing to have to say. Nor, with the lure of lucrative private practice before their eyes, were they notably attracted by the discipline and relatively low salaries of the Government Medical Service. Guggisberg was compelled to speak of these matters in his Address of 1921[2] and to appeal to young Africans to put their country before

[1] p. 89.  [2] *Debates*, 1920–1, p. 20.

their pockets in the early years of their service, deferring the hopes of private practice in addition to Government service until they were well established, and promising them identical treatment with Europeans in this, as in other respects.

But appeals and promises of this kind did not touch the main problem, which was the lack of local facilities for clinical experience to supplement overseas academic training; and in the long run of local facilities for at least the preliminary stages of the training itself; and it was to these problems that with the help of his advisers he principally addressed himself.

The Vision of Achimota was now accompanied in his mind by the Vision of Korle Bu. The Gold Coast Hospital at Korle Bu— the name of what was then an outlying district or suburb of Accra, to the west of the lagoon—has come to be bracketed in the public mind with the two other great projects of Guggisberg's governorship; so much so that his tombstone might well have been inscribed:

Sir Gordon Guggisberg
father of
Achimota—Takoradi—Korle Bu

But this would have been inaccurate. Achimota was his brain-child entirely. Takoradi had been thought of earlier in the century by others, but its construction owed almost everything to him. Korle Bu, on the other hand, he inherited from predecessors, who can claim credit for having been many years ahead of their time. His own contribution was to take hold of the modest idea of a modern native hospital—admittedly first-class by the standards of the day—and to transmute it into the vision of a future Medical School and, ultimately, a University Teaching Hospital. Even as an African hospital it profited from his energizing touch, for he suggested improvements to the original plans and made the mundane but vital contribution of keeping it at the head of the building programme.

A start had been made on the building in 1920 and Guggisberg had laid the foundation stone in January 1921; it opened its doors to patients on 9 October 1923, and was in full operation by New Year's Day, 1924. As might have been expected, it was immediately filled to bursting point. But while the building was in progress its purpose was being subtly changed from curing today's sick to training tomorrow's doctors, for the Governor was convinced that Africa's doctors must be trained in Africa, a point of view which needed to be conveyed somewhat delicately, since all the existing doctors had been trained elsewhere:

Although it had been very truly said that all judgements about the attributes of a nation or of a class are bound to be imperfect and must necessarily do injustice to exceptional individuals, nevertheless I must point out. . .

What he had to point out was that the doctors who had been trained overseas left something to be desired, and also that the overseas training could not cope with the growing demand in terms of sheer numbers:

To remedy this, we propose to include special instruction at Achimota College, and to follow this up by providing a proper medical school at the Gold Coast Hospital.[1]

The scheme he outlined, which would have to be subject to the approval of the General Medical Council in London, was a pre-medical training at Achimota followed by two years' clinical teaching and practice in the Hospital, on completion of which students would travel to England for their second professional examination; this to be followed by further university study in any university that would co-operate and that was prepared, above all, to continue the character training that Achimota would have started, through 'residence under supervision'. Residence overseas would thus have been shortened, and clinical experience gained in the diseases of West Africa and in the conditions then obtaining in the Gold Coast.

The Vision of Korle Bu went further still, for the training of medical staff was to be fully comprehensive, and on land which had been acquired near the Hospital there would be provision for improved training of sanitary inspectors, laboratory assistants, nurses, midwives and health visitors. Moreover the new Medical

[1] *Debates*, 1924–5, p. 84.

School would be available to the whole of British West Africa and not only to the Gold Coast, for it was about this time that the Colonial Office was first encouraging the four West African Governments to co-operate in technical and professional matters, and to take advantage of the obvious benefits of pooling knowledge and resources. At a West African Medical Conference held at Accra in December 1925, the Gold Coast representatives outlined the plans which centred upon Korle Bu, and invited such co-operation. The Conference agreed to recommend to their respective Governments that 'a College destined for the complete training of medical practitioners' should be founded as soon as possible, and that 'Gold Coast offers the best facilities for establishing such a College.'

But until such things could come about—and as we shall see in a moment they never did—Guggisberg was faced with the more immediate necessity of providing African Medical Officers quickly; on the explicit assumption, with which he fully agreed, that the Medical Service would not accept doctors, however well they were otherwise qualified, unless they had had clinical experience; and here he collided resoundingly with the African medical practitioners and their spokesmen in the 'Opposition'. For he approved a scheme, which was both sensible and generous, for giving the African medical graduate in the United Kingdom a short post-graduate course in tropical medicine at Liverpool or London, followed by clinical practice in the Gold Coast Hospital at £400 a year (1924 values); when the Director of Medical Services was satisfied with his performance in the wards he would be eligible for the Medical Service on an equality with Europeans; in other words he would have overcome his handicap *vis-à-vis* Europeans, arising out of their clinical experience and his own lack of it, by a three months' post-graduate course in England and a year or so in the wards of Korle Bu. During this probationary period he was to be known, perhaps unfortunately, as a 'Junior African Medical Officer'.

At once the storm clouds of suspicion gathered and the air was charged with the reek of racial discrimination. The African medical practitioners were 'aggrieved and humiliated'. This

was, on Guggisberg's part, 'an unveiled attempt to disparage or
hold to ridicule or contempt the African medical practitioner'.
Or so their inevitable petition purported to believe. Guggisberg
held his ground in Legislative Council with calm tenacity, for he
had been Governor now for over five years and was accustomed
to such animadversions, which arose in part from hypersensi-
tivity and in part from natural ebullience; and Caseley-Hayford,
when he came to set about the Governor in debate, appears to
have had his tongue a little in his cheek. He made some good
debating points:

I must say, Sir, it looks rather funny that a man who has been duly
qualified and granted a diploma by some of the best Universities
should have to depend ultimately for his daily bread upon a certificate of efficiency from the local head of the Medical Department.

And he was properly outraged:

. . . until we knocked and knocked and knocked the West African
Medical Staff was a closed door; they did not want us to get in . . .
human nature being what it is I suggest respectfully that it would
necessarily mean that the head of that Department would not in any
case be too anxious to encourage an aspirant.

But he finished by complimenting the Governor on the sound
policy that he had initiated, and he does not really seem to have
been very angry.

All these plans and negotiations fell most heavily of course on
the Director of Medical Services and his staff, and Guggisberg
was not so personally involved in them as he was in the other
great projects that we have reviewed. But even if he had taken
no initiative—and in fact he took a great deal—the Governor's
personal interest could make or mar what the medical staff were
trying to do, and there were many points, where politics and
medicine mixed, at which his intervention and support were
essential. As is shown, indeed, by the fact that the proposed
West African Medical School came to nothing, for:

. . . The final decision fell to a new Governor, A. R. Slater, who saw
his main duty simply as 'consolidation'. He claimed that there was
no evidence of any real desire on the part of the Gold Coast people

for this project, and agreed with the Governors of Nigeria and
Sierra Leone that it was premature (*blessed word*) as well as too expensive, in view of the recent fall in revenue. No protest was made
in the subsequent debate; and his advice was accepted by the
Secretary of State.[1]

There was another point at which politics and medicine met,
and where a Governor had to tread warily—in essence a matter
of quality *versus* quantity. Many European Medical Officers in
British West Africa were attracted, as was Guggisberg himself,
by the practice of the French colonial authorities of preferring a
close network of dispensaries and partly trained medical assistants to a few properly equipped hospitals and a handful of fully
trained doctors. In the French territories most people could get
some medical attention, even if much of it was not very good;
in the British only a very few people could get any at all. An
all-out drive to train large numbers of medical assistants had
obvious attractions, and seemed to be a sensible approach to the
problem as it actually existed in Africa. But in this matter
Guggisberg was unusually sensitive to the apprehensions of the
intelligentsia, perhaps because they accorded with his own
desire for excellence. With him, 'Only the best is good enough
for the Gold Coast' was more than a motto or a popular slogan;
it expressed how he genuinely felt.

So that although he also wanted medical assistants to be
trained in large numbers he put the brake on his medical
staff:

. . . not until we give Africans an opportunity of becoming fully
qualified medical men.

I have pledged my word to members of this Council that this Government would not support any scheme for the training of Medical
Assistants that did not at the same time include provision for the full
training of African Medical Officers.[2]

This was a subject on which Africans in the British territories,
rightly or wrongly, were extremely sensitive, and there were few
on which the suspicion of discrimination thrived so vigorously.
They respected Guggisberg greatly for his stand, though it is one

---

[1] Kimble *Political History*, p. 122.   [2] *Debates*, 1926–7, p. 149.

on which the most sincere and liberal of Europeans, then and much later, have disagreed with him.

Since Guggisberg was accused, seriously or not, of racial discrimination in his attempts to advance the African medical profession, it will be agreeable to end this chapter with the otherwise unedifying story of Dr. Tagoe,[1] a doctor who received such outstanding praise from his European superiors that Guggisberg directed that he should be posted to a station where he would have complete charge of a good hospital and operating theatre, and also be able to exercise administrative responsibilities. He was accordingly posted to the mining town of Dunkwa.

The twenty Europeans there—or those of them who were not civil servants—were outraged by this, and formally protested to the Governor, demanding a European doctor. Not content with this they had a question raised in the House of Commons, which the Secretary of State, Mr. Amery, dealt with summarily, testifying to his confidence in the Gold Coast Administration. The incident moved Guggisberg to unusual heights of eloquence and anger.[2] He began by saying:

It is difficult to deal in measured language with this Dunkwa petition.

He ended by saying:

There is only one word which describes the action of the non-official members of the European community at Dunkwa—namely, deplorable. As for the rest of Dunkwa, I congratulate them on having in Dr. Tagoe a Medical Officer of high professional qualifications and character.

In between, the dissident Europeans of Dunkwa felt the full blast of his wrath. E. J. P. Brown, an adversary of long standing,

[1] *Events*, p. 186-7.
[2] 'The only occasion on which I really heard Guggisberg lash out in Leg. Co. was when he replied to McKay's strong opposition to the posting of an African M.O. to a town with a considerable European population.' Private communication from Sir Andrew Jones to Mr. F. P. Cobb.

warmly congratulated him in the debate which followed, the last but one over which he was to preside.

Guggisberg's dreams for Korle Bu were unfulfilled, and one of the few visible signs that they ever existed is a framed plan in the Ministry of Health in Accra showing the proposed Schools of Anatomy, Physiology, Pharmacology and Pathology, dated 11 February 1928. But the building remains, as anachronistic, physically, in comparison with the new hospital buildings as is Achimota in comparison with the new University on Legon Hill. Both stand silent witnesses to the first age of faith in the Gold Coast—the age of Guggisberg. Recently it was proposed to pull down Korle Bu Hospital to make way for a building appropriate to the 1960s. Happily the decision was changed.

\*       \*       \*

The foregoing chapters have sketched the kinds of activity in which the Governor of an African colony used to be engaged. It was an extraordinary job, the like of which will probably not be seen again, certainly not in the story of the British race.

What is so interesting about Guggisberg's tenure of the office is that he was initiating in the 1920s reforms which were later to be announced with a sense of discovery, and implemented with pioneer pride, after the Second World War—planned economic development, higher education for Africans and the localization of the public service. In local administration and national politics his contribution was less distinctive. These are the five fields with which we have dealt, inadequately and in outline. A governor's activities, however, were protean, and the number of things in which he had to be interested was virtually unlimited.

A more balanced account of Guggisberg's work as Governor would need to give some attention to his absorption in the problems of land tenure[1] and taxation, and greater attention to certain departments of work in which, because of his professional training and interest, he intervened to an extent unusual with governors; especially in the areas of public works, public health and sanitation, surveys and mapping, railways and mining. But this book is not primarily a history of the Gold Coast between the years 1919 and 1927 but the story of the individual who gave those years a special flavour; and enough has been said to portray the man of action at the height of his power, in those areas of Government where his personal influence was most felt.

At this point some assessment of his life is not unjustified. Since he had still some years to live, and indeed another Governorship to hold, this may seem premature; but when he sailed from Takoradi on 19 April 1927, he left behind him the bulk of his public achievement and almost the whole of his private affections. The glory of the burning afternoon was over, and the twilight was to fall with tropical suddenness. It is perhaps fitting to recall him in the light of that afternoon.

[1] And more particularly of land registration, a perennial problem of great complexity on which experts in the Gold Coast disagreed and which was never satisfactorily solved. The accumulation of documents on this subject is forbidding in the extreme and it occupied much of the time of every governor. It was not, however, one on which Guggisberg left any characteristic mark.

# The Springs of Action

THE English language seems to lack a convenient word to describe the springs of action. We speak, colloquially, of 'what makes a man tick'; or, barbarously, of his motivations. Neither seems appropriate to the subtle manifestations of religion, race and sex which produced, in Gordon Guggisberg, an outwardly straightforward but inwardly rather complicated person.

The image that he presented to the world, in his fifties, was so perfect as to seem almost to caricature the expected attributes of a colonial governor. He was almost too good to be true. His presence was superb, and even in relaxed moments he carried with him the dignity of a King's representative. Always meticulous in his appearance, in his London club he enjoyed a mild reputation for being one of the best-dressed men about town. In the Gold Coast he insisted in public on formality and etiquette, and was a strict, though effortless, disciplinarian, for he had assumed the highest authority with surprising naturalness and ease. He was a regal governor, and had the royal gift for relaxing, particularly as a host, into informal gaiety and charm.

He had also, more importantly, a royal memory for names and faces, and stories abound of his recognizing obscure people after a lapse of years—a P.W.D. foreman standing by the roadside at Juaso who had served under him in France, or Achimota schoolboys, whom he remembered by name and family. He was a great all-round sportsman, for besides his cricket, which had been very nearly first-class, he played polo, tennis and golf with some skill. He had, as well, the hobbies appropriate to the versatile all-rounder; a gifted carpenter; a keen though average talent in sketching and watercolour; and a fondness for music which caused him to have a piano-player brought from England to Christiansborg Castle; a friend recalls his penchant for relaxing with it after dinner—'I can see him now sitting there and playing "In a Monastery Garden".'

Fraser spoke often of his capacity for quick human contacts, and especially of his free and natural relationship with Africans; though he was thinking of a time when European relationships with Africans were rarely free or natural, and Guggisberg's bearing towards the people whom he genuinely liked would perhaps not strike us as so surprising today. Among Europeans he made a good many enemies, some devoted admirers, few intimate friends.

Most of us dramatize ourselves a little, and Guggisberg certainly saw himself as a particular kind of governor; although the mental image oscillated a little between that of the father of a family and the captain of a cricket team:

It is as the head of a family that I wish to govern this country—a family of Officials, Merchants and Natives. My ear will always be open to any member; suggestions and helpful criticism will always be weighed; but once my decision is given I ask all those in the Family who do not agree with me to sink their private opinion and to give loyal support for the sake of their side.[1]

(In passing, these are somewhat remarkable words from one who had just stepped off the boat and who, but for an unexpected turn of fortune's wheel, would have done so as head of the Public Works Department.) Given that most families are quarrelsome and that their members dislike one another from time to time, this was perhaps a realized ambition, for while he was in the Gold Coast he occupied a patriarchal chair, and there was never any doubt where final authority lay. The Officials of the Family, apart from a few whose way of life he violently disturbed, adopted willingly the role of his children,

[1] *Government Gazette* (Extraordinary) of 13 October 1919, containing the Governor's address to a representative gathering in the Council Chamber on the day of his arrival.

and responded gratefully to his leadership.[1] Among the Merchants, or at least the European ones, he made many enemies, for they distrusted his expansionist ideas and doubted his commercial wisdom; but not all were opposed to him[2] and in after years they mostly thought of him with respect. As for the Natives, they understood fatherhood and family, and liked this way of speaking.

The press hailed him with rapture, as it was to do later, and more tragically, in British Guiana:

No Governor before him had outlined his policy so warmly and unequivocally on his first day in office. For weeks newspapers carried articles which hailed him as the 'New Messiah' who would lead the people out of the bondage of the Colonial Office; the incongruity of the situation apparently not appealing to their writers.[3]

The picture thus seemed idyllic, and no one, surely, could have doubted that Guggisberg was a happy and successful man. One has only, however, to listen to the reminiscences of his contemporaries, or to read the surviving fragments of his diary, to come to realize the tensions, doubts and disappointments which were the cause of the driving energy which he brought to his work; which in turn cured, or at least allayed, these tensions. For the work had a demonic quality which is not to be explained merely in terms of duty, though duty was a large part of his religion.

Even on the surface there were signs of tension. The frequent changes of mood, from aloofness to an almost excessive friendliness and charm, from wise moderation to bursts of quick temper, from strict discipline to a sometimes hilarious informality, do not suggest a man altogether at peace in himself. Deep down he was poised between the poles of arrogance and humility; he was not at ease, and was a man who needed to justify himself.

.        .        .

[1] See especially the remarks of Mr. Duncan-Johnstone, quoted on p. 97.
[2] Colonel Levey, his most intimate personal friend, was presumably a Merchant member of the Family, as he represented the Offin Rivers Estates Ltd.
[3] Kwaw-Swanzy, op. cit., p. 194.

A popular radio philosopher once said that no man who had made his mark in the world ever had a really happy domestic background. This is such obvious nonsense that one is tempted to dismiss it, yet an uncomfortable grain of truth remains. Guggisberg had made two unsuccessful marriages, and thus in an important aspect of his life he had failed. He was not a man who took kindly to failure.

We can, of course, know little of the facts of any marriage, but his first wife was very young and he, older and more experienced, had eloped with her. The responsibility for making the marriage a success rested to a large extent on him, and he was not a man to shirk his responsibilities; yet after a few years she left him. Whether or not the facts we have given earlier tell the whole story, which is improbable, the affair must have left him with a sense either of frustration or of humiliation, for never at any time in his life were his personal standards less than strict, and this cannot have been a mere episode to be forgotten after the first shock. Moreover she had borne him three children. It was not a wound that was ever likely to heal completely.

His marriage to Decima Moore survived an early burst of comradeship but never prospered. No marriage can contain two prima donnas, and Gordon and Decima soon began to play intolerably on one another's nerves, for in some respects they were too alike. She had ability as well as great vivacity. For example, she collaborated with Colonel Levey in mounting the Gold Coast stand at the British Empire Exhibition at Wembley in 1924, when she proved to be an efficient organizer as well as a hostess in the grand manner. Nor were her interests social merely in the fashionable sense, for the social problems of tropical Africa had interested her when she first encountered them at close range in the Ashanti bush, and in the developing Gold Coast she engaged in them at a more sophisticated level:

I have seen wonderful developments since I landed here in 1905 and I had a great deal to do with the inclusion of *women* in the Achimota scheme, as originally they were *not* to be included, and I had to work pretty hard for it, but got Aggrey, a wonderful *African*, on my side, and others, so they *were* included![1]

She had indeed many of the qualities of a successful Governor's wife, but lacked the vital one of being able to play second fiddle. The stage was in her blood and her place was in the spotlight, but though her sense of theatre was good her sense of protocol was rudimentary. One of the great occasions in her life as the Governor's lady was the visit of Princess Marie Louis to the country in May 1925, an affair which tried Guggisberg to the depths of his being, and which started with an incident both humiliating and preposterous. For as the Princess approached the official reception party Decima committed the unpardonable solecism of stepping forward to greet her, as to the manner born, in front of the King's Representative, and her husband was compelled to pull her back physically and push her into the background. Their conversation was widely overheard, caused deep embarrassment, and was the subject of lively conversation for some time to come. She spoke too freely to the press, and on one occasion at Plymouth, spoke of things she had no official business to know. Guggisberg also had to restrain her from flying the Governor's standard on her car. These would no doubt have been comparative trivialities if the marriage had been rooted in love and friendship but it is not evident that any bond existed between them that could have survived the initial attraction of two striking personalities, each in different ways looking for security. As we have seen from time to time in this narrative, her actions towards him became unfriendly, finally vindictive, and the marriage petered away to nothing.

The point need not be laboured. It cannot, however, be forgotten, for the relationship between them, and Lady Guggisberg's long absences in England, without the excuse of children to look after, were well understood and widely discussed in both

[1] Personal communication from Lady Guggisberg to Mr. Cobb's mother, 23 July 1953. This may throw some light on Guggisberg's unexpectedly 'advanced' attitude towards the education of women, and towards co-education. It is possible that he was under the influence of his wife in this matter, but if so there is no record of his having acknowledged it.

the European and African communities.[1] It does not help a man to be head of a Family of Officials, Merchants and Natives, when he is manifestly failing to be head of any family of his own. Wisely he did not try to make any secret of it, or even to avoid the subject, for when the Civil Service presented him with a memorial on his retirement, in the courtyard of the Old Secretariat, he openly requested that his wife's name should be omitted.

The situation was not only tragic, but supremely ironic. For Decima had undoubtedly played a very significant part in getting him a job which was beyond the wildest dreams of his imagination, and was then incapable of supporting him in it. While he for his part had to attempt the job without the help—indeed sometimes with the active hindrance—of the wife who should have enriched and completed it, and who had shown such persistent skill in helping to get it for him. In this situation her faults and failings are better known than his. It is doubtful whether he was entirely blameless, but this we cannot know, for people did not discuss him as they discussed his wife.

He was not, as we have said, a man who took kindly to failure, and it is certain that he sublimated the frustrations of his marriage in unremitting devotion to his adopted family. To put it simply, he lived entirely for his work, having little else to live for. But he could not have done so, being a conscientious and Christian man, without embarrassment and tension, and this needs to be understood in appreciating his Governorship of the Gold Coast.

Guggisberg was always sensitive about his name. Some people supposed that it was German, and during and after the First World War the British were more than a little hysterical about German names. Others supposed that it was Jewish, and people generally have always been a little unbalanced about this race. He owned to Swiss-Canadian descent, but preferred to think of himself as simply British.

But although for three generations the Guggisbergs had been

---

[1] Conversations with Sir Leslie M'Carthy and others in Ghana.

German-Swiss and Canadian, his Jewish great-great-grandfather was often in his mind in his closing years, though there
was no evidence to show at what time of his life he learned about
his ancestry. What is known is that on his first leave from the
Gold Coast as its Governor, in the summer of 1920, he visited the
villages of Guggisberg and Zimmerwald (from where the family
actually came) in some style, for he was driven by his African
chauffeur and received by a member of the Swiss Government.
He paid one other visit while he was Governor, and in a year of
comparative idleness after leaving the Gold Coast he was
strongly drawn to go again, but did not succeed in doing so.

There is something strange about a man on whom his ancestral village exercised this magnetic attraction, but who yet
maintained a life-long reticence about his forbears, even to his
wife. We cannot know to what extent Decima was ever in his
confidence, but her belief was that he was German:

No, Gordon Guggisberg was not a Jew, but of German extraction
from Stuttgart—*all* his people came from Germany and some of
them are now in Berne. His father migrated to Canada years ago and
was in business there.[1]

His family are equally imprecise in their knowledge of his
descent.

It is important here to emphasize that the account we have
given of his origins in the first chapter of this book rests solely
on what he said to his friend Colonel Levey in the closing days
of his life;[2] they were the confidences of a dying man who saw
no point in reticence any more, and who wanted to tell someone about himself.

How does all this bear upon his Governorship, and upon
Gordon Guggisberg as a person? In the 1920s, so soon after the
War, British people were possibly more ill-disposed to those of
German origin than at any time before or since, while those
of Jewish descent, however distant, have never altogether
shaken off the feeling of apartness which has been the legacy
of the long persecution of their race. Guggisberg was neither

[1] Letter from Lady Guggisberg, op. cit.     [2] See p. 9.

Jew nor German in any meaningful way, but could not altogether escape the tension inseparable from being thought one or
the other.

But in a deeper and more constructive sense his Jewish connection had a profound influence on the major work of his life;
this much he revealed to Colonel Levey towards the end.
Levey had been present at Christiansborg on a somewhat embarrassing occasion, when the Governor had before him an
erring chief from Keta, who had abused his magisterial office by
accepting bribes. On an occasion of this kind Guggisberg
could be rather terrifying, and the unhappy chief was subjected
to a dressing down which left him in a state of abject misery and
panic; suddenly the mood changed, for Guggisberg put his arm
round the miscreant, assured him that he would trust him in
the future, and told him, with perhaps forgivable exaggeration,
that King George was proud of the work which he was doing in
Keta. This improbable assertion raised the African from the
depths of misery to the heights of ecstasy, and he departed a
happy man, his devotion to Guggisberg life-long. This kind of
thing had often happened, and Levey and Guggisberg were
recalling it together. 'Why,' said Levey, 'could you never let the
sun go down on your wrath with any African, even when he had
tried you beyond endurance?'

'Levey,' was the reply—for this was a time when intimate
friends of their generation were happier with surnames—
'Levey, remember that the blood of an oppressed people runs
in my veins. I never forgot it. I understood the people of the
Gold Coast.'

There was in fact no mystery about Guggisberg's good relationship with Africans. It stemmed from the loveliest of virtues
—compassion.

We have seen already that Guggisberg was curious about
Fraser's unquestioning and sustaining religious faith, and we
shall see later that in the last months of his life he wrestled a
good deal with the problems of religion. The point of touching
on the matter here is not to suggest that he was an exceptionally

religious man, or to sustain any hypothesis that his driving energy in the service of the Gold Coast stemmed from the Christian faith, for we have already suggested that its origins were devious. It is simply that in his maturity—as a matter of plain fact—the problems of religion did occupy him a great deal; more, certainly, than they had done in his younger days, when a conventional kind of Christianity, rooted in personal decency and faith in the British Empire, had apparently satisfied him. With most people whose lives have any religious dimension at all it is perhaps more usual for the questing idealism of youth to mellow with middle age and success into an acceptance of a comfortable Mother Church; but Guggisberg's development was the other way round, for the older and more outwardly successful he became the more lively and questioning was his religious curiosity, and the deeper his dissatisfaction with the Established Church. He was not, of course, an inwardly successful man, and his life needed a key to its meaning.

Even allowing for the occupational optimism of the clergy in relation to their converts, it is no light thing for Fraser to have said:

He was a follower of our Lord for his last three years in the Gold Coast. He grew rapidly and was a fearless disciple, counting not the cost.[1]

And after he had left the Gold Coast he undoubtedly had promptings to become a missionary, though whether he ever seriously considered ordination in his late fifties is unknown. What is known is that he occupied himself in a most practical way with what might appear to be an improbable enterprise for a retired colonial governor. He was for some reason attracted to the inland waterways of Britain, and wanted to traverse them by boat, spreading the light to the bargees, and to any other inhabitants of these islands that he might encounter on the way. Whether this was to be the light of the Christian faith, as he told his daughter Rowena, or of the glory of the Empire, as he told Colonel Levey on his death bed,[2] is uncertain; in fact the two

---

[1] Private communication from Fraser to Mr. F. P. Cobb, 18 June 1958.    [2] p. 331.

were never far apart in his thinking, for he belonged to the school of imperialists who were sustained by a faith no longer credible to another post-war generation, that the noblest virtues which man could hope to achieve in an imperfect world had reached their ultimate expression in the British Empire.

When he died his daughters discovered to their consternation that a barge for this purpose, drawn to his most detailed specifications, with special places to take his most valued possessions (including an 'immense roll-top desk'), was actually in the course of construction, and the order with the boat-builder had to be hurriedly cancelled.[1] The thought of Sir Gordon Guggisberg navigating the Grand Union Canal and converting the passers-by to a belief in the British Empire, or to the Christian faith, is an agreeable one, and it is a matter for regret that he was not spared for this activity. More seriously, it is a comment on his rootlessness, since most governors do not contemplate retirement to a canal barge.

An aspect of Christian practice that fascinated him increasingly was humility, and its attendant simplicity. His own nature and his high office militated against both. He enjoyed power, or as he would have thought of it, command, and was inclined temperamentally to arrogance; but he was aware of conflict within himself and was not impressed with these characteristics in other people. He loved pomp and ceremony and deliberately exploited them in his work; but from time to time sought relief in their opposite.

Shortly before he was to take up his last appointment in British Guiana he invited Fraser to meet him at the Army and Navy Club for lunch, where he was to talk to the Reverend C. F. Andrews[2] in order to discuss labour and trade union problems among the Indian immigrants to his new country. C. F. Andrews was the friend of princes and statesmen and a power in British India, besides being at the time president of the Indian trade union movement. But he was a saint who did not altogether live in this world. Had he possessed a decent suit, which is unlikely, he would undoubtedly have given it away to the

[1] Information given by Miss Rowena Guggisberg.      [2] See p. 311.

first person whose need seemed greater than his own. On this occasion he turned up in Pall Mall in a frayed shirt, a tattered woollen cardigan, ancient flannel trousers, with a coat that had once been black but was now green with age; on his feet he wore what in those days were known as sandshoes. The porter, understandably, declined to let him in. Having been retrieved from the pavement by his host he was lunched in the place of honour and introduced to various generals and admirals who came over to congratulate Guggisberg on his appointment. After a long talk in the coffee room, during which the visit to British Guiana was arranged, Guggisberg saw Andrews to a taxi, paid the fare and stood looking down Pall Mall after it with bowed head. 'I feel,' he said to Fraser, who rescued him from his reverie, 'I feel as though I had been honoured to give luncheon to my Lord.'[1]

Guggisberg was one of the generation of men who were shocked into religious experience by trench warfare and mass slaughter, by the flower of comradeship that was plucked so strangely from these, and by their own survival. Hence the vow of service, which was made in various ways by so many of his contemporaries at the time, but which in his case deepened in its purpose, sustained him in private sorrow, guided him in public success, and caused him to go on seeking the answers to questions which most men of his age had shrugged off, since they didn't seem to be important any more.

In his private politics as in his religion, Guggisberg swam against the stream. In British life it has not been unusual, in privileged-left wing circles, for men to be socialist by conviction and conservative by temperament; desiring in their minds changes in society which would cause them nostalgic regret in their hearts. The converse of this, as seen in Guggisberg, has been less common, for by political conviction he was a true conservative, to whom 'the socialists' were potential betrayers of morality and destroyers of the Empire; but by temperament he was a political progressive, as his entire career as Governor

---

[1] Fraser–Cobb, op. cit.

shows. He would accept nothing without question; was a generation ahead of his time in believing in the possibility of eventual self-government; and was devoted to causes which most of his own European contemporaries in the Gold Coast regarded with the same kind of apprehension and distaste with which he contemplated the activities of the socialists at home.

The difference between the reactionary and progressive Conservative was curiously well illustrated in the contrast between Guggisberg and his principal European opponent in the Legislative Council, J. D. McKay. McKay had been an administrative officer for a few tours, but had left the Service to join a firm of solicitors whose business was almost exclusively with the mining companies, whom he represented in the Council, and with commercial firms. He was a persistent critic of Guggisberg's development plans, believing in particular that the loan debt on Takoradi Harbour would cripple the country's financial future, but he also attacked him ably and unremittingly on his measures for African advancement. Politically, at home, the two men might have had a good deal in common, and they were not without mutual respect. But at every point of Gold Coast policy their differences were profound, and McKay must have thought of Guggisberg, who couldn't stand the socialists, as a tiger let loose by the Fabian Society. This in spite of Guggisberg's avowed devotion to the chiefs and native institutions.

Such was Gordon Guggisberg, in appearance a British colonial governor out of a story-book, inwardly an insecure and troubled man, who for nearly eight years captured the devotion of a subject people. Shortly after he had gone the Governor of the day prescribed that the Legislative Council should adjourn in order to watch a cricket match, which was being played between the 'Secretariat and Civil Administrators' and 'All Other Departments'. One way and another it was quite a Guggisbergian occasion. The Chiefs of Legislative Council came in cloths on which portraits of Guggisberg were boldly printed, and underneath them were the words:

Guggisberg for ever Governor in the hearts of the Gold Coast people.

# II

## Guggisberg's Bequest

THE Romans governed Britain as a 'colony' for four hundred years and today the legacy of their Empire can be traced in their roads, their language and their legal system. Since the disappearance of Britain's brief empire in Africa many people have wondered what will survive of the legacy four hundred years from now. Some cherished illusions have already disappeared, and the cynical take refuge in saying that soon British culture will be discernible only in the whisky-soda at sundown, the cup of tea at half past four in the afternoon and the execrable bacon-and-eggs at the rest house breakfast. These interesting speculations are beyond the scope of this study, but it is relevant to the story of Guggisberg's life to see what his successors made of his bequest and what now remains of his influence, a mere forty years on.

To begin with an over-simplified summary, his Ten Year Development Plan, which was concerned with infrastructure rather than development, ran into difficulties in the economic blizzard of the early 1930s and was virtually brought to a standstill; some progress began to be made again towards the end of the decade, when new concepts of a diversified economy and external aid enlarged its scope. In education, Achimota weathered the economic storm and fulfilled many of Guggisberg's hopes, though some of its assumptions came to be questioned and new ones took their place; the wider education programme, on the other hand, was directly affected by the slump and it was not until after 1935 that there was any great progress in numbers in the schools, though this is not wholly relevant, as Guggisberg's policy had been based on quality before quantity, and on cutting out dead wood before new trees were planted. The 1925 Constitution did not lay the foundation of a long-term future, because it derived from thinking that came to be discredited after the revolution of 1948, but for twenty years it provided a basis for political advance that culminated in the Burns Constitution of 1946; while the Provincial Councils, after a slow start, achieved the substance of Guggisberg's hopes for them. In Native Administration, as represented in the Ordinance of 1927, his work was incomplete, and it was left to his successors to give it coherence, both in conception and detail; while municipal administration remained the Achilles' heel. In the Africanization of the public service his successors let him down; this fire died down with his departure, and when Ghana was born Africans who should by then have been competent to take over the Administration and the technical services were conspicuous by their absence.

It is worth saying a few more words about each of these matters, in order to put Guggisberg's work in perspective.[1]

His most enduring monument, in a physical sense, is Takoradi Harbour, even though his name was not mentioned at its official opening, for nothing short of nuclear war can now destroy it. It saw the Gold Coast through a vital thirty years and was a principal reason why Britain was able to hand over a relatively prosperous country to the first independent, ex-colonial government in Africa. Without it the Gold Coast's cocoa, timber and ore would have piled up in chaos round the surf ports, and overseas trade, on which the country was utterly dependent, would have been strangled. The harbour at Tema has supplemented but by no means replaced it, and if the statue of a Briton were any more acceptable in West Africa than the statue of de Lesseps at Port Said, then that of Guggisberg might well look out over the South Atlantic today. There was moreover a curious sense of fulfilment in its building, for nothing

[1] An account of the events of 1928–48, which will not be attempted here, is to be found in Bourret, op. cit., especially in Chs. V to VIII, to which acknowledgment is made. After 1948 all these matters assumed a new dimension.

could have been less probable than that the dreams of the young
surveyor in his early thirties would be turned into concrete
reality by his own efforts within a quarter of a century.

But he was, as we have pointed out, fortunate in the timing of
his Governorship, for he had entered into a relatively prosperous heritage, and although there was an economic recession
in its middle period trade was reviving before he left. His immediate successors were less fortunate, and both Takoradi and
the new railways, the spearhead of his communications policy,
were proving a deep financial embarrassment to the Government by 1930. In the first place the harbour soon proved technically inadequate, and a further loan of £1,170,000 had to be
raised at 4½ per cent to deepen it and build a berth for oil
tankers; secondly, the servicing of this loan and the original one
at 6 per cent was a serious burden on the revenue. His critics of
the middle 1920s might well have said 'I told you so.' Moreover
the new Central Province Railway never paid its way and the
proposed line to the North had to be abandoned; but by now it
was clear in any case that the lorries were winning in the struggle
of road *versus* rail, for which Guggisberg came in at the beginning, before sufficient facts were known.

The year 1930 was disastrous; the price of cocoa fell by more
than half and the general revenue by nearly a half. There was,
however, an accumulated surplus from Guggisberg's day of
over £2 million and the reserve fund which he had instituted
stood at £1·2 million; with drastic economies, including staff
retrenchments and salary cuts, the country managed to weather
the storm.

The Ten Year Plan had primarily been a plan to ease communications in order to get agricultural produce to the market.
The great priority of later years—diversification of the economy
—was never far from Guggisberg's mind, and he unceasingly
warned the country about the effects of relying too much on
the cocoa crop. But to him diversifying the economy meant
diversifying agriculture. No more than his predecessors (or
successors) did he think in terms of manufacturing industry or
the assembly of manufactured parts, and it may be that he did

not take sufficiently seriously the prophecies of those Africans who were beginning to make their voices heard, that the economic future lay in industrialization. Nor in his plans to improve the efficiency of agriculture does he seem to have given much thought to co-operative organization. But although it would be possible for economists today to criticize the Plan for these and other reasons, what mattered in those days was not so much what he proposed in detail as the fact that he proposed anything at all, for it was the first serious attempt to get away from a hand-to-mouth existence on a national scale. It was an essay in amateur planning a generation before the professional development planners arrived on the scene. The mere fact that he drove ahead with communications, electricity, water supplies and town improvements was an unquestionable gain to the country, even if the recurrent costs bore heavily upon the revenue, and upon the salary earners, in the years of slump; but that he should have done so in the context of an ordered plan, and that he never lost sight of the plan's objective, which was higher education and technical training, was of greater value still, both materially and psychologically, in a country that had traditionally lived from year to year.

As a physical monument, Achimota is the complement of Takoradi, though Guggisberg always saw it rather differently, as the harbour's ultimate purpose. It bridged the same gap of some thirty years in meeting the country's need, at any rate in part, for educated men and women; but since it was concerned with the human spirit and not with the import and export of commodities the ripples of its influence spread, and the name of this obscure and unimpressive little hill became a symbol of progress and freedom throughout Africa. Guggisberg, or rather Guggisberg-Fraser-Aggrey, built for thirty years in terms of bricks and mortar, for Achimota is no longer the University, but in addition to teaching Africans, many of whom were later to free their country from colonial rule, it implanted a tradition which, though temporarily overlaid, will outlive all other forms of British influence. Achimota gave the Gold Coast its supremacy in British Africa as the fount of education, and when it was proposed by the post-war Labour Government in Britain, in accordance with the Minority Report of the Commission on Higher Education,[1] that West Africa needed only one university, and that it should be at Ibadan in Nigeria, the pride of African and European alike suffered a deep wound. The Gold Coast ignored this odd advice and built its own University.

For the first decade of its existence, until the Second World War, when it became largely denuded of expatriate staff and partly commandeered for military purposes, it held to the rather curious course on which Fraser had set it[2]—an amalgam of kindergarten, primary, secondary, teacher training and intermediate university education. The ideas of the triumvirate about the English public school tradition; about teaching being based on native history and culture, and being given to some extent in the vernacular; and about everything to do with living, learning and teaching being grounded in the Christian faith—all this was firmly established. Much of it came to be criticized later on, as ideas in education changed, and there was resentment of its isolation from the rest of the educational structure of the country. During the slump, also, it was criticized for its costly material standards, and for its failure to find employment for its ex-pupils. Nevertheless, the Report of the Inspectors of the Department of Education had this to say in 1938:[3]

Achimota appears beyond doubt to be fulfilling the hopes of its founders as a training ground in which young men and women should learn to live as members of a community . . . we are confident that *what seemed an experiment of very uncertain prospects* has justified itself.

This inspection is interesting, for it arose from the fact that in 1930 Achimota had indeed ceased to be a Government institution, and was established under a quasi-independent Achimota

[1] The Elliot Commission, Cmd. 6655 of June 1945.

[2] Fraser retired, after a good deal of ill-health, in 1935.

[3] Quoted by C. Kingsley Williams, *Achimota; The Early Years*, op. cit., p. 99. (Author's italics.)

Council, as foreshadowed by Guggisberg at the formal opening; the power of inspection being one of the few that the Department of Education retained, though it was providing an annual grant of £48,000. Fraser[1] recalls that it had required a great deal of resolution on Guggisberg's part to make this speech, the substance of which was highly original in the context of the time. He spent a long time making up his mind, and finally did so in the knowledge that it would probably mar his reputation, such as it was, with the Colonial Office.

The significance of Achimota was manifold, but from the viewpoint of this account of its founder's life its main significance was that it was the greatest affirmation of faith in Africans ever made by a Briton.

In the broader field of education in schools and training institutions Guggisberg's work was less dramatic and bore less of his personal stamp. He had had to concern himself very largely with putting right what was wrong, and when coherent plans were eventually formed their first effect was to reduce—rather than to enlarge—*recuiller pour mieux sauter*—but when the time did come to leap forward economic conditions made it impossible to do so. Future Governors were to appoint other committees of educationists, for this is a subject in which ideas never take final shape and in which old discoveries go on being remade. Most comprehensive among them was the long war-time investigation of Sir Alan Burns' Administration and most spectacular the acceleration programme of Dr. Nkrumah in 1951. Guggisberg's contribution lay not so much in finding solutions as in killing for ever any sense of complacency about education, and in promoting it to the point where it became the purpose of all other activity. When we turn to assess his political bequest we are handicapped by the knowledge of hindsight, for we now know that there was (to use an apt colloquialism) no future in a good deal that he was trying to do. The ideas of Caseley-Hayford were to prevail and those of Guggisberg and his successors were to give way in matters of indirect rule, representative government, the role of native institutions and the

[1] In a letter to Mr. F. P. Cobb.

ballot box. Nothing that Guggisberg and his successors could have done would have altered this fact, for they, the Colonial Office and the British Government were misreading history and building for the wrong kind of future. It was incomprehensible to them, as it would have been to any of us, that several million family farmers—'real' people—were of less account to the country's political future than a handful of educated natives. Nor of course could they have foreseen that a second world war would telescope the expected political development of a hundred years into a decade; or that the world would shrink so that the journey to Moscow or Washington would become less arduous than the trek to Tamale; or that the tide of post-war nationalism would sweep aside every idea rooted in gradualism; or that in the lifetime of their own children the cry of 'one man one vote' would echo through the African bush. Least of all, perhaps, could they have foreseen the remarkable Report of the Watson Commission[1] following the disturbances of 1948, a report which threw overboard many of the assumptions and principles on which British colonial administration in Africa had been based.

Guggisberg's bequest in the constitutional realm was therefore made to the final generation of British administrators, who worked within the older concepts, rather than to the African nation that was to be. His prophecy that the Gold Coast would be developed through its chiefs and native institutions now seems incongruous, and his hope that an African way of life would prevail unsullied by bogus European institutions naïve— especially as he himself, through his economic and educational planning, was doing more than anyone else to ensure that the country would be drawn into the western world from which it had been isolated during most of man's material progress. Not that Ghanaians desire a 'bogus Europeanism' any more than he, but they are determined to be at the centre of world affairs, and the African personality on which they set so much store bears little resemblance to the cosy feudalism of the paramount chiefs, which seemed to Guggisberg commendable.

[1] Report of the Commission of Enquiry into Disturbances in the Gold Coast, Colonial No. 231 of 1948.

Nevertheless, his 1925 Constitution laid down the guide lines for another twenty-five years, and his Provincial Councils had a more important influence in helping to create a Gold Coast nation than at first seemed possible. The whole of his Governorship had been characterized by hostility between the chiefs and the coastal lawyers, and the latter, led by Caseley-Hayford, had vigorously opposed the Provincial Councils on which Guggisberg set so much store, and which he regarded as his greatest political achievement. This hostility did not die, nor did the Provincial Councils strike root, while he was Governor, and his satisfaction with them was based on hope rather than accomplishment.

Within a year or two of his departure, however, there were the beginnings of a *rapprochement*, and the Provincial and Municipal members of the Legislature came gradually to regard themselves as the joint representatives of Africans *vis-à-vis* the Colonial Government, instead of protagonists of internal vested interests. The matters which united them were more significant than those which divided them, for as has been pointed out[1] they both represented the privileged, wealthy and ruling class and there were many family connections between them. Co-operation was made easier when the three Provincial Councils of the Colony came together as a Joint Provincial Council in 1932 (a development which Guggisberg had foreseen and desired) and they found a common cause in some unpopular legislation in 1934,[2] and in the growing pressure from the official majority on the Council to introduce direct taxation. The threat of taxation in turn stimulated the growing desire for equal representation in the Council and for some representation in the Executive Council (at the time it went no further than this), and in the same year (1934) Ofori Atta and Caseley-Hayford, and the elements they severally represented, co-operated in a joint delegation to the Secretary of State in London to protest against grievances and to petition for further constitutional reform.

[1] Notably by Martin Wight in Ch. V of *The Gold Coast Legislative Council*.
[2] The Waterworks Bill (because it involved a water rate) and the Sedition Bill.

Although Guggisberg could not have foreseen—and possibly would not have supported—the causes which this delegation set out to sponsor, this reconciliation of the two dominant elements would have gladdened him, since it had always been his hope that his constitutional policies would bring them together and put an end to internal strife. It was largely the existence of the Joint Provincial Council that made this possible, though credit must be given to the foresight and magnanimity of Caseley-Hayford, who realized that co-operation with the Councils was more calculated to build a Gold Coast nation than personal isolation or collaboration with the declining, and now intransigent, A.R.P.S.

In another sense the Provincial Councils did not fulfil Guggisberg's hopes, for he had always intended that they should be much more than electoral colleges to the Legislature; that they should in fact both represent the Government to the people and the people to the Government, and that the Government should consult them and inform them of its policies. But in 1934, when the delegation was in London, Ofori Atta was complaining to the Secretary of State that the Government was not taking the Councils into consultation sufficiently often or sufficiently early, that many matters with which they were intimately concerned were settled over their heads, and that they learnt about decisions for the first time as *faits accomplis*. It is ironic that a constitutional device which was intended by Guggisberg to give the chiefs a fuller share in government, and to win their support for the Administration, should have succeeded in uniting African opposition to it.

However, the logic of the 1925 Constitution unfolded, and the meagre representative element, as we should consider it today, broadened down into the Burns Constitution of 1946; the last colonial constitution, but the first to contain an unofficial majority in the Legislature.[1] Guggisberg is remembered by Ghanaians with surprising warmth for this meagre dole of

[1] Though the Watson Commission thought little of this Constitution, which they believed to have been 'outmoded at birth', and to have been drafted to meet a situation which had long since ceased to exist. They thought the unofficial majority was meaningless, since real and effective power was in the hands of the Executive

representation, for it was the first the people of the Gold Coast ever received.

His immediate successors were more critical of his Native Administration policy (and Ordinance) than of any other aspect of his régime. They were a good deal influenced by Sir Donald Cameron's Political Memoranda of the time, in which he was describing the introduction of Indirect Rule into Tanganyika, for by contrast with this Guggisberg's policy in the Gold Coast seemed to be no policy at all, but a series of shifts and expedients. This was basically true, for it was a piece of unfinished business and the principles on which it was founded were uncharacteristically ill-formulated. In fact there had never been any clear thinking on this subject in the Gold Coast, for indirect rule, though largely assumed, had never been expressly enunciated. Various expedients had been allowed to congeal into a more of less workable system, but the system, such as it was, lacked the very essence of indirect rule. The chiefs had no real responsibility of an executive or financial kind, and what existed was in reality direct British rule exercised with the support of the chiefs rather than native rule exercised with the support and guidance of the British. Ransford Slater and Shenton Thomas became enthusiasts for the more orthodox doctrines of Cameron, and found their legacy from Guggisberg unsatisfying.

True, their own motives were mixed, for they seem to have been equally influenced on the one hand by the need to guard native institutions against undue westernization and to undermine potential 'agitators', and on the other hand by the need to raise local taxes by instituting native treasuries and powers of local taxation. But it is certainly true that the Native Administration Ordinance of 1927 had left the native authorities without treasuries and funds of their own, and the chiefs and their councils were without the embryo responsibilities of local government, and were still largely judicial tribunals.

It was indeed a somewhat vague and ambiguous piece of

Council, composed of official and nominated members. The Council, they thought, was a mere debating chamber, or at most a 'stimulant for intelligent discontent'. In their view also 'the star of the chiefs was on the wane'. They believed the Administration to have been wholly out of touch with reality.

legislation. However, Slater's proposals to introduce simultaneously an Income Tax Ordinance and a Native Revenue Ordinance, which were made under the extreme financial pressure of
the slump, encountered the kind of opposition customary in the
Gold Coast whenever direct taxation was proposed. The ensuing
story of disputation, protest and compromise is immensely
complicated, and it would be out of place to pursue it any
further here. The point is mentioned simply in order to record
that Guggisberg did not solve, even temporarily, a problem
which had occupied a great deal of his time, and his feeling
for principles seems to have been less sensitive in this than
in more rational and practical affairs. As we have seen, he
worked immensely hard, through many disappointments, to
get the 1927 Ordinance on the Statute Book, but what he
achieved was the shadow of indirect rule rather than its substance, and in terms of local government it represented neither
one thing nor the other. He himself seemed unaware of this, for
he expressed great satisfaction with the Ordinance, and it was
only in municipal affairs that he was conscious of a sense of
failure.

In the long run it did not matter very much, for indirect rule,
whatever may be said for or against it, is a colonial concept, and
the Gold Coast was not to be a Colony much longer.

In native administration and local government, therefore, he
left an indifferent legacy to his successors in Government House.
This could not be said of the last matter on which we shall
touch, namely the Africanization of the public service, in some
ways the most significant of all his contributions, the most
expressive of the purpose of his Governorship, and the one for
which he is held in most grateful remembrance. He had a sense
of mission to replace Europeans by Africans which was not
shared by later governors. Although they were liberally minded
men, whose general attitude to Africans was one of benevolence,
their approach to this matter seemed worldly-wise and cynical
in comparison with his eager optimism. They were also more
susceptible to local European opinion, to which Guggisberg,
in any matter which he thought he understood, could be blandly,

or sometimes coldly, indifferent. He had, as we have seen, laid down a policy and had had it approved by the Secretary of State; he had moreover drawn up an estimated schedule of African appointments twenty years ahead, and given specific instructions to departmental heads to adhere to it. But after his departure the pace slackened.

For example, almost exactly ten years after he had left the Gold Coast Mr. A. Korsah[1] was to complain in the Legislative Council:

... Government has failed to maintain that progressive programme of African appointments which was approved by the Secretary of State in the year 1926, and of which His Excellency Sir Gordon Guggisberg spoke to members of this Council.

According to this programme the year 1935–36 ought to have seen 148 Africans holding . . . what we call European appointments. Instead of that number we have 28. . . .

Even allowing for Guggisberg's excessive optimism about African ability in his own day, and for the fact that the educational programme had been hit by the slump in the early 1930s, the discrepancy between 28 and 148 is so great that it is impossible to believe that the European community did not heave a sigh of relief when he went, or did not revert to the comfortable belief that these things must come slowly, i.e. after the lifetime of everyone immediately concerned. (Over 1000 Africans were at the top of the grade immediately below the 'European' one, and some of them had been there for ten years.)

Ten years later still the Watson Commission was to report that of the 1,300 to 1,400 senior appointments in the public service, ninety-eight were held by Africans, Guggisberg's final projection (for the year 1945–6) having been 229. The Commission was very fair over this matter, and admitted in detail the many inadequacies in African civil servants that had come to their attention, and the poverty of the field of recruitment. Nevertheless, they believed that there was justice in the African complaint, which they summed up in these words:

You have not provided us with sufficient opportunities to learn. In

[1] Later Sir Arku Korsah. See footnote to p. 163. *Debates*, 1937, pp. 96–98.

cases where we have learned you have not given us the opportunity to show our capacity.

The Colonial Office, in its official riposte to the Watson Report, remarked complacently:

It is already an established rule that it must be shown to the satisfaction of the Governor that no suitable African is available before an overseas candidate is appointed to any post. . . . The Gold Coast Government will continue to observe this important principle.[1]

In the twenty years following Guggisberg's departure no more than sixty Africans were shown to the satisfaction of the Governor to be suitable. The Watson Commission did not accuse the Government of the Gold Coast of bad faith in interpreting the rule; it is however unlikely that Guggisberg's successors tried particularly hard, and it is difficult to imagine that he himself would have countenanced this rate of progress. The truth is, of course, that it was perfectly possible to observe such a rule in good faith, simply by waiting for Africans of outstanding ability to present themselves; but to lack the will to select, train and encourage them. The difference was between a positive and a passive approach, and this in turn reflected a difference between belief and disbelief in African ability, and between desire and reluctance to bring Africans forward in the Administration of the country.

Twenty years after Guggisberg's day colonial governors in Africa needed primarily to be politicians; if they existed today they would need primarily to be economists and sociologists. Guggisberg was primarily a surveyor and civil engineer, and in spite of Clifford's disbelief his training was not inappropriate to his day, for it was the first great age of construction in West Africa, when an engineer with drive met a more urgent need than an administrator with a philosophy. His capacity went beyond this immediate need largely because of his pecu-

---

[1] Colonial No. 223 of 1948. Statement by His Majesty's Government. Governor Arnold Hodson was apparently not even aware of this principle, for in addressing the Council in 1941 he said: 'My view is . . . that Europeans and Africans should hold the senior posts on a fifty-fifty basis. This has always been my policy. It will have to come gradually and by degrees and no good can come of trying to force the pace.' *Debates*, 1941, pp. 116–17.

liar and passionate belief in the people and the country; it fell short of the whole need because he never really got the measure of the coastal lawyers and did not foresee the inevitable effects of the higher education of which he was the supreme champion. But he served the Gold Coast well, and Clifford was wrong in thinking that his lack of 'administrative' experience would prove to be any kind of handicap.

It is interesting to speculate how he would have fared in the decade 1947–57. Sir Charles Arden-Clarke, the last Governor of the Gold Coast, was as appropriate to his own assignment as Guggisberg was to his, but the two assignments were worlds apart. Arden-Clarke, a talented amateur actor in private life, had the actor's gift for grasping a part. He took over the Gold Coast at a time of acute crisis, and his early speeches and actions showed little departure from conventional colonial assumptions. He was, however, a versatile man, sensitive to trends and atmosphere. He successfully felt his way into the role of conciliator, and helped to guide the country along the razor's edge to self-government, with different kinds of chaos awaiting him if he put a foot wrong. Guggisberg could not have done a job like this. He would have been armed with too many rigid principles, and would have been too dogmatically convinced of what was right to be done. But such speculations are essentially futile, because situations like this did not occur before World War II, and men like Guggisberg did not reappear after it.

Guggisberg gave the most creative years of his life to working for the ultimate independence of the Gold Coast, and alone among his expatriate contemporaries he would have comprehended that this might come about by 1957, thirty years after his own departure. Indeed, if he could have had his way, the country might well have become independent under the leadership of men less bitter towards Britain and more disposed to accept western democratic values. What his mind could not possibly have encompassed would have been the political régime in Ghana in 1966. He would have been delighted by the material progress, incredulous at the scale of expenditure in

contrast to the cheese-paring of his own day, and awed by the
Volta Dam, Tema Harbour, the University and the Teaching
Hospital. But the government and politics of the country would
have been either incomprehensible or repugnant. Fortunately
for his peace of mind he knew only the dawn, and was spared
the noon-day sun.

So great is the gulf between what Guggisberg stood for and
what now prevails that it is perhaps the greatest of all tributes
to him that the present rulers of Ghana, to whom the Gold
Coast of Guggisberg was equally repugnant, still hold his memory in respect. Naturally in Ghana today there is a reaction
against his name. It seemed important to gauge the strength of
this, and on a recent visit (June 1964) the author tried to do so.

In the first place it seemed that there was a conscious attempt
to diminish the *mystique* attaching to the name of Achimota.
Achimota is now in essence a primary school and a secondary
school, and one was made to understand that these were simply
two schools like any other. This, however, is understandable.
The University, of a scale and quality of building which would
have been unimaginable to Guggisberg, stands splendidly on
Legon Hill, a mile or two away, a monument to African pride
and vigour.[1] The Englishman, standing in the Legon playing-
fields and seeing the homely, agreeable tower of Achimota in
the middle distance, has natural feelings of British nostalgia and
pride, and would be pleased if Ghanaians looked on Achimota
still as the fount of higher education. But there is little reason
why they should, surrounded by so much of their own creation
at Legon, Cape Coast, Kumasi and in the new secondary
schools. Pride so deeply rooted in Nation and Party can hardly
be expected to embrace an emotional attachment to this now
modest creation of a foreigner, however deeply he loved the
people and their land, or to understand that thirty years ago the

[1] It was conceived and largely built before Independence, and many expatriates
in the Gold Coast Government deserve credit for their share in its creation, and in
particular for resisting the Colonial Office's original proposal that one university,
situated in Nigeria, should serve the needs of the whole of British West Africa. But
they would be the first to agree that the impetus was supplied by the then emerging
African leaders, and the whole magnificent structure, unlike that of other African
universities, was almost wholly built from local money.

Achimota buildings were considered thrilling and magnificent. Events have left the old Achimota behind, and what remains, as convenient school buildings, must be part of a system, devoid of caste or privilege.

Less acceptable, from the author's point of view, was the tendency among the younger generation, including those of Guggisberg's own nationality, to reinterpret the significance of his governorship. It must admittedly be difficult for democratic centralists to agree that anything commendable should derive from the activities of a colonial governor who in contemporary terms was both paternalist and imperialist. To them, no doubt, it is self-evident that the object of improving communications to the coast and of building a deep-water port was to increase the profits of the cocoa companies' shareholders; that the building of a hospital was to maintain the physical fitness of the workers; or that higher education had as its aim the middle-grade employees who were essential to the operations of the foreign capitalists. All this accords with the ideology. But to anyone who has tried, on however slender evidence, to understand Guggisberg's thoughts and attitudes, these seem to be odd conclusions, and at variance with the facts as far as they are yet known; and it will be surprising if, when the biography of Guggisberg can be written, he emerges as a stooge of British monopoly capitalism.

But the older generation of Ghanaians, however hard they fought the colonial power, whatever bitterness against the British lies in their inmost hearts, however committed they may be to the contemporary ideology of Ghana, do not share these thoughts. To them Guggisberg, colonialist though he was, was the man who first started to lead the Gold Coast out of colonial insignificance and to accord its people dignity in the twentieth century. To them:

Others abide our question, thou art free.

PART 3

1927–30

# 12

## Marking Time (1927)

GUGGISBERG was now fifty-eight and unemployed. It was a serious matter to him for reasons quite other than the need of a restless and creative man to get his teeth into a job of work. There was, primarily, the mundane matter of a pension. To earn a Governor's pension, under Colonial Office rules, he would have to have served ten years; he had so far served only eight, owing to the unusual circumstance whereby his first job in the Service was a governorship; when his leave pay expired, his Army pension, though reasonable by the money values of 1927,[1] would be embarrassing to him as a retired Governor, who had in fact drifted imperceptibly into a high standard of living. Moreover—and although he thrust the knowledge from him he must have known it—he was beyond the height of his physical powers, and becoming familiar with tiredness and depression, the first symptoms of what was to be a rapid physical decline. A job, and one that would last two years, was urgently needed. Finally, there was nothing else for him to do. Even if he could have managed financially he could not, like more fortunate men, have slipped quietly into domestic life, content with trivial tasks and occasional enjoyments, for he had no home and no domestic happiness. His relations with Decima were now impossible; she would make no plans, or even discuss the future rationally, and every contact with her was painful.[2] He could always live at Yateley, but it was not his own, and although he spent most of his time there on his return to England he seems to have become the kind of man, perhaps more familiar then

---

[1] It was £521. 10s. per annum.
[2] Much of the material for this chapter is gathered from a private diary, the only fragment of his personal papers to have survived.

than now, whose spiritual home was his Club. The Rag—the Army and Navy Club—was the place where he was most relaxed, and where he stayed on any plausible excuse.

He had arrived at Plymouth on a Saturday, 7 May 1927, and joined Miss Corry and his daughters at Yateley the same night. On Monday afternoon he was up at the Colonial Office, but 'Amery told me that although he was very pleased with my work in the Gold Coast, there were no other appointments vacant at present, and I might have to wait any time between three and four months and a year.' He waited, in fact, nearly eighteen months. Within three years he was dead. Unhappily, his last illness (after he had ceased to qualify for half pay as Governor of British Guiana) was not alleviated by a pension, which he missed by a matter of months.[1] These were curious circumstances for a man who had been the most popular and successful Governor of his day, and whose name is held in respect—even reverence—over thirty years later in a land where British rule has been decisively rejected and where even the British connection is regarded with cool objectivity.

As so often in such cases it is impossible to say that anyone behaved badly; higher officials in the Colonial Office were courteous, even friendly; just rules were justly applied; it was simply that Guggisberg committed the unpardonable error of not fitting into them. Since he was not a career colonial servant the Secretary of State had no responsibility towards him, other than a moral one[2]; yet Amery's conversation, in reference to Guggisberg's outstanding work, seems to imply that some responsibility was recognized. On the other hand, when he was appointed to British Guiana, the local press unanimously referred to him as having 'been brought out of retirement'. What is incomprehensible, to those unversed in the *arcana* of the Colonial Service, is that he was not allowed to continue in the

---

[1] But see footnote to p. 330.

[2] There is reason to suppose that at the end of his first term in the Gold Coast he was offered another governorship, and was warned by the Colonial Office that it would be in his own interest to accept it. He preferred to stay on. If the supposition is correct he may be said to have brought his unemployment on himself, and this may have been the greatest of his personal contributions to the Gold Coast.

Gold Coast, where his authority was now supreme, in order to see the opening of Takoradi Harbour, to earn his pension, and to fulfil his powers in what was now his natural habitat. In the light of hindsight it is perhaps as well that this did not come about, for he would have ended a further spell as Governor with those powers diminishing, instead of at the flood. But no one knew this at the time; it seems more likely that the normal rule about a third term was strictly and unimaginatively applied, regardless of the unique flavour of his governorship or of his personal circumstances.

Meanwhile, he was out of work. 'I left him [Amery] on the understanding that I would not keep worrying him for an appointment, but that I left my record of work in the Gold Coast as an evidence of my fitness for another Governorship.' Thus had the mighty fallen.

The next few months were occupied in a manner appropriate to his class and time. He was drawn into a number of conferences on colonial matters—on transport, on Colonial Regulations, on the embryo West African Medical School, on defence, on education; he attended official dinners, met distinguished people, lunched and dined with friends round London, engaged in village affairs in Hampshire and sought relaxation in carpentering; tried to write a little.

The social diary is at times impressive, 'Lunched with Lady Codrington at Eaton Square to meet the Duke of Connaught. He thanked me for my kindness to Princess Marie Louise.' Or again, 'Lunched with the Amerys, and in the evening attended the Government dinner at Lancaster House, sitting next to Austen Chamberlain, who talked well throughout the meal. I couldn't help being very much impressed by his evident and genuine belief in himself.' Had Chamberlain done less of the talking he might very well have returned the compliment, for Guggisberg, only a few weeks away from his triumphal leave-taking in Accra, was still at the top of his form, undimmed by the tribulations ahead. 'He is undoubtedly an able politician, but has been made able by his long experience of House of Commons and political work. I should say that he was a made statesman and not a natural one.' Guggisberg's knowledge of psychology was probably minimal, and he may not have realized that he was seeing himself in his neighbour at dinner. Of the Vice-Chancellor of one of the two older English universities, 'privately, I did not like the look of him'; and a glittering dinner party of dons at the other appeared to him as a company of 'pleasant men, but they left no particular *impression* on me!' But an interesting encounter at All Souls elicited a comment which may have reflected a little of his nascent bitterness. He lunched with Major-General Sir E. D. Swinton, then Professor of Military History in the University, who had joined with him at Woolwich on the same day in October 1886. Swinton had had a great deal to do with the introduction of tanks, and was labouring under a sense of injustice at not having been given credit due to him. He wanted to write to the press on the matter, but Guggisberg sought to dissuade him. 'Nobody nowadays—have they ever done so?—pays any attention to man's justification of himself.'

A Colonial Office committee which occupied more of his time than most, and which had introduced him to these pundits of the academic world, was the one concerned with the Tropical African Service Courses. Predictably, the eagle eye of Sir Ralph Furse had fallen upon him, for Guggisberg, apart from the fact that he was not out of the 'top drawer', was the personification of all that Furse admired, down to his devotion to cricket. He seems to have worked Guggisberg hard, and together they spent much time in Oxford and Cambridge on the Committee's business; Furse 'put me up to many of the "wheels within wheels" which revolve in university circles'. (Twenty years later Furse was still doing just that.) Guggisberg clearly enjoyed this work, and records the people he met and what he thought of them with his old zest. He was himself an ardent member of the Ralegh Club at Oxford, and addressed them at their annual dinner on 11 June 1927. 'These annual dinners and conversations are most inspiriting; one gives one's little and gets a lot.' He regretted the absence of such a Club at Cambridge, and was not alone in this. For a few weeks earlier, after a distinguished dinner at Brooks on the subject of West African Medical Schools, 'Lugard, Byrne and Cameron came round to the Rag afterwards, and we discussed the necessity for increasing the Empire spirit at Cambridge. I suggested to Lugard that we should try and get Cambridge to start a Club something like the Ralegh, and he is very anxious that this should be done.' Today it is agreeable, and a little moving, to contemplate this group of upright men in Pall Mall regretting the absence of the Empire spirit in the University of Cambridge. Alas, Cambridge was unmoved by their enthusiasm, for when they came to discuss the matter there the natives were agreed that such an enterprise could only 'evolve gradually', perhaps from the Probationers' Club which the T.A.S.C. Committee was hoping to recommend. Meanwhile, in Tropical Africa itself, the nationalists were beginning to put their heads together.

For the rest, Guggisberg filled his days in the manner customary to men who are really idle, but who are sufficiently distinguished and well known to fill their diaries, and thus sustain the momentum of engagements which has kept them going for a lifetime. It was unusually important to Guggisberg to do this, for under the surface activity of clubs, dinners and committees his personal life was unhappy, if not empty. His marriage, for years a tense, brittle and unhappy affair, was breaking down completely, and he could no longer turn a blind eye to his deteriorating health, which was diminishing what remained of personal ambition, though not yet his zest for African advancement and the imperial mission. Visits to Yateley from Aggrey and Fraser sustained him and took him back in spirit to his proud years, but even these were tinged with sadness, for Aggrey's death occurred a little later, and profoundly shook him, and he seems to have suspected that it would be his last meeting with his old friend Fraser. The Christian faith had always been a part of his life, but his beliefs, though sincere, were conventional and inarticulate, capable of sustaining him in success rather than in adversity. Fraser had helped him more than anyone in his private and religious life, and now Fraser was three thousand miles away. The most inspiriting event at this time was a letter from the Phelps-Stokes Fund in New York inviting him to visit America as their honoured guest.

Decima largely went her own way, among her own circle. For a few weeks after returning to London they had accommodation at the Metropole Hotel, but when in the first week he 'tried to have a friendly talk with her' about where they were to live his overtures were rebuffed. He asked her to accept Miss Corry's invitation to stay at Yately, but 'this led to a very trying scene, D. being absolutely obstinate in her attitude towards the whole question, especially making absurdly silly accusations about M. (Miss Corry) having come in to break up "our home" (which we have never had)'. He tried again a week later when 'she entirely refused to discuss anything whatever with me—a deadlock'. He was reduced to the humiliating and melodramatic course of writing a letter to her and leaving it on the mantelpiece of the hotel bedroom, but she got in first, for the following day both he and Miss Corry received 'outrageous' letters, and she did not return to the hotel. She wrote again, a week later, in a very 'uncompromising' mood—'signs of advanced megalomania I'm afraid'. Worse was to follow in the form of a letter inveighing against Miss Corry and his daughters, with 'rambling assertions that she has continually had to "save me from the Secretary of State".' He repeated his offer to take a house for them both, away from Yately Hall, but 'she burkes the point, so I let her go on.' 'It is very sad, but position quite impossible'. Finally, in early August, 'D. writes asking for a separation, or rather to say I may proceed with one. What's the good! Only spoil chances of a future appointment without real freedom. Declined.' The other side of the story is not known, but it must be remembered that he was not an easy man to live with, and that a quarter of a century earlier his first wife had found him intolerable. He was clearly not the perfect husband.

Another quietly nagging worry was his health. By July he was having trouble with his legs (as early as 1912 he had been temporarily crippled with thrombosis, and now the trouble was hardening of the arteries). In early August, at a country house party at Lady Loch's house in Suffolk (for England was England still in 1927) he contracted a fever, which he attributed to frequent inoculations on his legs—which, however, were doing him no good. Soon he was refusing to have them, in spite of his doctor's advice. By September he was deliberately inactive. A whole week was spent in the carpenter's shop at Yateley—'the only exercise that suits my legs; limit of walk is still about 200 yards, and that with an effort. Writing articles, or thinking of them, as a variation to woodwork.' (One of them appeared in the *National Review*, another in the *Financial Times*, both accounts of his stewardship in the Gold Coast, probably the only thing he was now capable of discussing.) His health began to affect him mentally. 'At present I have a curious apathy as to whether I am re-employed by the Colonial Office or not. Am so tired of being dependent on politicians. The only thing I do feel against not being employed as Governor is that it would be a waste of the experience I have gained. This perfectly modest, as I have no *personal* ambition left, except to do a job for Africa and the Empire. However, I'm not in the top notch as regards general health, and this may be influencing me. These legs are really damnable and one requires an effort to be cheerful.'

Before this, in June, he had greatly enjoyed a brief visit from Aggrey, en route for America, who had stayed a night with him at Yateley, and later his growing unhappiness was lightened by one from Fraser. Aggrey turned out to have his own troubles. Although still full of enthusiasm for his work and 'his people' he ventured for the first time to broach his family and financial troubles, these being of a familiar kind. The combination of supporting his wife and children in America, entertaining at Achimota and meeting the endless demands of his kinsmen in the Gold Coast was wearing him down. Guggisberg was able to help him a little, by persuading the Gold Coast Government to pay his steamer passage; this was apparently unusual in 1927, which may seem strange to Aggrey's successors at Legon in the 1960s. They talked far into the night over the fire (for it was an English June). 'Aggrey was simply glowing with kindness and enthusiasm. His honest brown face, shining in the firelight, his alert eyes, his gleaming teeth and his open smile were most

attractive. The man rekindled my tired interest in his people—
not that I have forgotten them, or that they are not my real
interest in life, but because I am tired, physically and mentally.'

The following day 'Took Aggrey to Farnborough station and
said goodbye.' This was on 8 June. On 31 July, on the eve of a
rain-spoiled Bank Holiday fête in the village, a telegram from
Chief Amoah in New York gave him the news of Aggrey's death.
'The fête being over, we had a hot sunny day. This continued
next day—summer at last! But the sun cannot remove my
depression over Aggrey's death.'

At the end of the month Fraser joined him for a week-end,
helped with yet another village fête, preached in the village
church and was seen off at Farnborough station. But Guggisberg's diary is strangely inarticulate about this visit, for Fraser
was off to Achimota, where Guggisberg had left a large part of
his heart, and he could hardly bear to see him go. After his
departure he read a West African novel which Fraser had given
him. 'Pretty bad, but interesting from a missionary point of
view; difficulty of weaning the native from his own God (a God
of fear who punishes and frightens him—thanks to the fetish
priests I suppose) to our God the Father of us all. Would the old
type of blood and hell Methodism suit him?' He took the opportunity—the last as it turned out—to have a long talk with Fraser
about his religion, his personal life and his marriage.

He was now spending more time at Yateley, preparing for his
American visit, the formal invitation for which had coincided
with Aggrey's arrival, and husbanding his strength. One of his
last visitors before his departure was Sir Joseph Byrne, recently
appointed Governor of Sierra Leone, who came to talk to him
about his new job. 'Says I helped him a lot'; but, alas, Guggisberg's abiding impression of him was of a man with two pensions, one from the Iniskilling Fusiliers and one from the Royal
Irish Constabulary, besides his salary as Governor. The question
of a pension was never far from his thoughts.

So began Guggisberg's first experience of being 'on the beach'.
Previously his leaves had been all too short, for whether as surveyor or as Governor he had used them as a continuation of his

work; and the brief enjoyments he had allowed himself were fully savoured in the knowledge of further creative work ahead in West Africa. This was the greatest test so far of his spiritual resources (though another, more searching one, lay ahead). For he was getting on in years, his unsatisfactory marriage stood out more starkly at home than during his years of responsibility as Governor; his health was slipping; he had no certainty of ever working again, and even less certainty every day of a pension that would support himself or make provision for his daughters. All this would have been unimaginable to the people of the Gold Coast, who knew little about Army pensions or Colonial Service rules, and who would suppose that a man as great as Guggisberg would in some undefinable way be exempt from the mundane worries of a slender bank balance. But it was an ever-present reality to him, and personal anxiety was never far away. No man can live on past reputation for ever, although some men try, and this particular reputation was something of a two-edged sword. The name of Guggisberg might arouse awe and affection in West Africa, curiosity in America and respect among his professional colleagues, but the people he had to impress were the senior officials of the Colonial Office, and they were singularly unimpressionable folk. It was not that he lacked appreciation in the months between his return to England and his departure for his American tour; but he must have known that what would survive the months would not survive the years.

Soon after his return to England Ofori Atta had taken the trouble to cable him, 'Ever unfailing gratitude to your Excellency for all you have done for me and my country.' European colleagues had expressed their thanks. Even a few British newspapers had given him a paragraph. But the occasion to give him most pleasure and satisfaction was the Annual Meeting of the Gold Coast Civil Service Dinner Club, which was held at the Connaught Rooms on 15 June. Guggisberg was not only, as Governor, the President of this Club, but had been its Founder. Sir John Maxwell had cabled on behalf of all serving officers their desire 'to place on record in this last year of your Presidentship the great and valued work which you have done for this

Colony . . . this work, the foundations of which you laid, continues to prosper'. But the principal guest and speaker was the Secretary of State, and Amery could be trusted to say the right thing well, even if he could not find Guggisberg a job. After reviewing the achievements of 1919–27 he concluded with words of great clarity and point:

He had one great quality which was useful, not only to a soldier, but to an administrator—the capacity of seizing on strategic points and making sure of them, confident that the details would adjust themselves if the strategic points were sure. Ten years of progress, Takoradi Harbour, the motor-roads, the Gold Coast Hospital, Achimota College and a system of native jurisdiction and its linking up with the legislature of the country—these were the great key points in development on which his reputation as an administrator will rest secure.

In his diary Guggisberg remarks, 'Amery spoke well and gave me much praise. I felt a bit sad at making my last speech at this Club, which I founded during my Governorship.' He was occasionally capable of understatement.

# 13

## American Interlude (1927)

AT the beginning of July 1927, some two months after his return, Guggisberg had received this letter from Dr. Jesse Jones, the Educational Director of the Phelps-Stokes Fund, who had been a member of the delegation to Africa some years before, and a guest at Christiansborg Castle:

> Phelps-Stokes Fund,
> 101, Park Avenue,
> New York
> June 17th, 1927

Dear Sir Gordon,

I am longing for the ability to express adequately all that I feel with regard to the great service you have rendered not only to Africa but to the British Empire and, indeed, to the cause of civilisation everywhere. Through Aggrey, Fraser and the British Press I have been receiving news of your remarkable achievements. The Gold Coast volume 'The Review of Events of 1920–26 and Prospects for 1927–28' is thrilling both in accomplishments and in a forecast of the future. Even though comparisons are odious, I cannot refrain from a comparison of the real significance of your achievements and those of our beloved Lindbergh. In permanency of human service, my vote is entirely for Sir Gordon!

But I must refrain, for always I must curb my Celtic fervour. Memories of the Accra Castle ramparts have become realities in harbors, hospitals, schools and civilisation. Were it not for Anglo-Saxon inhibitions hovering about me, I could carry on into greater eloquence.

My dear Sir Gordon, I have been thinking much of you and Lady Guggisberg during these last few weeks, and I am wondering whether you would find it possible to come to America some time next autumn. Your coming would be a real service not only to

America and to Africa but also the the friendship of the British
Empire and America. If you think such a plan would be possible for
you, will you please let me know so that I may endeavor to ascertain
whether we on this side can arrange a welcome that is deserving of
all that you are and all that you have done.

Always with appreciation to you and Lady Guggisberg, I am,

Very sincerely,

Thomas Jesse Jones

This somewhat gushing warmth was in strange contrast to the
restrained enthusiasm of Downing Street, and its author can
hardly have supposed that a British Government would soon be
leaving Guggisberg unemployed against his own wishes. It
must have given him considerable pleasure, though this would
not be deduced from the formal office minute which he recorded,
presumably from force of habit, at its foot: 'Ansd. & asked
for provl. progmme. & cost. FGG 28.6.27.' Later the Fund
agreed to place the sum of $1500 at his disposal towards the
expenses of the tour; it covered the bulk of them. He sailed for
Quebec on the *Montroyal*, faithful to a Canadian line, on 25
September.

The Trustees of the Phelps-Stokes Fund were anxious for him
to study the 'inter-racial movement' in the States, to rub
shoulders with the more advanced Negro communities, especially in New York, Atlanta and Chicago, and to observe at first
hand some aspects of Negro education. This last was perhaps
the main purpose, and although it involved visits to over thirty
educational establishments of one kind or another, including
Howard University, it was focused mainly on the two great
Institutes of Hampton and Tuskegee. The tour, in outline,
included Washington, Norfolk, Richmond, Charleston, Mont-
gomery, Nashville, Chicago, Detroit, Cleveland and back to
Washington. As a postscript, after returning to New York, he
visited Boston and Rochester.

Hampton and Tuskegee could have been relied upon to
impress him, since both conceived education in terms of hus-
bandry, manual skills, character, thrift, self-help and community service. To one who had fretted for so long against the
irrelevancies of English history, geography and the classics in

the school syllabus; against the snobbishness which this odd kind of education had generated in those Africans who experienced it; and against its uselessness for anything but the production of indifferent clerical labour—these Institutes must have brought balm and relief, as well as retrospective frustration. In Southern Virginia, where the influence of Hampton was spread over several counties, he saw Negro farmers working the land they owned in units of more than thirty acres, possessing their own cars and lorries, mixing their crops and stock production on rational lines. He was immensely struck by the standard of their home life, which owed much to the home economics teaching of the Hampton group of schools; impressed also by the support given by the U.S. Department of Agriculture.

Tuskegee made an even stronger appeal, for his latent capacity for hero-worship, which (Fraser apart) had never found a very satisfactory object among the European community of West Africa, could centre on a man who, shortly after the emancipation of the slaves, had set out to prove to the Southern whites, as Guggisberg himself had set out to prove to the Colonial Office and the British public, that the potentialities of the black man were as great as those of any other. Concerning Booker T. Washington he was handicapped by a shortage of superlatives. He was no less impressed with the Penn School on St. Helena Island, on the coast between Charleston and Savannah in South Carolina, as an example of 'what a school can do for a community . . . a perfect example of co-operation between school and countryside'. Had he been able to see all this some ten years earlier his influence on Gold Coast education might have been even deeper and more original (in the British colonial context) even than it was.

In the cities he encountered an urbane, well-informed and prosperous Negro community. He was, of course, on a conducted tour, and was shown the best. This he fully realized, and he makes it clear that he knew that in the background were the idle, the ignorant and the feckless Negroes in large numbers. But as always he was concerned to establish that the black man *could be* the equal of the white, an idea which in 1927 had not even the limited acceptance that it has today among Southern white communities. And what he saw had been achieved in sixty years after emancipation from slavery.

To reporters at Nashville, Tennessee, his enthusiasm for Tuskegee overflowed. 'It is the most magnificent training institute in the world, the greatest educational idea that has come to any man in the past century, and not to be surpassed. I was not surprised to see the picture of Booker T. Washington in every Negro cabin and school house that I saw during my trip over the South.' But as always, in speaking to the Press, he put in his word about British progress in West Africa and told them something of advances in the Gold Coast, concluding, as he frequently did, with these words: 'During my trip I have gained confirmation of my previous opinion, formed after twenty-five years in West Africa, that the Negro races are capable of the highest development.'

There was a certain amount of lionizing, for his hosts had prepared the ground well and heralded him as the maker of a country; he was not without honour, save in his own. He was received by President Coolidge, talked with Henry Ford, and visited Rochester as the guest of Eastman. He had from the start acquired a sort of stupefied respect for the benefactions of American millionaire philanthropists to the Negro cause, in particular of John D. Rockefeller and Julius R. Rosenwald, the Jewish owner of the Sears-Roebuck organization, comparing the size of their benefactions with the sums officially available to him for the social services of an African colony. At a final dinner at the Astor in New York—a 'Dinner in the Interest of Africa'— his hosts arranged for him to address seventy of the most distinguished figures in America in the philanthropic, missionary and educational worlds.

His health appears to have stood up to these demands. At least there is no direct evidence to the contrary, and his schedule was completed from start to finish. On the other hand photographs show a face noticeably more lined and cadaverous than of old, and a Charleston reporter had this to say, 'Sir Gordon spoke in a conversational tone, leaning forward with his hands on a chair in front. He is a tall man and rather frail, apparently about sixty-five . . .'; Guggisberg notes in the margin of his scrap-book 'Hard luck! This journey is apparently telling on me!' (He was fifty-nine.) The account goes on, '. . . of brown hair and eyes, short aquiline nose and prominent chin, soft voice and uses the broad "a". He is the realization of an American's notion of a high-bred English gentleman.' Thus was described the Canadian, of Jewish-Polish-German-Swiss descent, who was scarcely an Establishment figure.

The tour began in New York on 3 October and ended at Albany on 11 November. From there he returned by the route through which he had arrived, to Toronto, for a final sojourn in his birthplace. He had enjoyed every moment. He was back in the centre of the stage, immersed in the thing that interested him most, refreshed by new sights and sounds. Even at the level of the most innocent tourism it had been enjoyable. It is a little surprising to find this experienced and travelled man meticulously pasting picture postcards, newspaper cuttings and menu cards in his scrapbook. But this was presumably done back in England, when time again hung heavy.

He seems to have stayed some time in Toronto, for on 30 November he addressed his fellow-countrymen and officers at the Canadian Military Institute.[1] Here he was relaxed, bluff and soldierly, giving elementary and somewhat facetious instruction on the geography of West Africa and the White Man's Grave. It is interesting that he found this necessary; ignorance was virtually complete. He spoke of the days when Englishmen went to the Coast because of drink, death or divorce . . . 'But today a young fellow comes to West Africa . . .' and so on. He did in fact give some interesting figures of the improvement in health of Europeans since 1900, and said, to the general astonishment, that in his last tour of duty as Governor a senior European official had 'even brought two children to the Gold Coast for the school holidays'; he also remarked on the growing financial embarrassment to the Gold Coast Government of long-lived European pensioners, the oldest of whom were

[1] Selected Papers of the Institute 8.

currently 70, 80 and 91. In more serious vein he spoke—inevitably—of education. We were prepared to give the African
the best education, but on two conditions, '. . . the first, that he
shall be trained to be a decent chap, the second that he shall
remain an African and be proud of his country, and not become
a half-baked European'. 'Half-baked' was his favourite term of
derogation, and a man who was neither European nor African
his abiding *bête noire*. At the time he was speaking it was apparently difficult to give a man a first-class education and 'still
get him to retain a pride in his nationality, proud to belong to
one of these African tribes (sic)'. 'If we had managed this in
India, if we had not separated the Indian from the great masses
of his own countrymen, we should never have developed the
gulf between the educated and the uneducated—the gulf which
is the cause of all political discontent.' Finally, 'I think we have
caught it in time in the Gold Coast, and our system—he was
thinking of Achimota—may be the salvation of the country.'

'At the close of his address, His Excellency in his own charming manner answered many questions put to him by an interested audience. . . . One question which caused a ripple of
laughter was whether Canada had any exports to West Africa
other than engineers, officers and governors.'

One of the fruits of the American visit was a small book published in July 1929, by the Student Christian Movement, *The
Future of the Negro*. This had been planned by Guggisberg and
Fraser as a joint task, but distance prevented a proper collaboration, and it fell to Margaret Wrong of Toronto[1] to put together
and edit their separate and untidy notes, and to publish the first
two parts of the book under Guggisberg's name and the concluding part under Fraser's. Guggisberg was by now Governor
of British Guiana, and in an introduction written from Georgetown, after he had seen the proofs, he thanks Miss Wrong in a
charming sentence—'We are trying to believe that it was her
incurable modesty that led her to refuse to allow her name to
appear on the title page, and not her desire to avoid any sus-

[1] Daughter of the Canadian historian G. M. Wrong.

picion of association with us.' He had travelled a long way from the adolescent prose of *The Shop*.

It is not a work of any great significance today, but it was forward-looking in the context of the 1920s, and it is interesting in showing how Guggisberg's thoughts were shaping towards the close of his life. It was also the last time he wrote for publication, and is an appropriate concluding testimony to his passionate and abiding wish for better African education.

The first part is really a Report; it would have offended his soldierly mind to have accepted and enjoyed his American trip without giving some account of it, and in any case he had been so deeply impressed that he could not have done otherwise. For Hampton and Tuskegee were the living embodiment of all that he had been searching for in his Gold Coast years. They were the climax and justification of the admonitions in the Legislative Council, the thinking aloud of 'The Keystone', the years of struggle to express an educational philosophy, and to impose, as an amateur, an educational theory on suspicious and unwilling professionals. He was, perhaps, over-impressed, and may too readily have equated the westernized American Negro with his African charges. Yet he was moved and encouraged by the American Negro achievement in agriculture, business, the professions and the arts, and felt himself vindicated in his long years of fighting European scepticism in the Gold Coast and the Colonial Office. 'In committing my impressions of the American Negro to paper I hope . . . to encourage the civil servants and missionaries whose lives are spent among the fifty million Africans of the British Empire.' Whether he hoped also to encourage the Colonial Office is not recorded.

He was clearly surprised by the status achieved by the Negro in business in the main cities, partly the work of the then Principal of Tuskegee, who had founded the National Negro Business League and its offspring, the National Negro Finance Corporation. The value of Negro businesses was £300 million, at 1920 values, their insurance companies had over £50 million worth of policies in force, and their banks were transacting an annual business to the value of £20 million. The Negro had proved 'his capacity for handling large sums of money in a reliable and efficient manner', and his thoughts turned wistfully to the Gold Coast he had left behind. Negro farming, as promoted and guided by the Institutes, roused him to an equal enthusiasm. Only in the field of one of the arts did he express a reservation, in one of his rare essays into a mild, ironic humour:

I omit all mention of the Negro's bewildering contribution to the music of today—jazz—owing to my uncertainty as to whether it has a civilizing or a decivilizing influence. Perhaps the spirit from which it has been born has been warped in the process. If so I trust that, like the child's, its rickets may be curable.

This was the one field, perhaps, in which he was unable to identify himself, even objectively, with the folk he loved.

One says 'objectively', for his identification with them was never completely subjective. He did not, in the modern manner, dance, eat, drink, mix or relax with the Africans to whose welfare he devoted the thought and energy of a lifetime. They were always wards rather than friends, and judged by contemporary ways of thinking there were surprising limitations in his attitude towards them, for social equality had never appealed to him as being either desirable or possible. His passion was for equal rights and opportunities for the black man, not for intimacy with him.

Equal citizenship can be obtained without the social equality which the extremists (*sic*) say is essential to a full and free life. . . . If the aim includes – as the extremists claim it should – social equality such as inter-marriage and living in social intimacy with the white, then the sooner the claim is abandoned the better for the Negro's future. One has only to be a very short time in America to be convinced that that kind of social equality will not come in the present century. Today there are certainly occasions on which members of the two races meet for other than business purposes. . . . But when all is said and done these occasions are merely the exceptions that prove the rule.

His revolt against colour prejudice, which was deep and genuine, was in fact a revolt against the idea that the Negro was inherently less intelligent or able than the white man, and in this book he quotes much scientific evidence to rebut this idea; evidence that was apparently new to him at the time, though it is current coin today. Speaking of the founders and staff of Howard and Morehouse he says, 'A race that in such a brief span of time can produce such leaders must surely have begun to dissipate the strange notion that is prevalent both in England and America, that the capacity of the Negro races is limited.' But there he stopped.

Characteristically, much as he admired the fruits of the spirit as displayed in Tuskegee, the Hampton Institute and the Penn School, his concern was rather to understand the spirit of which the fruits were born, and which were personified for him in Booker Washington's life. Here was a man whom Guggisberg had no difficulty in venerating, for in that life were revealed the same austere values to which he himself had come to aspire, and which in some measure, often against the grain of his nature, he practised—humility, selflessness, service, belief in the dignity of manual labour, an emphasis on the practical. (It was the first of these that gave him most trouble.) 'Training for life and not for degrees' was Booker Washington's phrase, but Guggisberg had made it his own even before his American visit, and his association with Washington's successors stimulated him to renewed protestations, of the kind familiar throughout his Gold Coast years, on the central place of character training in education. He extols once more the simple values of the British public schools, the Boy Scout movement, of patriotism and of 'practical Christianity'; his enthusiasm for any other kind of Christianity was, alas, somewhat modified by the 'denominational keenness' which he had experienced as a colonial Governor—'the training cannot fail to suffer if the school is permitted to become the battle-ground of denominational enthusiasm'.

At the conclusion of the book, of which he wrote the major part, he reverts to the long familiar habit of laying down the law about Education (shades of the Legislative Council!). As of old, he metaphorically dons cap and gown, and works with pedagogic enthusiasm through a series of propositions, slipping unconsciously on one occasion into the old attitude of soldier-Governor ('The following points require attention in carrying out this policy. . . .' One pictures Heads of Departments hurriedly sharpening their pencils.). His propositions on this occasion number ten, not as in the Legislative Council of long ago, fifteen. They show the influence upon him of Fraser, as well as of his American experience. They are in one sense his final testament; in another his final orders to those concerned with education in African colonies. It is difficult in the book to disentangle Guggisberg from Fraser, and it may therefore be invidious to credit the more forward-looking propositions to their immediate author. But in the context of 1929 they were certainly enlightened—in the pleas, for example, to free school education from the bureaucratic control of Government, for educational research—'we have research in forestry, agriculture and medicine —why not in education?'—for universities with a degree of independence which would have pleased a University Grants Committee of a later generation in Britain. It is refreshing that a Colonial Governor should say in public, in 1929, 'A Government Department becomes an administrative machine, arouses popular suspicion, and is largely cut off from the enthusiastic co-operation of the public.'

Here Guggisberg deploys his educational ideas in their maturity, and since education meant more to him than anything else this book, however slight in bulk, is important in any appreciation of his life. Other convictions are revealed that have not altogether stood the test of time, or which are more controversial. As we have seen earlier, he was a traditionalist by temperament, and believed not only in the sanctity of native institutions, but that foreseeable development could take place through their agency, and that they would have an enduring political future. Even at this late date, and at the end of his American experience, he could write that 'the ballot box is not compatible with native institutions'. (Paradoxically he seemed to have admired the States Negro for being '100 per cent American', and described him as being a 'new species of the genus African'.) But in affirming his belief in development through native institutions he spoke of 'those which should be discarded, retained or blended with those of the West', rather as though this could flow from a deliberate act of will. He underrated, or had not sufficiently considered, the erosive effect of western institutions.

True, the 'blending' which he foresaw is coming to pass, some forty years later, as certain western political institutions become adapted to the 'African personality'; as, for example, 'non-party democracy' acquires its own rationale and philosophy. But his notion that West Africa could borrow the West's technology and reject altogether its social and political influence or attitudes was naïve. Gandhi had a similar vision of an indigenous culture, but knew that western technology would open the door to every other kind of western institution and so tried to wean his followers away from the factory to the spinning wheel. But in this he could gain no support from Indians.

In these last pages we have quoted rather freely from what Guggisberg actually wrote; our excuse must be that these were his last published words; no apology is needed for this final quotation, in which is contained the explanation and justification of his whole career:

Our task today is infinitely more difficult [than pioneering], including as it now does moral and intellectual, as well as material, development. It is precisely because we have this dual task that we want more and more the best that England can give; not only the best in science and the professions but men and women imbued with the real Christian spirit—the spirit of the life and teachings of Jesus, love of mankind and a desire for service. And the best share we can take in the task is to present to the African, through our political officers, agricultural and forestry officers, businessmen, bankers, in fact through everyone with whom the African has to do, an example of decent Christian life. As in the case of schools in our own country, the example of the men and women who are teachers counts for far more than the spoken lesson.

The test of our administration, of the education we provide, of the Christianity we take to the African, lies in the success with which the African people acquire the knowledge to realize and control the changes which are coming so quickly, and the art of discrimination between what is good and bad for them in our civilization. After twenty years of West Africa I may be biased in my view, but I am convinced that there is no greater work that an Englishman can do for mankind than to go to the help of these mighty African races, now in the throes of the greatest change of their history.

# 14

## British Guiana—Anti-climax

IN the late summer of 1928 the Secretary of State offered Guggisberg the macabre assignment of the Governorship of British Guiana, vacated by Sir Cecil Rodwell on his appointment to Southern Rhodesia. One uses the adjective not to disparage the Colony or its people, but to describe a situation which would have daunted a vigorous, adaptable man of high intelligence and capacity, and which now had to be faced by an ageing, ailing man, whose very reputation was perhaps his greatest handicap, and who was no longer adaptable. In the first few months of his governorship, by a tremendous feat of will-power, he managed to summon up reserves of energy which gained him an immediate reputation for drive and enthusiasm; but he achieved little else. On 1 July of the following year, after less than eight months in the Colony, he was driven to his ship in an ambulance through a small and silent crowd, unregretted and soon forgotten, except by a handful of officials who had the privilege of working at his side.[1]

British Guiana was a somewhat smaller colony than the Gold

[1] For much of the material of this chapter I am indebted to private communications from the Rev. Winslow A. Beckles; Sir Frank McDavid, C.M.G., C.B.E., formerly Financial Secretary and later a member of the 'Interim' Government (1954–7); Mr. W. A. Macnie, C.M.G., O.B.E., formerly Director of Land Development and once a Police Officer and A.D.C. to Guggisberg; Mr. Vincent Roth, O.B.E., formerly a Survey Officer and now Director of the British Guiana Museum and Zoological Gardens; and above all to Mr. H. R. Persaud, then Government Archivist and now Permanent Secretary to the Ministry of External Affairs, who not only gave me a connected outline of Guggisberg's administration but was good enough to collate a number of contemporary newspaper accounts. I acknowledge also a conversation with Mr. M. B. Laing, C.M.G., O.B.E., formerly Clerk to the Legislative Council and later Commissioner for Local Government, who was for a time Guggisberg's Private Secretary. I have acknowledged the names of these gentlemen in appropriate footnotes.

Coast, with a considerably smaller population, estimated in 1928 at a mere 300,000, and belonged to a different world. The Gold Coast was potentially a homogeneous country in spite of tribal differences, but virtually the whole of the population of British Guiana had been imported, the majority being the descendants of slaves or indentured labourers. Indians, known as East Indians, and Africans, forthrightly and indeed until very recently known as 'Blacks', were the principal ethnic groups, each numbering about forty per cent of the whole; ten per cent were of 'mixed race' and four per cent European, mostly Portuguese. There was also a small Chinese element. The original inhabitants—'aborigines' or 'Amerindians'—numbered only three per cent, and were mostly in the less accessible inland areas. The internal racial problem, as between Indians and Africans, had not then achieved its later prominence, but nation-building, as Guggisberg understood it, was hardly a serious possibility. Among the primitive and unsophisticated there was little on which to build, while the merchant and educated classes along the coast were wholly cosmopolitan, and of a 'western' and slightly aggressive kind of sophistication to which Guggisberg was unaccustomed. 'British Guiana was politically precocious, but educationally backward. It consists of a congeries of races from all parts of the world, with different instincts, different standards and different interests.'[1] The productive part was confined to the narrow alluvial coastal strip, no more than seven per cent of the whole country, while the vast hinterland with its forest and mineral wealth, as well as its splendid scenery and waterfalls, was hardly penetrated and almost uninhabited; though the gold and bauxite miners had once worked up most of the rivers.

But the greatest difference between the two countries, from a Governor's point of view, lay in their economic situations. Guggisberg had taken over the Gold Coast at a time when cocoa was booming and when reserves had accumulated during the War; he had a good start and was undoubtedly lucky. The economic and financial situation in British Guiana was

[1] Report of the Wilson-Snell Commission—see below.

utterly forbidding, and the Administration seemed to have lost heart and initiative in trying to deal with it. In the seven years before Guggisberg's appointment the economy had stagnated; in six of these years there had been a budget deficit, totalling £682,000, and reserves were less than a sixth of this amount; revenue had been static at a little above or a little below £1,000,000; public debt stood at over £4,000,000, of which over £1,640,000 was represented by advances from the Crown Agents for public works. For British Guiana had the abnormal handicap of a coastal plain which lay below sea level, and which was a bottomless pit of expenditure necessary for sheer survival, on drainage and irrigation; while the public services of Georgetown and the other coastal towns, especially the supply of pure drinking water, had to be maintained and improved at all costs, the alternative being the certainty of epedemic disease.

No one had any solution to propose to this potentially disastrous situation. Economic stagnation was matched by a stagnation of spirit, and the Government, owing to an ancient Constitution inherited from the Dutch, was virtually unable to govern. 'The Colony had stood still, without exaggeration, practically ever since the British took it over from the Dutch a hundred years ago. Financially, its condition was rotten; adminstratively, even worse.'[1]

'The Constitution—a patchwork resulting from a trading company assuming political functions—provided for two bodies, a Court of Policy and a Combined Court. The former consisted of eight officials and eight elected members, but since the Governor, who presided, had the casting vote, it was officially controlled. It controlled policy but not the purse. The Combined Court consisted of the Court of Policy and six (elected) "Financial Representatives", and was thus controlled by the elected members. The combined Court controlled the purse but not the policy. This division of powers provided ample opportunity for quarrels between Government and elected members, most of whom constituted themselves into an elected

---

[1] Guggisberg: private letter to his friends—see final chapter.

opposition.'[1] This Constitution presented a classic example of
the divorce of responsibility from power; it meant moreover
that the Government could never plan ahead financially for
more than twelve months, the whole fiscal system being thrown
annually into the melting-pot.

It is not wholly true to say that no one had any solution, for
the British Government had resorted in 1926 to the classic
device of sending out a Commission of Inquiry.[2] Its terms of
reference were 'to consider and report on the economic situation
of the Colony, the causes which have hitherto retarded and the
measures which could be taken to promote development, and
any facts which they may consider to have a bearing on the
above matters'. This Commission spent a month in the Colony.

Its fundamental, and long-term, conclusion was that the
future health of the economy depended on opening up the
'interior', which represented eighty-seven per cent of the land
area, by road and railway, particularly with a view to developing a timber industry, as well as assisting the existing gold and
diamond undertakings; but that this would be a distant dream
until the preposterous financial situation was cleared up. The
first essential steps were to balance the budget, to plan for the
proper funding of loans and to give the Government the
financial power to implement a policy. The last, which meant
an overhaul of the Constitution, was the first in order of priority
and the Commission recommended that a locally appointed
body should be set to work upon it.

This was April 1927, when Guggisberg was leaving the Gold
Coast. In July of the following year, about the time of Sir Cecil
Rodwell's departure from British Guiana, a new Constitution
was promulgated, in readiness for the next Governor who would
lead the country into the promised land. It largely followed
conventional colonial lines, with Legislative and Executive
Councils; the former had the usual official majority of two ex-
officio, eight nominated official and five nominated unofficial;

---

[1] Persaud.
[2] The Wilson-Snell Parliamentary Commission, whose Report is contained in
Cmd. 2841 of 1926.

the latter departed from what was customary at the time, as it included three unofficial and two elected members, alongside six officials, all being members of the Legislative Council. Here at last, in the colonial context of the time, was an instrument with which the Government could govern, and through which, incidentally, the Secretary of State could make his wishes felt.

One says 'in the colonial context of the time', but it is doubtful whether the Colonial Office was wise in imposing this particular Constitution on British Guiana. The former one was admittedly a sad muddle from the point of view of planned development. On the other hand it was far more responsible from a democratic point of view, since the Court of Policy was half elected and the Combined Court was controlled by elected members. As a consequence, the processes of government attracted men of stature, who were by no means lacking in the Colony. The new Constitution was a typical colonial one, with an African pedigree, and the Colonial Office seem to have been insensitive to the effect of this on a relatively sophisticated people. Nor did it apparently occur to them that they might do better than turn the elected element into an automatic opposition, which was the inevitable effect. Both in Guggisberg's Gold Coast, and now in British Guiana, it is possible that a more liberal constitution in the 1920s would have evoked more responsible leadership than that which was to emerge a generation later. The word 'responsible' was apt to be construed by nationalists as meaning, in the minds of the British, 'pro-imperialist', and there was some justification for this. But accepting the British Government's own premises in this matter, it seems strange that they were not prepared to place more trust in moderate men of substance and position, who would certainly have given them more support and loyalty than the extremists who succeeded them, and to whom political power was ultimately given.

But although, for good or ill, the constitutional jungle had thus been cleared, the problems facing the new legislature, and above all the new Governor, were intractable. The Colony shared a weakness with the Gold Coast, namely its excessive dependence on one export crop, sugar taking the place of cocoa; but here again Guggisberg was lucky in the Gold Coast and unlucky in British Guiana, for whereas cocoa prices were rising when he went to Accra sugar prices were low when he came to Georgetown, and the crop had suffered catastrophically in a prolonged drought in 1926. The industry itself was well organized, both technically and, at least by contemporary standards, in its labour and social policies, but it was fighting against subsidies in competitor countries, and was dangerously dependent on Imperial Preference. It was estimated that if preference were discontinued seventy-five per cent of those employed in the industry would be thrown out of work, and 'chaos, financial and economic, would prevail'.[1] The other crops, notably rice and citrus fruits, were of poor quality, largely because of the lack of research and experiment, and there was an urgent need for an agricultural bank to stimulate production. Education was in a pitiable condition, and here Guggisberg's knowledge and enthusiasm might have led to some improvement if he had been able to escape from his obsession with the fiscal problem. As it was, some sharp remarks about its condition on the very day of his arrival earned him unpopularity without achieving anything. Not that anything could have been too scathing to describe the state of the schools and the profound irrelevance of their syllabuses. A British Inspector of Schools, invited by the Guianan Government, had reported on the position in 1924, with recommendations; two years later 'not a single one of his recommendations had been carried into effect'.[2] Outside the capital city, public health provision was rudimentary, although the Colony was riddled with all the diseases associated with the tropics on the one hand, and with dirt, apathy and ignorance on the other. There was no effective Public Health Department, for although it existed on paper it had no executive authority over the entrenched public health powers of the village authorities,

---

[1] Guggisberg—private letter. Incidentally he came to develop a firm belief in the future of a rice industry, if only it could be sustained by research and by capital loans.                                    [2] The Wilson-Snell Commission.

which did not exercise them, having neither the knowledge the staff nor the financial resources. The death rate was in the neighbourhood of thirty per thousand.

A railway to open up the interior was thought, rightly or wrongly,[1] to be an urgent necessity, psychologically as well as economically, but although a good deal of survey work had been done nothing had happened, nor could anything be expected to happen in view of the Colony's public debt, and its small resources and population. The improvement of Georgetown Harbour, the development of river transport and of course roads were essential, but no one could see the way forward. Commenting on this situation the Parliamentary Commission (p. 34) said, 'We should view the matter differently if the Imperial Government were prepared to shoulder over a period of years the interest and sinking fund obligations which a railway development loan would involve.' It would never have occurred to them, in 1926, to propose grant-aid, for, alas, this was before the days when the 'Imperial Government' regarded financial aid to its under-developed territories as a normal obligation of power. Colonies were supposed to provide for their own financial needs, and Guggisberg was sent out with specific instructions from the Secretary of State to balance the budget as a first priority.

In the background was the urgent and unfamiliar problem of under-population, since it was hopeless to think in terms of developing a country of this size with a population of 300,000. Since the abolition of slavery the sugar planters had recruited labour from all over the world, but notably and most satisfactorily from India; but in 1917 the Government of India had put a stop to emigration to British Guiana, and were only prepared to consider re-opening it on very onerous terms, involving large capital expenditure in settling Indian families on the land. Two controversies were raging at this time—whether schemes of immigration should be centred on indentured labour or on family farm settlement; and whether the immigrants should come from far afield, or mainly from the overcrowded West

[1] Its usefulness has since been questioned, and it has not in fact been built.

Indian islands, particularly from Barbados. The new Governor
became heavily involved in these controversies.

   This was the unpromising background of Guggisberg's assignment. He tackled it with a will, but quite apart from the fact
that his body was no longer equal to the will's demands he
made serious errors of judgement. He had always been 'every
inch a Governor', but now he seemed to welcome pomp and
circumstance for their own sake, to have developed a manner so
regal as to be embarrassing,[1] so authoritarian as to make
enemies of the only people who could have helped him. Every
ceremonial and ritual of traditional colonial legislative procedure was instituted and rigidly adhered to. Sir Frank McDavid
recalls:

The official members of the Legislative Council were ordered to
attend all meetings of that body in the regulation white civil service
uniform with its gilt buttons and oak leaf gorgets although as a concession without 'swords'. Thus, somewhat uncomfortably attired,
they became (under a procedure quite new to the colony) the
'bearers' of formal 'Messages' from his Excellency the Governor to
the Legislature (whose autocratic president he also was); and, as one
official of the old school unhappily remarked to a colleague—'we
official members are now only a lot of uniformed messenger boys'.

   The display may have been a reaction from his obscurity in
England, but it was oddly at variance with the professed decline
in ambition, his fundamental humility, and his cherished
canons. Moreover, after a time, he made the elementary mistake of comparing British Guiana too often with the Gold Coast,
to the former's disadvantage, and of bringing African terms
into his conversation and speeches. Beyond question his heart
was in Africa, and there may have been a subconscious resentment at being sent to this strange, unkempt, cosmopolitan and
lethargic hot-house. The 'professionals'—the civil servants who
worked closest to him—saw through this outward show and
learnt to respect him, for even in his decline he was a force to

[1] For example, he issued to the press daily a Government House Circular,
describing all the comings and goings in the manner of the Court Circular (Roth).

which they were unaccustomed—a Governor willing to grasp the nettle, anxious to take hold of each refractory problem in turn and try to make some sense of it. But 'Guggisberg of blessed memory', the idol of the people, did not survive.

It is important to remember that Guggisberg was himself a man under authority, and that he was not given a free hand as to what he might do in British Guiana. To balance the budget, to retrench the civil service, to bolster the economy—these were orders from Downing Street. He was not expecting popularity and he did not get it, and this may have accounted to some extent for his determination to impress his authority. On the very day of his arrival, 7 November 1928, in a speech to an audience of representative citizens in the Council Chamber, he said:

I am afraid that if I land here in twelve months time I shall not receive the warm welcome I received today. . . . I know the Government will meet with a considerable amount of opposition and dislike in carrying out some of their reforms. . . .

Again, he was badly served by the publicity that preceded him. It had become generally known that in his eight years' service in the Gold Coast the country's revenue had doubled and that there had been expansion in every direction. All this had been written up in the local press. He was regarded as a miracle-maker. 'People's hopes sky-rocketed. A Saviour had at last arrived to turn to fact their dreams of good.'[1] And Sir Frank McDavid recalls:

It is difficult to appreciate now what profound hopes were founded on the appointment of Sir Gordon Guggisberg as Governor by the people of the Colony. . . . Sir Gordon's fame as a great and successful administrator had preceded him and he was heralded as the saviour of the country. I recall a well-known old European resident who had made British Guiana his home—the late Mr. Ulric White— shouting triumphantly at his work place when the news came through—Guggisberg is coming!—Guggisberg is coming! He will pull us through.

And Mr. A. R. F. Webber, in the *Centenary History and Hand-*

[1] Beckles.

*book of British Guiana*—'He came with an exalted reputation
. . . the crowds on the day of his arrival were wild with enthusiasm. Always the pitiful faith in the power of a Governor.'

It must be confessed that Guggisberg played up to this situation by the manner of his arrival, in which he gave free rein to
his theatrical instincts. The ship docked among those on the
quayside precisely at the appointed time, but only the captain,
officers and crew were to be seen; passengers apparently had
been confined to cabins.[1] Suddenly, in a hush of expectation,
the great man, in full regalia, appeared upon the bridge. He had
modestly brought out with him a Rear-Admiral as A.D.C.[2]
and a Brigadier-General as Private Secretary; these retired
officers, in the full-dress uniform of their rank, followed on his
heels. Decima could not have arranged it better, but Decima
was not there. The crowd, by far the biggest ever known on such
an occasion, were wild with enthusiasm. In the 'short, slow
drive to Government House . . . some temporarily broke through
the Police, trying to shake his hand. Some succeeded, and one
woman in doing so touched his hand and shouted "Our Father,
our Saviour has come" .'[3] ('For some time after he came the
unemployed daily congregated in the shade of St. Andrew's to
see him journey to the Legislative Council meetings; the sayings
credited to him were told and re-told at the street corners.
Hero-worship was general.')[4] It was perhaps not the best start
for a sick man faced with an impossible task.

On this day, then, the leading citizens assembled in the
Council Chamber not so much to greet a Governor as to pay
homage to a Messiah; it was of some importance what he said to
them, and this in fact left them a little puzzled. 'I am not'—
almost his opening words—'a believer in autocratic government
*no matter what my past experience may have been.*' What he believed

[1] Macnie.

[2] Rear Admiral F. C. Fisher. To do Guggisberg justice, one reason for this
appointment was that Fisher's wife, formerly Ella Craigie, was the daughter of one
of Guggisberg's step-sisters, Lady Tudor, by her first husband, Admiral Craigie.
This rather remote kinswoman came to Georgetown to act as hostess at Government House, in the absence of the natural incumbent. See p. 309 below. I am
indebted to Lady Davson for this information.

[3] Macnie.                                          [4] *Daily Chronicle.*

in, it appeared, was co-operation, but he thought it necessary to define this word, since next to 'education' it was the most misused word in the language:

My definition of the word is this; that from full knowledge gained of the needs of the people and the country a Government should adopt a definite policy and base on that definite policy smaller policies governing our activities in every direction.

The press could make little of this, believing that co-operation meant something quite different, and to a close though somewhat critical observer 'it soon became evident that by "co-operation" Sir Gordon meant that he was Sir Oracle— that "when I open my mouth let no dog bark" '.[1] This was perhaps unfair, though as Sir Gordon elaborated his point the view certainly seemed to emerge that if the Government made its policy crystal clear to the meanest intelligence everybody would naturally want to co-operate, and that opposition, unless stated with as much cogency and intelligence as the policy itself, would be irresponsible. This view, which thirty years later was to find acceptance in his own beloved Gold Coast, did not altogether go down well. It presupposed a degree of docility which was foreign to the inhabitants of British Guiana, who were disposed to be cantankerous and individualist. Some of them suspected already that this was 'African talk'.

Dealing with priorities, it is significant that he should have said, 'Standing head and shoulders above all others, by far the most important policy in this country and the one to which the Government intends to devote the utmost energy, is that of population.' He had not yet met the Government, but he had on the voyage from England prepared Memorandum No. 1, containing Fourteen Principles, for the Government's instruction! He followed this with Health, 'since it is no use making a population if you are not going to keep them alive'. Education came third, and here his familiar view on academic education was even more sharply expressed than usual: '. . . not the education of what I call the degree, and what I am afraid is very often the education that leads to following the vocation of the

[1] Beckles.

parasite . . . but all that good citizenship means in knowledge of books, skill of hands, devotion to duty and service to fellow-men.' He reserved for his fourth priority, though he was under instructions to put it first and it is the thing for which he came chiefly to be remembered by the mass of people, economy, and the retrenchment and reform of the civil service.

One thing in Georgetown he found to be an improvement on Accra—the established custom on an occasion such as this of repairing to the Cathedral to ask God's blessing on the Commission of the new Governor; and it was with a high sense of purpose and dedication that he knelt before his Maker and paid homage to his King. 'At the conclusion of the service . . . the people could not be kept under any longer and cheered His Excellency even in the Cathedral. . . . Never in the history of the Colony was a Governor the recipient of such an enthusiastic welcome by the people.'

It is appropriate at this point to say a word as to how Guggisberg's physical appearance impressed his people on this memorable day, for one is aware of a slight undercurrent of apprehension. 'He was a tall, gaunt old man, who would easily have passed as the brother of Abraham Lincoln, so close was his resemblance to the late American President.'[1] '. . . our new Governor appears to us sixty years old. He bears the brand of African service. He is lean, angular, grey-haired and unyouthful. This must not be interpreted as meaning that he is aged or decrepit; far from that . . . but the West Coast of Africa is unkind to those who serve it well. Sir Gordon Guggisberg looks an ascetic (sic) almost cadaverous.'[2] Of more significance was an incident recorded by his A.D.C. Later on the day of his arrival there was an engagement in the Town Hall, which necessitated climbing two flights of stairs. 'He told me that owing to hardening of the arteries he experienced some difficulty with long stairs, but overcame this by pausing at regular intervals to speak to whoever was near to him, or to look out at the view; and he asked me to pause and look back as I walked

---

[1] Beckles.                         [2] *Daily Chronicle*.

ahead of him.'[1] Mr. Macnie also recalls the interesting point that he produced invitation cards, printed in London, for his first Reception at Government House, and that they bore Lady Guggisberg's name as well as his own. He explained that she had decided not to accompany him to British Guiana 'shortly before he left the U.K.' She felt he was not strong enough, had played his part in public service, and should have remained in retirement; in which of course she may have been right from a physical point of view, though it may have puzzled Georgetown society that she did not therefore consider it more, rather than less, urgent to be with him. Clearly there had been the familiar difficulties in the background; the fact that the cards were printed, and that he did not have them reprinted, indicates a last-minute scene, but suggests also that there was temporarily sufficient *rapport* for her to have agreed to go with him.

To what extent Guggisberg was deceiving himself about his health must always be obscure. That an element of self-deception existed can hardly be in doubt. According to the *Daily Chronicle* he announced publicly on the day of his arrival that he intended to serve the full six years of a governorship; and to a friend in the Colony he had written before his arrival:

I hope to have about ten years of life left, and these I want to devote to a work besides which my work in West Africa was mere child's play. [2]

He must have known that this was, to say the least, improbable; but eight months later, when inflammation of the liver and possibly sprue were added to his arteriosclerosis, and he was virtually a hospital case, he could still say on his last public appearance, 'I have got nothing wrong with me except a chill on the liver with its usual accompaniments', and that he was simply taking his leave early so that he could return fighting fit in October. An attitude either heroic or childish, according to one's point of view. The probable truth is that life had almost literally nothing for him but his work; he would have worked

---

[1] Macnie.

[2] The Bishop of Guiana—Address at Memorial Service, 28 April 1930.

himself into his grave in any circumstances, given the chance, and his financial stringency when off the active list encouraged him still further to turn a deliberately blind eye to his physical weakness. The one certain thing is that the lasting impression he left on friend and foe alike in British Guiana was a complete and unswerving devotion to duty. Those who suffered from his policies and those who for any other reason disliked him were united in paying him this tribute.

In spite of the doubts and criticisms which his forthright and unconventional debut had raised in certain minds (though not, on the whole, in 'official' minds) his first speeches and acts had been impressive. In spite of his age and health he brought into the country a new and energizing spirit. An air of expectancy and excitement prevailed.

Three weeks after his arrival (on 28 November) he opened the first Session of the reformed Legislature. He reserved his fire for the December Budget Session, but said enough to keep expectancy alive and tingling. In December the Government would 'clear the decks of the debris of 1928 and prepare for the action of 1929', and in a typical flourish he announced that in December, and year by year onwards, he would deliver to each Budget Session of Parliament an 'Annual Message', in which he would summarize the progress made in carrying out the Government's policies and deliver 'an account of the Government's stewardship'. He saw himself repeating, for as many years as God allowed him, the Headmaster's Annual Address at Speech Day, with which the Gold Coast Legislative Council had become so familiar. He seemed to exude confidence and vigour.

He added a few further details of 'his' policy. Of recent years we have become so familiar with the spread of representative government in former British dependencies, and with the Governor as constitutional monarch, that we need to remind ourselves of the immense personal power that a British colonial governor wielded at this time. Guggisberg's frequent confusion (as it may now seem to us) between the Government and himself was normal and acceptable, and Guggisberg differed from other governors only in that he was generally trying to do far more than they, and possibly had less hesitation, not only about being in control, but about being manifestly seen to be in control. Co-operation did not mean to him what it would now mean to us—development from below, progress by team-work, with the Governor *primus inter pares* (an idea Guggisberg could never have understood); it meant *informing* the people of what Government was doing, and *consulting* the experts at every stage. A cynic might have added that it meant also informing the Government of what *he* was doing. If this seems an inadequate definition of co-operation to us, it was considerably in advance of the concept of the time.

A month later, on 21 December, he deployed his policies and plans more fully.[1] To give British Guiana the population it needed (his target was two million in fifty years) he was going to start in 1930 an experimental colonization and land settlement scheme. To ensure success, a land settlement scheme was first going to be started for people already in the Colony. The future, he decided, did not lie in resuming the traditional policy of indentured labour, but in settling family farmers on productive plots, provided with essential services. (In this he was probably somewhat starry-eyed, and was no doubt harking back sentimentally in his mind to his old friends the cocoa farmers of the Gold Coast. But they, however small their farms, had a cash crop to sell, which they could supplement by growing their own food. In British Guiana the small peasant farmer might very well have starved.)

A Colonization Committee was appointed and preparatory work was soon to be begun, and in an attempt to solve the thorny problem of Indian migration he proposed, imaginatively, to seek advice from the Rev. C. F. Andrews.[2] He passed on,

---

[1] Governor's First Annual Message to Legislative Council, supplemented by notes from Mr. Persaud.

[2] Perhaps the most eminent English Christian missionary in India in this century. Friend of Gandhi, and Adviser to the Government of India on racial disputes, concerning Indian nationals, in South Africa and Kenya, and on indentured Indian labour in Fiji. Andrews did actually visit British Guiana after Guggisberg's departure.

over the whole gamut of agriculture, forestry, mining, land, communications, public health, and came to education.

At this point in his career everything that he could say about education was predictable, but he said it in full. We have referred earlier to the shabby and inadequate system which he inherited, and he now proposed to have it examined and overhauled from top to bottom; it was already in his mind, wisely or unwisely, to invite Fraser to come over from Achimota for this purpose. But it was in speaking of education that he had to sound the first jarring note, for whatever utopian future there might be for it the immediate and unavoidable necessity was a reduction of expenditure in primary schools, involving a progressive reduction in grant-aid to the religious bodies, calculated to extinguish it by 1933. This brought him to the principal, and painful, section of his Message, and to the point from which he started to make enemies. His pronouncement on finance was to bring disillusionment to those who had been naïvely waiting for the conjurer to perform his magic, and to rescue them painlessly from the financial swamp into which the Colony was sinking.

A cursory examination of the finances had convinced Guggisberg that it would be impossible to comply with Amery's instruction to eliminate the estimated deficit which faced him on arrival. The most he could do was to reduce it from $410,000 to $200,000, with the proviso that this would be the last time that the Government would budget for a deficit. The Secretary of State accepted this. The price was to be a systematic examination and reorganization of the public service, involving rationalization of departments, retrenchment of staff and overhaul of appointments, promotions and increments; departmental expenditure was to be reduced by something between twelve per cent and fifteen per cent. To this unpalatable and unpopular task the Governor proposed to devote his personal attention throughout 1929. 'Every question of filling appointments, making promotions and granting increments . . . will, during 1929, be settled by the Governor personally in conference with the Head of Department concerned.' He acknowledged that it was not customary for a Governor to engage in this kind of activity, but that he was determined to do so because—in effect —he didn't trust anybody but himself. 'Although it is possible that I shall utilize the services of an advisory committee, I feel it is highly desirable that these subjects should receive my personal attention during this period of transition. . . .'

It was in fact his principal preoccupation throughout his Governorship, and hardly one which was likely to win him much applause. He could not rid his conscience of the burden of this duty, and so plunged of his own free will into the most tedious, unrewarding and distasteful of activities, one which both earned him unpopularity and prevented him from attempting more constructive tasks. It was obvious, however, that he was still seeing his work in British Guiana in terms of a long span of years; this was the necessary, destructive work which would enable him to build more constructively in the long run. By the time he left the Colony the hard times, he hoped, would have been forgotten, and he would be remembered, as in West Africa, for his creative achievement in education, health, transport and political advance. Even so, his courage at this point should not be underrated.

His unpopularity was never universal. The elected members of the Legislative Council, for example, deprived of the power that they had enjoyed under the old Constitution, stood poised to oppose the new Governor. 'But he completely stole their thunder. In the Combined Court, the elected members had spent a great deal of time reducing, or attempting to reduce, establishments. Now this was to be done from above, so to speak. And while he was about it, he made the position of the elected members under the new Constitution quite clear. He wanted their advice and their co-operation, but the final decision was to be his.'[1]

For the first time for many years in this country, Government is in a position to govern . . . we shall give the unofficial members of this Council every opportunity of co-operating with us and advising

[1] Persaud.

us. . . . In the last resort, however, when opinions are divided, some one body will have to decide and act. . . .[1]

'All of this made a terrific impression. For the first time in the history of the Colony (so it was said) a Governor had made a thorough investigation of its problems and had formulated a clear-cut policy; for the first time the people had been taken into the confidence of the Government. Here was open diplomacy, frankness and plain speaking. The Governor had shown unprecedented interest, conscientiousness and devotion to duty. He was going to put British Guiana on the road to economic solvency and political progress.'[2]

But this, of course, was not the view of 'the retrenched', or of their friends and relations. In time, as the Governor worked his way systematically from one department to another, amalgamations resulted in redundancy, and redundancy in compulsory retirement; the number of posts on the Fixed Establishment dwindled month by month. Thirty-one teachers were retired and the number eligible for pension reduced from 960 to 300; magistrates, police, post-office officials, doctors, nurses and other hospital staff were pruned. In the Unfixed Establishment reductions were wholesale, and this was more upsetting for the politicians than the relatively small number of senior appointments. Mr. Beckles, a somewhat uncompromising critic but a first-hand witness, was able to write recently, 'The medicine which Sir Gordon was supplying to his patients was so drastic that many persons actually prayed for his return or death. Poor, hungry people could see no relationship between a great, sudden increase in unemployment among junior civil servants, and progress, and their opinion of Sir Gordon was that he was an enemy rather than a friend of the people of British Guiana.' Minor amenities in Government offices were also cut, office hours extended by an hour a day, and leave for locally appointed civil servants reduced. Discontent spread as, on the one hand, the retrenched and their families suffered unemployment, and, on the other, the public had to put up with fewer doctors, post offices, police stations and public amenities.

[1] Guggisberg—First Annual Message.                    [2] Persaud.

The Governor had not merely to work in this atmosphere; he had courageously assumed personal responsibility for creating it. But he never at any time 'pulled his punches'. He offended the Negro community by telling them straight that they should go back to the land if they did not want to be left behind, '. . . they will have to wake up to the fact that the vocation of farming is just as honourable as that of a lawyer, a doctor or a clerk'. He offended the Indians by saying that they must drop their exclusiveness, modify their traditions and regard themselves as Guianese. When it was urged that this might prevent further Indian immigration he replied, 'If a decision such as I have just made [concerning Hindu and Muslim marriages and the Income Tax Ordinance] . . . is sufficient to debar immigration from India, then I do not want to see immigration from India.'

Although pinned down in Georgetown to a greater extent than he would have wished, by his reorganization of the public service, he managed to tour the alluvial belt of the Colony as conscientiously as any of his predecessors, and in doing so set a new standard of rigour and efficiency. He was not disposed to share the Wilson-Snell Commission's view that opening up the interior was a high priority; the alluvial belt must be developed first and must 'earn the money for opening up the interior'. His insatiable thirst for local knowledge became a byword, and local officials in all departments got down to their homework on being warned of an impending visit, in order to have at least some answers at their finger-tips.

He complained constantly about the inadequacy and inaccuracy of the maps and, going back to the early days of his own service, thought seriously of asking the Home Government for a detachment of Royal Engineers. The one departmental activity outside Georgetown on which he managed to keep a personal eye was the experimental land settlement scheme—the pilot scheme which was to precede large-scale immigration. According to the chief surveyor of this scheme he 'inaugurated a Colonization Scheme and organized a careful survey, topographical, geological, forestry and soil, of the north-west portion

of the North-West District. I was in charge of the main framework for this survey, for which the Governor issued personally
very technical and detailed instructions as to how it was to be
done.'[1]

It was, no doubt, a partial relief to the Governor to get back
on to his home ground; it meant a change from the chores of
reorganization, with its depressing corollary of retrenchment;
but it was an example also of his old fault of being unable to
keep his fingers from matters which he should have delegated.
As in Accra he found an ingenuous pleasure in the role of
*grand seigneur*, dispensing favours. A characteristic story is told
by Sir Frank McDavid:

Sir Gordon paid a formal official visit to the Treasury late one
afternoon, and was received by the Treasurer, the late Mr. Thomas
Millard, C.M.G. . . . Mr. Millard led Sir Gordon into the little
screened-off apartment that was his private office. Sir Gordon took
one look and walked out. 'Is *that* where you live?' said he. 'We must
build you an office—out there—pointing to the eastern wall of the
Public Buildings. After the Governor had left I asked Mr. Millard if
he was serious in suggesting that a structure should be added to the
Buildings in order to provide a private office. 'Yes,' he said. 'The
Governor will ask the P.W.D. to prepare a drawing and get on with
the job at once!' I was, and appeared, incredulous. So my chief
explained 'If Sir Gordon thinks that it is desirable to move those
stairs'—pointing to the main central staircase—'and re-erect them
outside the building, he would order it to be done.'

The excrescence proposed by Guggisberg, which would have
ruined the building aesthetically, was in fact circumvented by a
little civil service intrigue and tact.

It is understandable that when the millennium failed to arrive,
and when the most conspicuous feature of policy was retrenchment, the Governor should fall somewhat into disfavour with
the masses. What of his relationship with their leaders? 'He
was', says Mr. Beckles, 'a man of restless energy for his age',
and any kind of tranquillity, either for senior civil servants or
politicians, had disappeared. The civil servants, on the whole,

[1] Roth.

took this well, for most of them admired and respected Guggisberg. The political leaders, of whatever race, enjoyed the experience less, because he was often openly critical of them. Matters came to a head when they counter-attacked, informing Sir Gordon that 'they were not the kind of people he had left behind in Africa, and they resented his dictatorial attitude towards them. Sir Gordon calmly silenced his critics by informing them that it would be a real pleasure to him could he find in this country men as distinguished as some of those he had found in Africa.'[1] His negrophile reputation, his known admiration of Aggrey, and his appointment of leading Negroes to the Legislative and Executive Councils, did in time win him the support of leaders of African descent, but his relationship with the unofficial Indians and Europeans was not always happy; and his tactless harking back to the Gold Coast grated on others besides the political leaders—on an education committee, for example, his unthinking use of the word 'Mission', which was not customary in British Guiana, caused needless irritation.

Guggisberg's strategy was perfectly clear. The first eight months of 1929 were to be a time of spade work, reorganizing the public service and producing detailed schemes to give effect to the policies announced at the Budget Session. He would call a meeting of the Legislature in August, at which these schemes would be presented; he would stay on to tidy up details, but would go on leave in October for a month, returning for a meeting of the Legislature in November. On 1 January 1930, the order would be given to advance. Specifically, the pilot resettlement scheme would then begin, together with another pilot scheme—in local government.

The latter—the District Administration Scheme—touched off a controversy that continued long after he had left British Guiana,[2] and it is necessary to say a little about it. Guggisberg's determination to reform local government was typical of his general strategic approach. In the Gold Coast and British Guiana alike he started by establishing his paramount aim, to

[1] Beckles.    [2] McDavid.

which all other aims were subservient. In the Gold Coast the paramount aim had been education; the whole apparatus of Takoradi Harbour, the railway extension and the road-building programme existed to facilitate the transport of cocoa; the purpose of this was to increase the revenue in order that money might be available for Achimota and the schools. In British Guiana the paramount aim was to increase the population by land settlement and immigration, and the whole apparatus of surveys and public health existed primarily for this. But land settlement and immigration would, in his view, be impossible without a reform of local government. 'I say quite frankly that if the present system of local government was bound to continue I should not touch anything to do with land settlement, even of the existing population.'[1] What existed could hardly be called a system. Outside the coastal cities it was simply a network of 'Village Authorities', self-perpetuating, apathetic and lacking in resources, and subject only to remote control by a 'Local Government Board'—'a body of men meeting once a month or so in Georgetown'. British Guiana and the West Indian islands in general had been outside the main stream of imperial administrative thought, which had found its apogee in the doctrines of Lugard and Cameron; the conventional provincial and district administration, with a 'political officer' in charge and a team of departmental officers under his broad surveillance, was unknown. What existed was inherited from Dutch and British immigrants, who had thought in terms of their own needs, and was not established by an administrative cadre for the purpose of governing a backward people.

Local administration in the Gold Coast had been rudimentary enough, but at least there had been a coherent chain of command through Provincial and District Commissioners, the absence of which in British Guiana removed all Guggisberg's familiar bearings. This could hardly be quoted against him as an instance of Gold Coast nostalgia, for no reformer could plan for national development in a country at British Guiana's stage of development without some such administrative framework.

[1] Final speech to the Legislative Council, 28 June 1929.

Whether he was once more tactless in referring too explicitly to West Africa is another matter—there is evidence that he was. He had also burnt his fingers at the outset by introducing the matter prematurely, before he had sounded local opinion and gauged local prejudice. He had not explicitly dealt with it in his own December 'Message', but his Colonial Secretary, Mr. (later Sir) Crawford Douglas-Jones, had presented a scheme[1] to that session of the Legislature, and Guggisberg had been compelled to withdraw it, to his somewhat obvious chagrin. In the early months of 1929 he determined to return to the attack:

I am therefore gong to introduce into the Legislative Council in November a scheme to replace the one which I withdrew—a scheme of District Administration. Whatever may have been the merits or demerits of the scheme which was withdrawn there is no necessity to talk about it.[2] I hope that the new scheme which will be introduced will go through in all its points, and that we will give it a test in 1930.[3]

He had in mind a system of 'County' administration, with a Commissioner in charge of each County and an engineer, competent in drainage and irrigation, an agricultural officer and an *immigration officer* on his strength, though officially responsible to their respective Departments. The Local Government Board would remain, but would be largely fused with the County Administration through the presence of the County Commissioners and Immigration Officers at their meetings. Later the Counties would be subdivided into Districts and the whole scheme brought together under a new Local Government Ordinance. In other words the normal system of African administration. He had already given his personal attention to the selection of the first Commissioners.

I have devoted myself to picking out the best officers in the Government service for this work. I have not got all I want, so there may be one or two vacancies . . . but I have got officers to start it with on January 1st, 1930.

[1] Associated also with the name of Sir Harry C. Moorhouse, C.M.G., D.S.O.
[2] A reference to his continual complaint that members of the Legislative Council gossiped, exaggerated and leaked confidential information to the press—'I put British Guiana in the top of her class for false rumours.' [3] Final speech, 28 June.

He went on to discuss the qualities he was looking for in such men, in terms sufficiently familiar to Sir Ralph Furse, Lord Lugard or Sir Donald Cameron:

If he is not a success he will go back to where he came from. It is not every man who has the sympathy, the strength of character, the tact and the powers of leadership that make a Commissioner, but above all I place the quality of having absolute sympathy with the people first. I see no reason why you should not have sympathy and be firm and strong and just, but sympathy comes first.

Presumably Guggisberg regarded himself as possessing tact.

The District Administration Scheme, which to Guggisberg was elementary common sense, and essential for the development of the country, was criticized 'on the ground that it would bring about tyranny and oppression'.[1] Basically people were objecting, as they object always and everywhere, to anything new, while the Local Government Board and the Village Authorities were touched on the raw by the obvious implication that they were no use. In the end, although District Commissioners were duly appointed, District Administration in the Gold Coast sense never became a reality.

These, then, were the preoccupations of the first months of 1929, the year in which the ground was to be cleared for the great advance in 1930. Time passed rapidly and the Governor's health grew worse. On 17 June his doctors finally confined him to his room. Facing facts, he revised his plans for a Legislative Council in August and a month's leave in October; he booked a passage home on 1 July and summoned a special Informal Meeting of the Council on Friday, 28 June, which he was resolved to address, doctors or no doctors. When it came to the point he flatly disobeyed their orders and got himself out of bed, thus raising an interesting constitutional question as to who, if anyone, may exercise compulsion on a Governor and Commander-in-Chief in *mens sana*, if not *corpore sano*.

I have therefore determined to go home on Monday (1 July) and return in October, We can then have the meeting on the Legislative Council in November or December.

[1] Persaud.

Whether this was bravado or self-deception, or whether he really believed what he was saying, we can never know. On any showing it was heroic, for he literally rose from his sick-bed to address the Council and collapsed on it when it was over.[1] It was on this occasion that he said 'I have got nothing wrong with me except a chill on the liver. . . .' In his speech he looked forward eagerly to the November or December meeting, 'probably the most important meeting that has been held of the law-giving body of this country'.

On this occasion he referred quite openly to criticisms of himself:

I am told by my advisers that the elected members of the Legislative Councils have received the impression from various utterances that I have made in public that I am going to carry through all these schemes in an autocratic and high-handed manner. This is perfectly untrue. Rumour on this occasion, as on every other occasion, is a lying jade.

He went on to outline his familiar thesis, based on his horror of the 'half-baked', that schemes must be virtually beyond criticism before they are submitted for criticism. Of course he welcomed criticism, provided it was 'helpful'; one wonders, regretfully, whether 'helpful criticism' and 'humble gratitude' were not synonymous in his mind. The last words he ever spoke on a public occasion were these:

I think you have probably found out by now that I am not afraid of criticism of any sort, but I do look forward to, *if there can be such a thing in this world,* something in the way of helpful criticism, and I may say straight out that I have had a very great deal advanced in the columns of the local press for which I am very grateful. [There seems to be some confusion here, but it was the muddled expression of a weary man.] There are others for which I have not been quite so grateful, but still one takes the fat and the lean together. [Author's italics]

The body of his final exhortation covered now familiar ground. Apart from its advocacy of District Administration it centred on land settlement, the prelude to renewed immigration. The last six months had brought to light some gloomy facts—

---

[1] Laing.

far worse than he had realized in his initial optimism; for
example, that only a quarter of the existing farming population
had large enough farms to make a living, and that the other
three-quarters needed to be resettled before there could be any
just possibility of settling foreign immigrants on prepared plots.
But eagerness soared within him as he spoke, especially when he
came to describe the problem from an engineer's and surveyor's
viewpoint, and any man is interesting when speaking of the
subject he really understands. He had already sent a despatch
to the Secretary of State asking for a party of Royal Engineer
Survey Officers, and for an engineer with experience of Holland
or Egypt—'one who will come out here but *not* on a visit.
Gentlemen, we have had enough of visitors'—words which have
found a heartfelt echo throughout the under-developed world
a quarter of a century later.

Alas, at a meeting of the Legislative Council in October 1930,
his successor, Sir Edward Denham, pronounced the predictable,
dreary words:

. . . I feel confident that the Colony will owe in the future a great
debt of gratitude to him [Guggisberg] for his initiatory efforts in
this important direction, but I think it will be advisable to wait a
little longer. . . . The Colony offers an admirable field for Colonization . . . but we are now so deeply concerned with our own problems of unemployment . . . etc.

In Guggisberg's eight years in the Gold Coast he had gathered
a richer harvest than is given to most men in a lifetime; his
personality and achievement are stamped indelibly on the
country and can be discerned even in the revolutionary Ghana
of today. In his eight months in British Guiana few of his seeds
bore fruit, and to this day many who are familiar with Guggisberg of Achimota, Takoradi and Korle-Bu are surprised to
learn that he was ever in British Guiana at all.

The speech over—he spoke for an hour and a quarter—he
was virtually carried to his bed; even after a week-end's rest
his doctors thought it advisable that he should go to the dock-
side by ambulance, and he was taken on board on a stretcher.
There were no demonstrations, but of course the silence of the

small crowd could be interpreted as sympathy or indifference. 'The crowds that saw the Governor off were silent, not hostile', remarks Mr. Persaud, who then goes on to give a horrifying glimpse of what once lay in store for unpopular Governors of British Guiana—'They did not throw bricks or sticks of "offal from the slaughter-house", as they had done to a previous Governor (Sir Philip Wodehouse). The people did not demand his recall as they had done in the case of Sir Walter Egerton. On the contrary, when he left, there were not many people who did not wish him to return.' In the circumstances this seems to have been as much as he could have hoped for.

The *Daily Chronicle* wrote a long and almost excessively respectful leader. The Government settled down again under Crawford Douglas-Jones. The Colony went its slightly self-pitying way. Nothing, it seems to have been generally accepted, could ever go right for British Guiana. Guggisberg twice came back into the local news—in January 1930, when he threw up the sponge and retired; and three months later, when he died. It will be convenient to record at this point the impression which he left on his last battlefield.

During the autumn of 1929 the Colony had been able to reflect on the stature and quality of the man who had gone, untroubled by his zealous and disturbing presence. On 16 January 1930, the *Daily Argosy* paid him a long tribute; after the customary note of self-pity ('. . . as is invariably the local custom, the chapter closes on a pronounced note of disappointment'), it prepared the way for his successor, Denham, by informing the world that the position of the Colony could hardly be worse, that the new Labour Government in Britain could not be relied upon to continue the development policy of the Conservatives (contrary to what was later to become accepted dogma), and that Denham, 'an official somewhat past his prime', would find it difficult to measure up to Guggisberg. After this cheerful opening, it said this of Guggisberg:

His memory will be cherished locally as that of a man who possessed the courage of his convictions and who was not deterred, at an age when he could have honourably retired on his laurels, from attempting valiantly to tackle the difficult problems of a Colony which has proved the graveyard of more than a single reputation. Further it is an undeniable fact that he restored both the dignity and the prestige, not only of the Office of the Administrator of the Colony but also of the Legislature—the latter of which had sunk to a pretty low ebb. In addition he instilled into the officials of the Civil Service an alertness and 'esprit de corps' which was highly desirable and which it is hoped will not now again disappear.

His policy for the development of the Colony, however much its wisdom in regard to specific items of detail was open to question, was ambitious, to say the least of it, and was marked by a distinct breadth of vision. The methods by which he hoped to achieve his aims may not always have met with the unanimous approval of the community but even those in disagreement with him could not but be impressed by his tenacity of purpose and his faith in the ultimate future of the Colony. Above all, his restless and untiring energy, his keen grasp of affairs, and the indomitable courage with which he trampled on his physical disabilities all marked him for what he was —a strong man possessed of the courage of his convictions.

The *Daily Chronicle* was equally fulsome. The Legislative Council spoke of his 'zealous attention to detail, his self-sacrificing devotion to duty, his keen insight into the problems of the Colony, to find a solution to which has baffled the ingenuity of so many previous administrators'. Everything that was said and written was of a piece—disagreement with him over many aspects of policy, but praise of his devotion to duty. 'His measures had caused a lot of suffering, but people generally agreed that he meant well and had the interest of the country at heart.'[1]

When, three months later, the news came of his death, the emotion which stirred throughout the Colony was perhaps expressed best by an artless but spontaneous letter from an anonymous contributor to the *Argosy*:

With all Sir Gordon's faults, the result of over-zealousness, he has been to us an ideal Governor, a thorough optimist and opportunist (*sic*), strong in his own conviction, prompt in acknowledging and remedying his errors, dignified but not haughty, broad-visioned and courageous. We therefore love him still and shall revere his memory.

[1] Beckles.

The official tribute was paid at a memorial service at Christ Church, where he had worshipped during his Governorship. The Bishop of Guiana faced quite openly the ex-Governor's failure: 'He was not popular; none of us can pretend that he was. He was not successful; the Colony is in a more distressful condition than when he came. . . .' But the Bishop had taken as his text the story of Mary anointing the feet of Jesus, and how the disciples complained of the waste, and he went on:

. . . and now the alabaster box is broken. What is the odour? I think we can say that any offering such as he deliberately offered was one of sacrifice. He knew that he was in bad health and deliberately offered for the last ten years of his life to do what he realized was a harder job than he had ever tackled, surely breaking the alabaster box. I think such a sacrifice is a very precious possession for us—looking beyond all personal feelings, beyond all personal favour, and giving us an inspiration to do something of what he did. That spirit of sacrifice, the spirit of a wise and forward look, is really a very precious possession for us here and now.

Those who remember that Guggisberg ended his career in British Guiana customarily speak of his Governorship there as an anti-climax. This hardly does justice to the facts. Viewed objectively, it was no small achievement to dispel indolence, to arouse excitement, and even merely stimulate conflict, in a Colony where apathy and self-pity had been the chief enemies of progress. Subjectively, and in terms of the dramatic quality which was so engaging an aspect of his life, the struggle of a sick man to fight stubbornly to the end, in the toughest assignment that an unsentimental Colonial Office had to offer, has a pulse-quickening quality. What other Governor has been carried to his ship on a stretcher, straight from a fighting speech in the Legislature? Had this been done in the theatre, instead of in life, there would surely have been a hush as the slowly falling curtain gradually shut off the gangway from the audience's sight; then the moment of silence before the gathering applause. The climax in *Lear* is not poorer because it presents the King in utter defeat.

Let Mr. Persaud have the last word:

He did not accomplish much, but certainly more than his predecessors had accomplished in much longer periods. He roused the Guianese (or Guianians, as he called them) from their indolence and apathy, taught them the dignity and value of labour, and held before all the prospect of a glorious future. This, perhaps, was his greatest work.

# 15

## The Curtain Falls

Author's note: On 25 February 1930, two months before he died, Guggisberg, now too weak to write, managed to dictate a letter to his friends, which was printed and circulated by his friend and doctor, Cecil Le Fanu. A copy of this was kindly shown to me by Mr. Laing. It is tempting to reproduce the letter as it stands, but it is headed 'For private circulation among the friends of Brigadier-General Sir Gordon Guggisberg. Not for publication.' The use that I have made of it in the first part of this chapter is perhaps scarcely less a breach of confidence, but by using it obliquely and restricting verbatim quotations to a minimum I trust that I have avoided offence; especially after the passage of thirty-five years. Two short quotations, of a less personal kind, have already been given in the previous chapter.

As he was carried up the gangway at Georgetown, Guggisberg looked back to wave to the members of the Legislative Council who had come to say goodbye. '. . . I took a last look round on the sea of faces, now grown so familiar and friendly, black, white, brown, yellow. *Shall I see them again?* Of course, why not? The medicos say that I will be up and working after ten days at sea.' If the 'medicos' did in fact say this they were meeting a traditional problem in a traditional way, for their patient's condition was now serious. Amoebic liver—not, as was thought for many years, sprue—was the condition that was killing him, with low blood pressure, hardened arteries and recurring fever. He travelled by way of Montreal, taking the Cunard liner *Aurania* to Liverpool. By a happy coincidence he was cared for on the voyage by an old nursing sister from his Gold Coast days, Miss Vecock, then Matron of a West Indian hospital. His destination was a nursing home in Devonshire Street, where from 28 July he passed through what he describes as 'six weeks of torture', not so much from his physical condition but because of the hot weather which caused the windows to be kept open, letting in the petrol fumes, motor horns and the yelling of children in the London street. He had become abnormally sensitive to noise; even the street noises of Georgetown had worn him down, and he had seriously considered building a quiet house for himself on the coast. He was well looked after, but on 9 September he was able to move, to his profound relief, to Sister Agnes' famous Nursing Home for the King Edward VII's Hospital for Officers, reopened after its summer cleaning. For three and half months he did not leave his room.

It was here that he conducted his final dealings with the Colonial Office. They came to see him, in the persons of Mr. Darnley, the official in charge of British Guiana affairs, and later Sir Samuel Wilson, the Permanent Under-Secretary, and an old friend. Although they both discussed the possible date of his recovery and his future employment, the conversation, on their side if not on his, must have had an air of unreality. So far as Guggisberg is concerned it is, to the end, impossible to determine whether he continued to delude himself, or whether unreasoning optimism was a feature of his condition. He 'warned' Mr. Darnley that he would not be fit to go back to the tropics for at least five months. Later, in talking to Wilson, he was 'in a position to tell him' that on the advice of the specialist it would be unwise for him to go back to the tropics at all, and that it would be another six months before he could commit himself to anything. Wilson, presumably to humour the invalid, murmured sympathetically about the possibility of a governorship in a healthier climate about the middle of 1930.

Guggisberg could apparently persuade himself to build on this, for he writes, in matter-of-fact terms, 'As to the future, I have not yet made up my mind. If the appointment which the Colonial Office *proposes to offer me* in May is in a healthy climate, I may possibly take it for a year in order to . . . —and here perhaps is the real explanation of his self-deceit—'in order to

complete my service to Governor's pension. . . . ' For the only
real help which the Colonial Office could have offered him was
financial, and this it rigidly failed to do. When Darnley first
called to see him he said he would receive full pay from 1 July
to 14 September, which was his entitlement; thereafter he
would go on half pay for *one month only*, until 14 October; the
Office would then have finished with him, unless or until he was
again employed. Guggisberg protested that Colonial Regulations allowed a man a maximum of six months' half pay on
medical certificate, but Darnley regretfully informed him that
this did not apply to governors! 'Nothing ever does, it seems to
me, that would be to their advantage.'[1]

It is interesting, if unprofitable, to ponder the meaning and
logic of this odd provision; was it that governors were supposed
to be above such material considerations? Or that it was *infra
dig.* for them to receive sick benefit? But if so, why offer him sick
pay for one month? If ordinary mortals may receive it for six,
and if governors are to be regarded as different from other men,
surely twelve months would have been more logical. The rule
probably had some obscure aristocratic origin and acquired the
status of a principle, although it was plain nonsense. But worse
was to follow. He was still a few months short of the ten years'
service which would qualify him for pension; but although he
had given his health to the tropical dependencies, no formula
could apparently be found to bridge this gap. £700 a year—
the sum at stake—dangled tantalizingly a few months away.
He never got it, and from 14 October onwards until his death
his income remained £521. 10s. a year from the Army. As
things turned out he hardly needed it for his own comfort, and
it would not have accrued to his wife or daughters. But if, as he
probably supposed in his heart, he had a few years to live quietly
in England, the difference between £520 and £1,220 would have
meant modest luxury for himself and a chance to leave a
respectable sum to his daughters, instead of barely paying his

[1] In fact, the Colonial Office seem to have relented, for they now tell me that he
was granted further extensions on half pay which did not terminate until 31 March
1930, i.e. a few weeks before his death. Guggisberg does not mention this.

way. 'However . . . there I was stranded, having so far failed, according to Colonial Office officials, to qualify for my Governor's pension by several months.[1] Under the circumstances, Wilson recommended me to resign from British Guiana, and to take my chance of a Governorship next May. I had no option but to accept the suggestion; indeed I think it was for the best, for if I had returned to British Guiana and broken down again, I should, apart from my own health, have inflicted an injustice on the people I was administering.' In point of fact, a decision about British Guiana had already been taken, for the King had approved the name of Sir Edward Denham as his successor. His own pride apart, this gave Guggisberg satisfaction—'the very man I would have chosen, if asked'. The date of his retirement, technically, was 15 January 1930.

Although life in Sister Agnes' nursing home was a relief after Devonshire Street, 'as time went by it naturally lost its charm', and he was pleased when they decided that he was well enough to spend Christmas at 'home' (Yateley). But no good came of this, beyond a temporary feeling of escape, and it was decided that he should be taken to Switzerland on 24 January. It is known that he had developed a sentimental urge to re-visit the village of Guggisberg, but whether these two reasons were connected is not apparent. However, when the time came no doctor would take responsibility for the journey, and instead he set out on a shorter one, seventy miles by road, to his final earthly destination. This could hardly have been less appropriate, for it was a seaside boarding house in a Victorian street in the respectable resort of Bexhill-on-Sea. Presumably it matters

---

[1] These frequent references to 'several months' or 'a few months' are apparently misleading. He served as Governor for seven and a half years in the Gold Coast and eight months in British Guiana. But according to the Colonial Office his pensionable service was considerably less than his actual service as a Governor owing to the exclusion of certain periods of leave which were in excess of the leave which would have been granted to a senior civil servant in the territory (the leave of a Governor being at the discretion of the Secretary of State, but being roughly equivalent to that of a senior civil servant). The Colonial Office in fact maintain that his pensionable service was less than eight years. Guggisberg either did not know this or turned a blind eye to it. I am indebted to the Colonial Office for giving me these facts, but I have left the original draft unaltered as I am reporting Guggisberg's state of mind as shown in his diary.

little where a man dies, yet somehow one feels a sense of loss. For the first time dramatic propriety is overthrown, and Guggisberg is found in a setting with which he seems to have no affinity. The probable explanation of this move is that Dr. Cecil Le Fanu, who had been a Medical Officer in the Gold Coast during the Régime, had retired there, and made it his business to take charge of his old chief. Indeed, Guggisberg writes of him as being 'in loco parentis', with a Dr Webb in medical attendance and two nursing sisters to look after him. However this may have been, a life of adventure, authority and achievement drew to its close in the mild, genteel surroundings of No. 27 Cantelupe Road, Bexhill-on-Sea. He was not by any means forgotten or neglected. He was touched by the kindness and frequency of letters; he was visited at a number of week-ends by his old friend Colonel Levey (to whom he told the story of his forbears recounted on page 13); and once his daughter Rowena took him out in a bath-chair along the seafront, which proved to be his last glimpse of land or sea. But mainly he fought the last fight in a hired room of a cheerless boarding-house in a strange town.

Here he lay for three months, growing weaker and reflecting on the past. At first, and before he finally accepted defeat, his mind strayed back to Africa. He toyed with the idea of offering himself, for some nominal remuneration, to a mission or school. No doubt this was little more than the fruitless day-dreaming of an unoccupied and exasperated invalid, but he committed it to writing none the less, '. . . I must get back to Africa to try to do some more work for the African races. In order to do this I am willing to forgo my pension, serious as the result would be for me financially, but as you know my heart is in Africa, and I believe that away from the trammels of the Colonial Office there is opportunity for me to do something useful both for the Empire and for the natives of Africa.' Another idea which engaged his frustrated mind, and which he poured out to Colonel Levey, was that he would travel by barge through the inland waterways of England, converting its inhabitants to a a belief in the Empire.

After a time he gave up. Inevitably he wrestled, as others have done before and since, with the problem of why it had to happen. He had the kind if unsubtle mind which could still attribute physical affliction to divine punishment for sin, and searched his conscience for shortcomings in his service over the last ten years (it did not occur to him for a time that life had any meaning apart from spending oneself in service). In all sincerity he could find nothing of which to be ashamed. 'And yet, in the middle of the task where I was most needed, I was struck down.' Gradually he sorted the problem out and achieved some peace of mind. Most people who profess faith in Christ, as Guggisberg did, know that worldly success is less important than inward grace, but manage to suppress this knowledge as long as they are being successful. Only when further success is no longer possible do they allow this knowledge into the forefront of their minds, to find too often that faith has weakened through neglect, so that they are left at the end with nothing. Guggisberg was no exception. His diagnosis of his own spiritual disease was acute, for he had constantly in mind a saying, the authorship of which he could not remember, 'All profound thought has recognized that if we occupy ourselves exclusively with the world, even for the purpose of serving it, we become worldly, superficial, unreal and ineffective.' 'I recognized that fact for a long time and fought against it, but slowly and insidiously its truth has been proved.' He admits that three times during his final illness, since leaving Georgetown, he thought that death had come, in August and December, and again during his first week in Bexhill. (Between August and December he was arguing with Sir Samuel Wilson about a governorship in a healthier climate.) 'On the third occasion I confess that I passed through the worst week of my whole life; I entirely lost all faith.'

Yet he died a happy man, with faith restored. Two things brought this about. The first, a book. Guggisberg was no great reader, except of maps and memoranda, and his intellectual tastes were unsophisticated; but some years earlier Fraser had given him a book with the awesome and uncompromising title of *Sin, Suffering and Sorrow*, written by Bishop Walter Carey of Bloemfontein. This work apparently spoke to Guggisberg's condition. 'It gives a clear, and to my mind satisfying, argument as to why these things must be.' An engaging comment from a dying man, wrestling with eternal truth, rather as though some difficult query in a survey report had been satisfactorily explained. The other influence was the kindness, patience and personal sacrifice of Cecil Le Fanu and the two nursing sisters. With Bishop Carey to guide him in the theory of Christian resignation, and these three to exemplify 'practical Christianity' (for example 'putting up with my vile temper') life made practical sense, and faith was restored.

He died, a physical shadow, on 21 April 1930. It is said that he died propped up among the pillows, wearing his Achimota blazer. It is impossible to discover whether this is true or not; what can be said without qualification is that this is precisely what *ought* to have happened, for he was an Achimota man to the end, and it would have been the gesture, soldierly and theatrical, with which he would have chosen to make his bow. The cause of death was recorded as syncope, chronic myocarditis, arteriosclerosis and amoebic hepatitis. Only the doctor and nurse were present at his death.

The funeral was not unworthy, by the unambitious standards which the British set themselves in these matters. Five women represented the family, his wife and daughters and his wife's two sisters; twenty or thirty other people were present, including his successor in British Guiana; the right interests were properly represented; some forty wreaths accompanied his body to the cemetery, among them one inscribed 'In affectionate memory from Elinor Glyn'; another from Decima significantly worded 'In memory of 1905'. Only to Messrs. J. W. de Graft Johnson and I. J. Amorin, representing the Gold Coast Students' Association, and accustomed to a somewhat more spacious conception of family and funerals, did the proceedings appear wholly inadequate. It was admittedly a small group that stood around the grave, but it was not denied the touch of theatre appropriate to his departure. From a modest position in the wings, as the coffin was lowered, or, so to speak, as the curtain fell, Decima swept forward to centre stage, and placed her wreath of lillies to accompany Guggisberg into the ground.

The Borough Cemetery at Bexhill-on-Sea is a pleasant place, on slightly rising ground, looking across a landscape of suburban calm, a fringe of farmland and a hint of sea. Here, under the conventional mound of earth, he lay. Nobody put up a headstone. The years passed. The mound grew shabby.

But this was not to be the end of the matter. The world might forget Guggisberg, but not the Gold Coast. The traditional tributes paid in Georgetown have been freely quoted, for these were the proper appraisals of a controversial reputation after death. But there was nothing controversial about his reputation in the Gold Coast, or formally restrained about the tributes paid that April in Accra, the Colony and Ashanti. It is indeed unnecessary to quote from them at all, for it is enough to say that they were tributes to a king. His friend Ofori Atta in particular was unlikely to rest until he had paid homage at the grave.

This opportunity occurred in August 1934, when the Paramount Chief had affairs in England,[1] of which a pilgrimage to Bexhill-on-Sea was not by any means the least. One Saturday afternoon, on 10 August, a surprising party descended on the town, when, as it is agreeable to reflect, the holiday season was at its height. Sir Ofori Atta's party arrived at Bexhill railway station in a special coach, and were met by the Deputy Mayor (Alderman Mrs. Meads, J.P.), six members of the Town Council, the Superintendent of Police, the Deputy Town Clerk and Mr. and Mrs. Albert Cartwright.[2]

The Chief was attended by Yao Boaffoa, his State Umbrella Holder, and Jones Osare, his little awoso, or 'soul-bearer', who carried a sword in a leopard-skin sheath. Members who accompanied the delegation included:

[1] The deputation to the Colonial Office described on p. 263.
[2] The former editor of *West Africa*, and a notable figure in African affairs, also living in retirement at Bexhill. A possible alternative explanation of Guggisberg's going there is that the Cartwrights were in touch with him.

The Hon. Dr. F. V. Nanka Bruce
The Hon. K. A. Korsah
Akilagpa Sawyerr (Accra Town Council)
Dr. J. B. Danquah
Mr. E. O. Asafu Adjaye
Mr. H. K. Ageyman (Secretary to the Kumasihene)

A wreath of carnations, roses and lilies was placed on the grave:

> In everlasting memory of Governor Sir Gordon Guggisberg
> from the people of the Gold Coast and Ashanti.

Dr. C. V. Le Fanu, of Fairmont Road, formerly of the Gold Coast
Medical Service, who attended Sir Gordon in his last illness joined
Sir Afori Atta as he walked to the grave.[1]

The Bexhill party was a little taken aback, as they had not
quite realized that their municipal cemetery was the resting-
place of so eminent a man. Their surprise, however, was nothing
to that of Ofori Atta and his party, as they gaped incredulous at
the shabby grave. 'But'—stammered the Paramount Chief,
hardly able to speak—'but . . . but . . . he was a Great
Man.'

After a time, a considerably chastened party continued the
pilgrimage, whose next objective was No. 27 Cantelupe Road,
to the perturbation of the proprietor—it was by now under new
management—and of the guests.

They gazed reverently on this shrine, and were apparently
admitted to the entrance hall. Here it was Sir Ofori Atta's turn
to supply the touch of theatre without which no Guggisberg
occasion was complete, but this time, for a change, it was bedroom farce. He was quite determined to see himself the very
room in which Guggisberg had died. Nobody knew exactly
which this was—Le Fanu, if he was present, must have forgotten. Somebody thought it might have been a particular
room, and tentatively pointed it out up on the landing. The
Paramount Chief of Akim Abuakwa, by now somewhat impatient, shot incontinently up the stairs and into the room. The
unprepared spinster lady who occupied it, and who was *en*

---

[1] *The Bexhill Observer*, 11 August 1934.

*deshabillé* at the time, is said never to have recovered from the incident.[1]

The special coach was attached to the 4.54 p.m. to Waterloo, Ofori Atta's ambition fulfilled, but his mind deeply disturbed by the weed-grown mound in the municipal cemetery. It was left to him and to the Africans of the Gold Coast to do what his family could not afford, and what his fellow-countrymen would never have thought of doing. Today a handsome and seemly headstone is inscribed:

TO THE EVERLASTING MEMORY OF
GOVERNOR SIR GORDON GUGGISBERG,
WHO DIED IN 1930 AT BEXHILL.
THIS MEMORIAL WAS ERECTED BY THE
PARAMOUNT CHIEFS AND PEOPLE OF
THE GOLD COAST AND ASHANTI.

In spite of his admonitions to his young first wife, Guggisberg had not been a prudent man in domestic finance. As a Governor, considering his uncertain pensionable position, he had spent too freely and entertained too well, and had managed to save little from a salary which for over nine years had been substantial. It is true that his spending had generally been in furtherance of his work, but he began to think too late not only about his own retirement but about provision for his dependants. He left (to his daughters, in a will made in 1926) the sum of £1,934. 6s. 6d.; and nothing whatever besides. His management of his private affairs had always been as unsatisfactory as his public image in the Gold Coast had been successful. The Government of the Gold Coast came to his aid by voting, *ex*

---

[1] This story was told to me by Mrs. Meads herself, who was of course present. She also supplied some of the other impressions that I have tried to transmit. Mrs. Meads died in January 1964, at the age of ninety-five.

*gratia*, modest pensions to his widow and daughters, which the present Ghana Government maintains.[1]

His last letter to his friends is a poignant but not a sad or pathetic document, for it is an account—in some ways a military appreciation—of the ultimate problems of a man of stature. It includes, however, one note of pathos. It is cross-headed 'Written from Bexhill-on-Sea'; but in the top right-hand corner are written the words

> Permanent address:
> The Army and Navy Club,
> Pall Mall, S.W.1

[1] Lady Guggisberg died on 18 February 1964, at the age of ninety-three.

# INDEX

*Note:* (GC) indicates that the subject has reference to the Gold Coast only.